Jonah

**Seeing God's Perspective
A Crucial Paradigm Shift**

CLINTON'S BIBLICAL LEADERSHIP COMMENTARY SERIES

**J. Robert Clinton, D. Miss., Ph.D.
Úna F. Lucey**

BARNABAS PUBLISHERS

Copyright © J. Robert Clinton, August 2002
All Rights Reserved

No Part of this publication may be reproduced, stored in a retrieval system, or transmitted in any form or by any means - electronic, mechanical, photocopy, recording, or any other - except for brief quotations embodied in a critical article or printed reviews, without prior permission of the publisher.

Barnabas Publishers
P.O. Box 6006
Altadena, CA 91003-6006
ISBN No. 0-9741818-9-7

Printed in the United States of America

Series & Title Cover Design: D.M. Battermann, R&D Design Servies
Book Design & Layout: D.M. & R.D. Battermann, R&D Design Services

Jonah

CLINTON'S BIBLICAL LEADERSHIP COMMENTARY SERIES

Seeing God's Perspective—

A Crucial Paradigm Shift

J. Robert Clinton, D. Miss., PhD.
Úna F. Lucey

ISBN No 0-9710454-6-1

Copyright © J. Robert Clinton August 2002

Table of Contents

Contents	Page
Abbreviations	v
List of Tables	vi
List of Figures	vii
Introduction to Clinton's Leadership Commentary Series	ix
Preface	xi
General Reflections on Jonah	1
Overview	3
Leadership Topics and Leadership Lessons	5
1. BIOGRAPHICAL GENRE	5
2. GOD'S SHAPING PROCESSES	6
3. BROKENNESS	6
4. SOVEREIGN	7
5. FOCUS/ BEINGNESS	8
6. SPIRITUAL AUTHORITY	8
7. GOD'S CONCERN FOR ALL HE CREATED	9
8. ETHNIC PREJUDICE	9
Jonah Commentary	13
For Further Study	18

Leadership Articles (bold faced items appear in other commentaries as well): 23

1	***Biblical Framework—The Redemptive Drama***	24
2	*Bible Translations and Hebrew Poetry;*	40
3	***Biographical Study in the Bible, How To Do***	44
4	***Figures and Idioms in the Bible***	50
5	*Getting God's Perspective, A Leader's Necessity—Jonah's Dilemma*	57
6	***God's Shaping Processes with Leaders***	61
7	***Isolation Processing —Learning Deep Lessons from***	65
8	*Jonah, Biographical Sketch*	73
9	*Jonah, Brokenness*	77
10	*Jonah, Contextual Flow—Seeing the Flow*	81
11	*Jonah, Desperate Praying*	84
12	*Jonah, First Foreign Missionary?*	86
13	*Jonah, God's Shaping Activities*	88
14	*Jonah, Hebrew Poetry*	93
15	*Jonah, Eight Important Ideas to Communicate*	100
16	*Jonah, Sovereign Guidance*	107
17	*Jonah, Obedience Testing*	112
18	*Learning Vicariously From Other Leaders' Lives. (Heb 13:7,8)*	117
19	***Leadership Eras In The Bible, Six Identified***	121
20	***Leadership Genre—7 Types)***	125
21	***Left Hand of God, The***	128
22	***Macro Lessons—Defined***	131
23	***Macro Lessons: List of 41 Across Six Leadership Eras***	134
24	*Nineveh*	137
25	**Paradigms And Paradigm Shifts—Illustrated in Habakkuk and Jonah**	139

26	*Pivotal Points*	144
27	***Prophetic Crises, 3 Major Biblical Times***	149
28	***Six* Biblical Leadership Eras, Seeing the Bible with Leadership Eyes**	156
29	**Spiritual Authority Defined—Six Characteristics**	171
30	*Testing Patterns*	174
31	*Transparency With God*	177
	Glossary of Leadership Terms	183
	Bibliography	195

Abbreviations

Bible Books

Genesis	Ge	Nahum	Na
Exodus	Ex	Habakkuk	Hab
Leviticus	Lev	Zephaniah	Zep
Numbers	Nu	Haggai	Hag
Deuteronomy	Dt	Zechariah	Zec
Joshua	Jos	Malachi	Mal
Judges	Jdg	Matthew	Mt
Ruth	Ru	Mark	Mk
1 Samuel	1Sa	Luke	Lk
2 Samuel	2Sa	John	Jn
1 Kings	1Ki	Acts	Ac
2 Kings	2Ki	Romans	Ro
1 Chronicles	1Ch	1 Corinthians	1Co
2 Chronicles	2Ch	2 Corinthians	2Co
Ezra	Ezr	Galatians	Gal
Nehemiah	Ne	Ephesians	Eph
Esther	Est	Philippians	Php
Job	Job	Colossians	Col
Psalms	Ps	1 Thessalonians	1Th
Proverbs	Pr	2 Thessalonians	2Th
Ecclesiastes	Ecc	1 Timothy	1Ti
Song of Songs	SS	2 Timothy	2Ti
Isaiah	Isa	Titus	Tit
Jeremiah	Jer	Philemon	Phm
Lamentations	La	Hebrews	Heb
Ezekiel	Eze	James	Jas
Daniel	Da	1 Peter	1Pe
Hosea	Hos	2 Peter	2Pe
Joel	Joel	1 John	1Jn
Amos	Am	2 John	2Jn
Obadiah	Ob	3 John	3Jn
Jonah	Jnh	Jude	Jude
Micah	Mic	Revelation	Rev

Other

BAS	Basic English Version
CEV	Contemporary English Version
fn	footnote(s)
KJV	King James Version of the Bible
NEB	New English Bible
NLT	New Living Translation
N.T.	New Testament
O.T.	Old Testament
Phillips	The New Testament in Modern English, J.B. Phillips
TEV	Today's English Version (also called Good News Bible)
Vs	verse(s)

List of Tables

Page		
38	Jnh 1-1	Bible Books Related To Chapters of the Redemptive Drama
40	Jnh 2-1	Bibles and Poetic Format
41	Jnh 2-2	Some Help In Noting Parallelism In Printed Poetic Format
44	Jnh 3-1	Four Types of Biographical Sources
51	Jnh 4-1	11 Figures in the Bible Defined
52	Jnh 4-2	13 Patterned Idioms
54	Jnh 4-3	15 Body Language Idioms
55	Jnh 4-4	14 Miscellaneous Idioms
59	Jnh 5-1	Other Macros Seen in Jonah
62	Jnh 6-1	Early Shaping Processes Identified and Defined
63	Jnh 6-2	Middle Ministry Shaping Processes—Identified, Defined
63	Jnh 6-3	Latter Ministry Shaping Processes—Identified and Defined
66	Jnh 7-1	Isolation Results
67	Jnh 7-2	Common Happenings in Isolation
67	Jnh 7-3	Job and Type I Isolation
68	Jnh 7-4	Moses and Type II Isolation
68	Jnh 7-5	Elijah's Type I Isolation Experience, 1Ki 17:1-6—Some Observations
69	Jnh 7-6	Elijah's Type II Isolation Experience, 1Ki 19 —Persecution— Running
69	Jnh 7-7	Jonah's Type III Isolation Experience—Need for Perspective
69	Jnh 7-8	Habakkuk's Type III Isolation Experience—Need for Perspective
70	Jnh 7-9	Nine Observations from Paul's Isolation Experiences
73	Jnh 8-1	References to Jonah in the Scriptures
77	Jnh 9-1	Biblical Examples of Brokenness
89	Jnh 13-1	Positive Testing Pattern
89	Jnh 13-2	Negative Testing Pattern
97	Jnh 14-1	Basic Procedure—Analyzing Extended Hebrew Poetry
103	Jnh 15-1	8 Key Ideas From the Book of Jonah
109	Jnh 16-1	Components of the Guidance Diagram.
111	Jnh 16-2	Jonah and Components of the Guidance Diagram.
113	Jnh 17-1	Positive Testing Pattern
113	Jnh 17-2	Negative Testing Pattern
122	Jnh 19-1	Basic Questions To Ask About Leadership Eras
123	Jnh 19-2	Six Leadership Eras in the Bible—Brief Characterizations
125	Jnh 20-1	Six Leadership Eras in the Bible
126	Jnh 20-2	Seven Leadership Genre—Sources for Leadership Findings
129	Jnh 21-1	Some Occurrences of the Left Hand of God
130	Jnh 21-2	God's Left Hand Working Through Cyrus
132	Jnh 22-1	Leadership Eras and Number of Macro Lessons
132	Jnh 22-2	Top Three Macro Lessons in O.T. Leadership Eras
133	Jnh 22-3	Top Three Macro Lessons in N.T. Leadership Eras
140	Jnh 25-1	10 Examples of Biblical Paradigm shifts.
142	Jnh 25-2	Needed Paradigm Shifts; If Leaders Are to Impact the Post-Modern Era
146	Jnh 26-1	Before and After Paradigm Shifts
152	Jnh 27-1	The Restoration Era Crises And Related Biblical Material
153	Jnh 27-2	The Restoration Era Crises And Related Biblical Material
157	Jnh 28-1	Six Leadership Eras Outlined
158	Jnh 28-2	Six Leadership Eras in the Bible—Definitive Characteristics
158	Jnh 28-3	Seven Leadership Genre—Sources for Leadership Findings
164	Jnh 28-4	Six Leadership Eras,On-Going Impact Items, Follow-Up
167	Jnh 28-5	Transitions Along the Biblical Leadership Time-Line

168	Jnh 28-6.	Moses' Transition/ Lessons/ Implications
168	Jnh 28-7.	Jesus' Transition/ Lessons/ Implications
172	Jnh 29-1.	Six Characteristics of Spiritual Authority

List of Figures, Diagrams and Charts

25	Figure 1-1.	Overview of Redemptive Drama Time Line
32	Chart 1-1	The History Books—Major Content
34	Chart 1-2	Differences in Palestine—Close of O.T., Beginning of N.T.
45	List 3-1	All Who Finished Well (Mini, Midi, Maxi Types)
45	List 3-2.	Some—Not Sure About Their Finish (Mini, Midi, Maxi Types)
45	List 3-3.	Some Who Did Not Finish Well (Mini, Midi, Maxi Types)
46	List 3-4.	Critical Incident Types
51	Figure 4-1	11 Common Figures of Speech
62	Figure 6-1	Some Major Shaping Processes Across The Time-Line
66	Figure 7-1	Three Types of Isolations
66	Figure 7-2	Isolation Sovereignty Continuum
89	Figure 13-1	Ministry Task Continuum—Luke 16:10 in Action
94	Figure 14-1	Tree Diagram Giving Overview of 3 Types of Parallelisms
108	Diagram 16-1	Guidance Diagram
113	Figure 17-1	Ministry Task Continuum—Luke 16:10 in Action
122	Figure 19-1	Tree Diagram Categorizing the Basics of Leadership
131	Figure 22-1	Leadership Truth Continuum/Where Macro Lessons Occur
145	Figure 26-1	Pivotal Points Characterized
146	Figure 26-2	Prime Critical Incident Diagrammed Functionally
150	Chart 27-1	The History Books—Major Content
165	Figure 28-1	Leadership Eras— Rough Chronological Length In Years
166	Figure 28-2	Overview Time-Line of Biblical Leadership
167	Figure 28-3	Two Major Transitions—The National Transition and The Great Divide

Introduction

This leadership commentary on Jonah is part of a series, **Clinton's Leadership Commentary Series.** For the past 12 years I have been researching leadership concepts in the Bible. As a result of that I[1] have identified the 25 most helpful Bible books that contribute to an understanding of leadership. I have done eleven of these commentaries to date and am continuing on the rest. I originally published eight of those leadership commentaries in a draft manuscript for use in classes. But it became clear that I would need to break that large work (735 pages) into smaller works. The commentary series does that. Titus was the first in the series. Haggai was the second of the series that is being done as an individual work. Habakkuk was the third. And this one, Jonah, will be the fourth done in the series.

This is a leadership commentary, not an exegetical commentary. That means I have worked with the text to see what implications of leadership are suggested by it.

A given commentary in the series is made up of an *Overview Section*, which seeks to analyze the book as a whole for historical background, plan, theme, and fit into the Bible as a whole. In addition, I identify, up front, the basic leadership topics that are dealt with in the book. Then I educe leadership observations, guidelines, principles, and values for each of these leadership topics. This *Overview Section* primes the reader to look with leadership eyes.

Then I have the *Commentary Proper*. I use my own translation of the text. I give commentary on various aspects of the text. A given context, paragraph size, will usually have 3 to 4 comments dealing with some suggestions about leadership things.

The *Commentary Proper* suggests *Leadership Concepts* and connects you to leadership articles that further explain these leadership concepts. The emphasis on the comments is not exegetical though I do make those kinds of comments when they are helpful for my leadership purposes.

The *Leadership Articles* (in Jonah, there are 31 totaling 155 pages) in the series carry much of what I have learned about leadership in my 38 years of ministry. In one sense, these articles and others in the series are my legacy. I plan to publish all of the articles of the total series in a separate work, **Clinton's Encyclopedia of Biblical Leadership Insights,** which will be updated periodically as the series expands. I think a person at almost any level of leadership can be helped greatly by getting leadership perspectives from these articles.

I also include a *Glossary,* which lists all the leadership concepts labeled in the comments.

Other books in the series, to be released over the next five years, include:

---

[1] These "I's" refer to Bobby. "We" includes Una.

1,2 Timothy—Apostolic Leadership Picking Up the Mantle,
1,2 Corinthians—Problematic Apostolic Leadership,
Daniel—A Model Leader in Tough times,
Philemon—A Study in Leadership Style,
Philippians—A Study in Modeling,
John—Jesus' Incarnational Leadership.

All of the above were previously done in the large manuscript and used in classes. And they are available as the original single work on CD in pdf format. Now I will break these out as individual commentaries in the series. And then I will do other books anticipated in the series over the next five years. Some of these will be done as I can get to them:

Nehemiah—Focused Leadership,
Malachi—Renewal Lessons Needed to Face Nominality Head-On,

And my long-term thinking includes developing the following:

Acts—Apostolic Leadership in Transition Times (a multi volume project),
Deuteronomy—A Study in Moses' Inspirational Leadership,
Numbers—Moses, Spiritual Authority, and Maintenance Leadership,
Mark—Jesus' Power Ministry,
Joshua—Courageous Leadership,
Matthew—A Study in Leadership Selection and Development,
1,2 Samuel—3 Leaders Compared and Contrasted (a multi volume project).

I (Bobby) have already done a study of each book in the Bible from a leadership standpoint and have identified and written up a number of leadership topics for each book. This analysis is captured in my book, **The Bible and Leadership Values**.

In an age of relativism, we believe the Bible speaks loudly concerning leadership concepts offering suggestions, guidelines, and even absolutes. We, as Christian leaders, desperately need this leadership help as we seek to influence our followers toward God's purposes for them.

J. Robert Clinton
Úna F. Lucey
November 2002

Preface

Every Scripture inspired of God is profitable for leadership insights (doctrine), pointing out of leadership errors (reproof), suggesting what to do about leadership errors (correction), for highlighting how to model a righteous life (instruction in righteousness) in order that God's leader (Timothy) may be well equipped to lead God's people (the special good work given in the book Timothy to the young leader Timothy) .
(2 Timothy 3:16,17– Clinton paraphrase – slanted toward Timothy's leadership situation)

The Bible--a Major Source of Leadership Values and Principles

No more wonderful source of leadership values and principles exists than the Bible. It is filled with influential people and the results of their influence--both good and bad. Yet it is so infrequently used to expose leadership values and principles. What is needed to break this *leadership barrier*? Three things:

1. A conviction that the Bible is authoritative and can give leadership insights;
2. Leadership perspectives to stimulate our findings in the Bible--we are blind in general to leadership ideas and hence do not see them in the Bible;
3. A willful decision to study and use the Bible as a source of leadership insights.

These three assumptions underlie the writing of my leadership commentary series. **Jonah** is one of a series of books intended to help leaders cross the *leadership barrier*.

Leadership Framework

Perhaps it might be helpful to put the notion of leadership insights from Jonah in the bigger picture of leadership in the Bible. Three major leadership elements give us our most general framework (cross-culturally applicable as well) for categorizing leadership insights. The study of leadership involves:

1. **THE LEADERSHIP BASAL ELEMENTS** (The *What* of Leadership)
   a. leaders (we are dealing primarily with this element in the book of Jonah)
   b. followers
   c. situations (God sets up a special situation to deal with a leader and a value)

2. **LEADERSHIP INFLUENCE MEANS** (The *How* of Leadership)
   a. individual means
   b. corporate means

3. **LEADERSHIP VALUE BASES** (The *Why* of Leadership)
   a. cultural (we are dealing with a major cultural value that Jonah held)
   b. theological (Jonah must learn the practical realities of a theological concept)

Preface

It is these elements that enable us to analyze leadership throughout the whole Bible. Using these major notions we recognize that leadership at different times in the Bible operates sufficiently different so as to suggest leadership eras--that is, time periods within which leadership follows more closely certain commonalties than in the time preceding it and following it. This allows us to identify six such eras in the Bible.

Six Bible Leadership Eras

The six leadership eras include,

1. **Patriarchal Era**

2. **Pre-Kingdom Era**
   A. Desert Years
   B. The War Years
   C. The Tribal Years

3. **Kingdom Era**
   A. United Kingdom
   B. Divided Kingdom
   C. Southern Kingdom

4. **Post-Kingdom Era**
   A. Exilic
   B. A Foothold Back in the Land

5. **Pre-Church Era**

6. **Church Era**

For each of these major eras we are dealing with some fundamental leadership questions. We ask ourselves these major questions about every leadership era.[1] Usually the answers are sufficiently diverse as to justify identification of a unique leadership era.

Where does Jonah fit?

The book of Jonah obviously fits in the third leadership era, *The Kingdom Era*. In fact, it occurs in Part B of that leadership era—*The Divided Kingdom*. It is a time of difficulty for leadership. The Assyrian empire has not yet destroyed the northern kingdom. But it is going downhill rapidly. And the Southern Kingdom is not far behind.

---

[1] The six questions we use to help us differentiate between leadership eras includes: 1. What is the major leadership focus? 2. What are the influence means used? 3. What are the basic leadership functions? 4. What are the characteristics of the followers? 5. What was the existing cultural forms of leadership? 6. Other? I comment on each of these in the **Clinton's Encyclopedia of Biblical Leadership Insights**.

But the message of Jonah is not about the Northern Kingdom and its demise. Other prophets will work on that. The book of Jonah deals with Jonah as a leader. Along with Job and Habakkuk Jonah is in the Bible to demonstrate how God shapes a leader. And it shows two of the most important lessons that leaders have to learn—how to go through difficult paradigm shifts and the crucial nature of a leader getting God's perspective on things. Habakkuk shows both of these lessons also. In Habakkuk the emphasis is on the perspective with the paradigm shift being secondary. But in Jonah the emphasis is on the paradigm shift with perspective being a close second.

And so God not only uniquely shapes Jonah by giving him dramatic sovereign demonstrations to bring about the paradigm shift in his situation but also opens up Jonah's perspective on the sovereignty of God and God's concern for other peoples of the world beside the Jews. And we, present day leaders, benefit. We learn the importance of getting God's perspective, even if it means cherished paradigms must go. And we learn that God is sovereign.

What does Jonah say?

Before we can look at leadership insights from Jonah we need to be sure that we understand why Jonah is in the Scriptures and what it is saying in general. Having done our homework, hermeneutically speaking, we are free then to go beyond and look for other interpretative insights--such as leadership insights. But we must remember, always, first of all to interpret in light of the historical times, purpose of, theme of, and structure of the book.

One way of analyzing the structure, that is, the way the author of Jonah organizes his material to accomplish his purposes would be:

Structure
I.   (ch 1:1-17)   Jonah's Disobedience and Discipline
II. (ch 2:1-10)   Jonah's Deliverance
III. (ch 3:1-10)   Jonah's Obedience
IV. (ch 4:1-11)   Jonah's Reaction

The overall thematic intent of this short book could be represented by a subject, which permeates all of what God is doing through the book of Jonah and several ideas about that subject. Here is our analysis of such a theme.

Theme   **JONAH'S RELUCTANT OBEDIENCE**
- was prefaced by initial disobedience,
- was necessitated by God's discipline,
- brought about timely deliverance for Nineveh and
- was used by God to show His concern for non-Jewish peoples.

It is always difficult to synthesize statements of purpose when the author does not directly and explicitly give them. But it seems reasonable to imply that the following are some of the purposes of this small four-chapter book in the Old Testament.

Preface

- to illustrate God's missionary purpose, i.e. to show Israel's true purpose as typified by Jonah,
- to show God's concern for individuals and His intervention in their lives for their good: the sailors, the Assyrians, Jonah.
- to cause a major shift in thinking about God being exclusively just for Jewish people,
- to demonstrate God's processes for bringing about a major shift in thinking.

Having done our overview of the book, hermeneutically speaking, we can look into how God shaped this prophetic leader in a critical time in his life. And we see how that leader who knew God and refused to obey God was lovingly disciplined in order to move on with God's perspective and purposes.

General Reflections—Jonah

With this background in mind, we can now proceed to the leadership commentary including its *General Reflections*, *Leadership Lessons*, *Commentary Notes*, *Articles*,[1] and *Glossary*.

Today, we live in the church leadership era.[2] It is difficult to place ourselves back hundreds of years into the 3rd leadership era—Kingdom Leadership. God has taken a people and made them into a kingdom. But the kingdom has split into a northern segment, Israel, and a southern segment, Judah.[3] So most modern day pastors and parachurch leaders do not bother to go back and study this period of time in the Bible. Judah, the Southern Kingdom, is on a rapidly destructive path. The Northern Kingdom is still alive but will soon feel the discipline of God's *Left Hand* (the Assyrians).[4] God has His hand on a prophetical leader, Jonah, to speak to the northern kingdom. But it is not Jonah's ministry to the northern kingdom that we see presented in the book of Jonah. Instead we see God's working in Jonah's life. Why is it included in the Bible, you say? It is an example for us, present day leaders. We can learn how God works in a leader's life.[5]

All leaders at one time or other will face an obedience issue in which they do not want to obey or at best only want to give a reluctant obedience. Jonah was that way and with good reason. So God deals with this inner heart attitude so that Jonah will learn to obey God from the heart. And the example stands for us too so that we can learn the lessons, vicariously, that God taught Jonah. We can learn about God's sovereignty, His love for other peoples and His loving discipline.

Suggested Approach for Studying Jonah

Read through the overview to get a general feeling of what Jonah is about. Note particularly the *Theme* of the book and its *Plan* for developing that theme, i.e. the outline for developing that theme. Then note the various purposes that we suggest the book of Jonah is seeking to accomplish. Then read through each of the leadership findings that we suggest are in the book. This is all preparation for the first reading of the text.

---

[1] Numbered articles are included in this commentary on Jonah. Unnumbered articles occur in other commentaries. You are alerted to their existence if they relate somewhat to the material. You may want to follow-up on them later. Numbered articles related directly and should be studied.

[2] See **Articles**, 19. *Leadership Eras in the Bible, Six Identified; 28. Six Biblical Leadership Eras, Approaching the Bible with Leadership Eyes*. This is probably an important pre-requisite for you before approaching the commentary.

[3] See **Article**, 1. *Biblical Framework—The Redemptive Drama*. This is another important pre-requisite giving important background information setting the situation in which Jonah's incident happens. See also **Article**, 27. *Prophetic Crises, 3 Major Biblical Times*, which pinpoints the crisis Jonah was facing.

[4] God's *left hand* refers to the use of people other than Israelites to accomplish His purposes.

[5] See **Article**, 18. *Learning Vicariously From Other Leaders' Lives*.

General Reflections—Jonah page 2

Read the text itself, all four chapters at one sitting, without referring to any of the commentary notes. Just see if you can *see what of the overview information* and the *leadership lessons* are suggested to you as you read the text.

Then reread the text, probably a chapter at a time and note the comments we give.[6] From time-to-time, go back and read a leadership lesson again when it is brought to your mind as you read the text and the commentary. Also feel free to stop and go to the **Glossary** for explanation of leadership terms suggested by the commentary. And do the same thing with the **Articles**. These articles capture what we have learned about leadership over the years as we have observed, researched, and taught it. It is these articles that will enlighten your leadership understanding. Obviously because of the uniqueness of the book, dealing primarily with a leader and not the leader's direct ministry, there will be some unusual leadership articles.

We have provided some *note space* at the conclusion of the Jonah commentary where you can jot down ideas for future study. Have fun as you work through Jonah, and by all means learn something about *paradigm shifts, God's perspective,* and *obedience*. Let this book inspire you to obey whole-heartedly that which God reveals to you. Learn the important lesson of learning vicariously by studying other leader's lives.[7]

Read through the overview, which follows. It gives a summarized version of the hermeneutical background studies for Jonah.

---

[6] From time-to-time in the comments, I will use the abbreviation SRN. SRN stands for Strong's Reference Number. Strong, in his exhaustive concordance, labeled each word in the Old Testament (dominantly Hebrew words but also some Aramaic/ Chaldean) and New Testament (Greek Works mostly) with an identifying number. He then constructed an Old Testament and New Testament lexicon (dictionary). If you have a **Strong's Exhaustive Concordance** with lexicon, you can look up the words I refer to. Many modern day reference works (lexicons, word studies, Bible Dictionaries and encyclopedias) use this Strong's Reference Number.

[7] The old adage, experience is the best teacher is true, if you learn from it. Personal experience is a great way to learn. But in terms of leadership, you will never have enough time to learn all you need to know for your leadership. by personal experience alone. I suppose that is why God gave us the leadership mandate—Hebrews 13:7,8 emphatically reminds us that vicarious learning is crucial for our leadership. And we have three whole books (Job, Habakkuk, Jonah) in the Bible devoted exclusively to illustrating God's shaping of leaders. And that is their main purpose for being in the Bible. See **Article**, 18. *Learning Vicariously From Other Leaders' Lives*.

Jonah Overview

***BOOK* JONAH**	**Author:** Probably Jonah?	
Characters	Jonah	
Who To/For	Israel (northern kingdom) but applicable to both.	
Literature Type	mostly narrative; select incidents focused on a crisis time in Jonah's life; there is a Hebrew Poetry section in chapter 2, which shows the depth of feeling Jonah has in his crisis.	
Story Line	Jonah, a prophet (2 Kings 14:25), received a commission from the Lord to go and preach, a prophetic judgment, to the Assyrians in Nineveh. This great warlike nation was an enemy of Israel (and eventually defeated them and took them into captivity). Jonah did not want to obey this word from the Lord. So Jonah determined to run away—go somewhere where he was not known. He took passage on a ship. The Lord brought a storm. The crew determined that someone on the ship was the cause of their trouble. They cast lots and it fell on Jonah. When questioned he admitted he was running away from God. He and they determined that to save the ship the best thing to do would be to throw Jonah overboard. This they did. God sent a large fish which swallowed Jonah whole. During the three days Jonah was in the fish's stomach he desperately called on the Lord for deliverance. The fish vomited Jonah onto dry land. Again the Lord gives the command. This time Jonah obeys (with some reluctance in his heart). His message is well received. The Assyrians repent. Jonah is displeased because he had hoped they wouldn't and that God would destroy them. Jonah waits to see if anything will happen to the Assyrians. God shows Jonah that He is sovereign and has concern for the Assyrians as well as the Jewish people. The narration ends here but it is clear Jonah got the message since he actually wrote up the testimony,[8] which certainly puts him in a bad light.	
Structure	I. (ch1:1-17) Jonah's Disobedience and Discipline II. (ch 2:1-10) Jonah's Deliverance III. (ch 3:1-10) Jonah's Obedience IV. (ch 4:1-11) Jonah's Reaction	

---

[8] Or related his experience to someone who did write it.

Jonah —Overview

JONAH continued

Theme — **JONAH'S RELUCTANT OBEDIENCE**
- was prefaced by initial disobedience,
- was necessitated by God's discipline,
- brought about timely deliverance for Nineveh and
- was used by God to show His concern for non-Jewish peoples.

Key Words — prepared (4 times) this indicates the sovereign control behind the things happening to Jonah; big, great (14 times); Other important words include: 1:2 (city), 1:4 (wind), 1:10 (fear), 1:12 (storm), 1:16 (fear), 1:17 (fish), 3:2 (city), 3:3 (city), 3:5, 3:7 (king and his big ones), 4:1 (anger), 4:11 (city).

Key Events — see the story line

Purposes
- to illustrate God's missionary purpose, i.e. to show Israel's true purpose as typified by Jonah,
- to show God's concern for individuals and His intervention in their lives for their good: the sailors, the Assyrians, Jonah,
- to cause a major shift in thinking about God being exclusively just for Jewish people,
- to demonstrate God's processes for bringing about a major shift in thinking.

Why Important — This book more clearly than any other portrays God's missionary concern in the Old Testament. His purpose, all the way from Abraham on, was to bless the nations through Israel. The book is intended to teach His people the lesson of the inclusiveness of God's government, and to rebuke the exclusiveness of their attitude toward surrounding peoples. This is a book, which teaches us much about God and how He deals with leaders.

Where It Fits — It is not exactly certain where Jonah fits specifically but generally it fits leadership wise in Phase B, the Divided time of Kingdom Leadership.[9] And in God's redemptive drama it fits in Chapter 2, The Destruction of A Nation[10]. It occurs a good number of years before the actual destruction of the northern kingdom by Assyria.

---

[9] See **Article**, 28. *Six Biblical Leadership Eras, Approaching the Bible with Leadership Eyes*. This is probably an important pre-requisite for you before approaching the commentary.

[10] See **Article**, 1. *Biblical Framework—The Redemptive Drama*.

Jonah —Leadership Lessons   page 5

Leadership Lessons

1. **BIOGRAPHICAL GENRE.**[11] The actual events from Jonah's life are concentrated in a relatively small time frame—perhaps as much as six months of his life or as little as two or three months. However, the period taken as a whole forms a pivotal point in his life with a major change in his perspective as the eventual outcome of God's shaping processes. Like Habakkuk and Job, the critical happening involves a change in paradigm with regard to God's working in the world. Other shaping processes involve the notion of *ministry task*, *God's sovereign guidance*, *obedience check*, a *life crisis* and *paradigm shift*.[12] This is a pivotal point in the life of Jonah. A pivotal point[13] is a critical time in a leader's life in which something happens, sometimes inadvertently, or a decision is made which, can: 1. curtail further use of the leader by God or at least curtail expansion of the leader's potential. 2. limit the eventual use of the leader for ultimate purposes that otherwise could have been accomplished, 3. enhance or open up the leader for expansion or contribution to the ultimate purposes in God's kingdom or 4. serve as a guidance watershed which forever changes the direction of the leader's life and ministry. We do not have biblical information to determine the result of the pivotal point in Jonah's case—except that we do have the book. What we do know about Jonah[14] is that he was a prophet from Gath-Helper who prophesied in the reign of Jereboam II in the northern kingdom of Israel. His major prophesy about Jereboam II came true. We see again in this very incidental note in 2 Kings 14:25 that God was still working on Israel's behalf, even though Jereboam II was not following God. And we surmise from the book that Jonah was a patriot with a view common to Jewish people that excluded God's working on the behalf of other nations. We know also that he was a poet. And finally we know that he was an honest man who wanted his learning experience with God to be used to help others, even though it might apparently reflect poorly on his own walk with God. We do have the book.

Leadership Observations/ Principles/ Values Suggested by this concept:
   a. Biblical leaders' biographical information should be studied to learn lessons vicariously (see Hebrews 13:7,8; 1 Co 10:6, 11; Ro 15:4).[15]
   b. Leadership emergence is a lifetime process in which God intervenes throughout in crucial ways to shape that leader towards his purposes for the leader. This incident in Jonah's life is a very special intervention by God.

---

[11] Biographical genre is the major source of leadership information in the Old Testament. The other six leadership genre include: Direct Leadership Contexts; Indirect Leadership Contexts; Leadership Acts; Parabolic Passages; Books as a Whole; Macro Lessons.

[12] In leadership emergence theory, we have identified some 51 shaping activities. We label these shaping activities with the phrase, process items. They are items God uses to process a leader. See *process items*, **Glossary**.

[13] See **Article**, 26. *Pivotal Points*.

[14] I am assuming that the Jonah mentioned in 2 Kings 14:25 is the same as the Jonah of this book. Other scholars do not necessarily hold this view.

[15] The principle of intentional selectivity plays a vital role here. That something of a biographical nature is included in Scripture, out of all that could be included, signifies something special about the entry. It should be studied carefully. See **Article**, 3. *Biographical Study in the Bible, How To Do*.

c. When viewed from a whole life perspective it can be seen that God's intervention or shaping is intentional.[16]
d. Leadership emergence can be thwarted.
e. The flow of this pivotal point in Jonah's life illustrates an obedience continuum[17] moving from a combination of willful disobedience/misperceived obedience to reluctant obedience to willful obedience. Jonah moves as far as reluctant obedience in the book itself but to willful obedience in post-reflective analysis (at least in attitude).
f. The essential ingredient of leadership is the powerful presence of God in the leader's life and ministry. Jonah had this.

See **Articles**, 6. *God's Shaping Processes with Leaders; 13. Jonah, God's Shaping Activities; 25. Paradigm and Paradigm Shifts; 20. Leadership Genre—7 Types; 17. Jonah, Obedience Testing; 30. Testing Patterns; 26. Pivotal Points.*

2. **GOD'S SHAPING PROCESSES.** The *shaping macro lesson* is certainly in view in this little book of Jonah. A <u>macro-lesson</u> is a high level generalization of a leadership observation (suggestion, guideline, requirement), stated as a lesson, which repeatedly occurs throughout different leadership eras, and thus has potential as a leadership absolute. The *shaping macro lesson* was first seen in the Patriarchal Leadership Era in God's interventions in Abraham's life. It is a simple observation: *God shapes a leader's life and ministry through critical incidents.* In Jonah's case the central shaping process is that of a *paradigm shift*, a major change in Jonah's thinking about the Assyrians and God's concern for non-Jewish people. Before the paradigm shift Jonah held a fairly typical Jewish view of non-Jewish people, which assumed that God exclusively deals only with Israel in order to bless. Jonah claims to <u>know</u> that God was all-loving but he didn't want God to be that. God is basically against non-Israelites. After the shift Jonah saw that God's mercy is not reserved exclusively for Israel. He has concern for all He created—to show His mercy and grace to all who repent. The means for getting at the paradigm shift included a series of processes: (1) a *ministry task*, that is, a special assignment from God, (2) an *obedience check*, which was failed, (3) followed by remedial action, which included a *life crisis*, (4) a repeated *obedience check*, which was passed, and brought with it God's blessing in ministry and (5) a time of *isolation*. Finally, the end result of the process was reflection[18] on what had happened and a challenge to see it from God's perspective, which led to the paradigm shift. For Jonah the pattern that took him through to the paradigm shift included: apparent obedience (misperceived), initial disobedience, reluctant obedience, willful acquiescence (seen long after the fact in the transparency involved in writing the book as a testimony of what happened).

---

[16] While we do not have the breadth of perspective on Jonah's life, it is clear even is this one short period of time in Jonah's life, that this is an intentional divine intervention. God is moving Jonah to see God's perspective on the Assyrian situation.

[17] See **Article**, 17. Jonah, *Obedience Testing.*

[18] Some of this reflection takes place in the final chapter as God deals with Jonah. But we are assuming that most of it took place after the events in Jonah and resulted in Jonah's writing the book to show God's concern for Assyria.

Jonah —Leadership Lessons page 7

Leadership Observations/ Principles/ Values Suggested by this concept:
a. God shapes a leader's life and ministry through critical incidents.[19]
b. Often leaders will need paradigm shifts in order to align with God's perspective.[20]
c. Leaders are given ministry tasks for their own development in addition to the development of those to whom they minister.
d. God's shaping processes develop leaders' character and theology.
e. Isolation processing can solidify a leader's call to and conviction about ministry.

See *ministry task, obedience check, corporate crisis, life crisis, critical incidents* and *paradigm shift* in the **Glossary**.

3. **BROKENNESS.** Sometimes in order for God to get the attention of a leader, He has to take the leader through a brokenness experience.[21] Such was the case with Jonah. Jonah's brokenness experience was emphasized in his isolation processing.[22] The prayer/song from the midst of his life crisis shows that Jonah had gone through a brokenness experience and was committed afresh to God for His deliverance and aftermath.

Leadership Observations/ Principles/ Values Suggested by this concept:
a. Brokenness can have different levels.[23]

---

[19] A critical incident is a special intervention (could be a series over time) in which God gives a *major value* that will flow through the life or will give *strategic direction* to narrow the leader's life work. In this case it is an important value.

[20] Job, Habakkuk, Peter, and Paul are examples of leaders needing paradigm shifts in order to align with God's purposes. Others could be cited.

[21] Brokenness is a state of mind in which a person recognizes that he/she is helpless in a situation or life process unless God alone works. It is a state of mind in which a person acknowledges a deep dependence upon God and is open for God to break through in new ways, thoughts, directions, and revelation of Himself that was not the case before the brokenness experience.

[22] Isolation processing refers to the setting aside of a leader from normal ministry or leadership involvement due to involuntary causes, partially self-caused or voluntary causes for a period of time sufficient enough to cause and/or allow serious evaluation of life and ministry. In Jonah's case the fish incident in ch 2 was an involuntary cause. The hillside experience in ch 4 was voluntary. In both cases, though short periods of time, they were intensified by the events. In isolation times leaders are forced to go deep with God and learn things that could not be learned at any other time (or perhaps ways) in their lives.

[23] In Jonah's case a life crisis threatens in such a way as to drive Jonah immediately to recognize his utter dependence upon God. This is a level 1 brokenness resulting from recognition of God's intervening action deserved by the recipient. In this case, fear of loss of life. The affect is prominent. Later in Chapter 4 Jonah is broken again. This is a level 2 brokenness resulting from conceptual agreement with God. This brokenness has the cognitive dominant followed by the conative. His anger with God showing mercy to the Assyrians is met by God's perspective on the situation. That we have the book at all shows Jonah was broken—He has been broken again and has gone through a paradigm shift agreeing with God about God's actions in Nineveh. See *affect, cognitive, conative*, **Glossary**.

b. Transparency with God often has the affect learning domain dominant. It is important, permissible, and perhaps even necessary for a leader to express his/her emotions.
c. A leader should learn to be transparent with God in appropriate cultural ways.[24]
d. Brokenness involves full-orbed learning (affective, cognitive, conative and experiential) though usually one learning domain is dominant.
e. The heart of brokenness is utter dependence upon God. This often can only be learned by a first-hand experience. But the very fact that the book of Jonah is in the Bible shows that leaders can learn aspects of brokenness vicariously. The book has that as one of its purposes.
f. Dependence upon God must be an ultimate value for a leader.

See *learning domains, affect, cognitive, conative, experiential*, **Glossary**. See **Article**, *9 Jonah, Brokenness; 7. Isolation Processing — Learning Deep Lessons from God*.

4. **SOVEREIGNTY.** The book clearly shows that God is behind the scenes in the shaping of a leader. Numerous sovereign interventions are pointed out: there was a boat ready, a storm comes up, Jonah is chosen by the lots, there is a fish ready, there is an overwhelming response of repentance by the Assyrians, there is the sun, the vine. All leaders must learn to see God in the experiences of their life and to believe that He is using them to shape his/her leadership. A <u>leader</u> is a person with God-given capacity and a God-given responsibility who is influencing a specific group of people toward God's purposes for them. For a leader to do this, that leader must be able to get guidance from God. A stepping-stone for a leader to get guidance for a group is learning how to get guidance for himself/herself. One aspect of guidance, seen so vividly in Jonah, is that of sovereign guidance through circumstances. It is a tremendous asset for a leader to believe in a sovereign God who can control circumstances. Now guidance through circumstances alone is not totally safe. But it is part of the process.[25]

<u>Leadership Observations/ Principles/ Values Suggested by this concept:</u>
a. One aspect of sovereign guidance involves God's intervention in the circumstances of a leader in such a way that the leader can be convinced that God is speaking through those circumstances.
b. Sensitivity to God's working in circumstances must be developed.
c. Circumstances alone are usually not a safe means of determining God's guidance.
d. Getting God's guidance personally is a stepping-stone for getting God's guidance for groups being influenced.
e. A lack of sensitivity to God's working in personal circumstances will become a barrier to seeing the Left Hand of God.
f. Biblical leaders who had effective ministry, like Jonah, were sensitive to God's working in circumstances.

---

[24] In Jonah's case and Habakkuk's case, both men use Hebrew poetry to express their inner most feelings as they interact with God. Poetry is a most affective medium.

[25] See **Article**, *16. Jonah, Sovereign Guidance; 21. Left Hand of God*.

Jonah —Leadership Lessons   page 9

5. **FOCUS/ BEINGNESS.** God's ministry to a leader is often more important than God's ministry through the leader. What we are is fundamental to what we do. If a typical missionary were to report back to the sending group concerning the events of Jonah, they would report on what happened in Assyria, the great revival, the turning to God. But God's emphasis is on what is happening to Jonah. Jonah had an intimate relationship with God. This intimate relationship allows for transparency with God. Chapter 4 certainly underlines this. Note Jonah's accusation to God. Note his anger. Note his transparency about what happened to the Assyrians. And, eventually Jonah is transparent with others. We have the book.

Leadership Observations/ Principles/ Values Suggested by this concept:
    a. Ministry flows out of beingness. Character is at the heart of beingness.
    b. An intimate relationship with God allows one to be honest with God about life and ministry and opens one up to further perspective on life and ministry.
    c. Transparency with God flows from a leader whose ministry flows out of beingness.
    d. Transparency about failures as well as successes allows others to learn vicariously.
    e. Transparency allows integrity[26] to be seen—that is, the consistency between inner life and outer life.
    f. Leaders are given ministry tasks for their own development and not solely the development of those they lead. In this case, the main emphasis in the book is on Jonah's shaping. The secondary emphasis is on Jonah's prophetical preaching to the Ninevites, which brought about their repentance.

6. **SPIRITUAL AUTHORITY**. A <u>macro-lesson</u> is a high level generalization of a leadership observation (suggestion, guideline, requirement), stated as a lesson, which repeatedly occurs throughout different leadership eras, and thus has potential as a leadership absolute. The *Spiritual Authority Macro Lesson* first seen in the Pre-Kingdom Leadership Era in Moses ministry is certainly in view here in Jonah. *Spiritual authority is the dominant power base of a spiritual leader and comes through experiences with God, knowledge of God, godly character and gifted power.* Jonah demonstrates spiritual authority in his ministry with the Assyrians. And the whole book demonstrates how a leader goes through a deep experience with God and gains knowledge of God and His ways. This is a pivotal point, which deepened Jonah's spiritual authority.

Leadership Observations/ Principles/ Values Suggested by this concept:
    a. Spiritual authority ought to be the dominant power base in a leader's ministry.
    b. Jonah demonstrates how a leader experiences God and gains knowledge of God.
    c. Jonah demonstrates spiritual authority in his ministry to the Assyrians.[27]

---

[26] Integrity is the top leadership character quality. It is the consistency of inward beliefs and convictions with outward practice. It is an honesty and wholeness of personality in which one operates with a clear conscience in dealings with self and others. See **Article**, *Integrity—A Top Leadership Quality; 31. Transparency With God.*

7. GOD'S CONCERN FOR ALL HE CREATED. Since the call of Abraham in The Patriarchal Era and the development of the Jewish nation, God has communicated His concern for all those He has created. God's intention was for Israel to be a conduit of God's blessing to His creation. Over time, the people of God exchanged this perspective for the assumption that God exclusively blessed Israel. In spite of His people's assumption, God remained faithful to His initial promise to bless all the nations and enlists Jonah to be an agent of blessing to the Ninevites. In Jonah's case, he gave cognitive ascent to God's love, faithfulness, and slowness to anger. However, the practical application of this truth ended up being the point of contention between Jonah and his God. And, if God was concerned solely about the ministry task of preaching to the Ninevites, He conceivably could have moved on to another prophet. However, since God desires that His people embrace His concern for His creation He keeps enlisting His prophet in hopes that he'll embody God's interests.

Leadership Observations/ Principles/ Values Suggested by this concept:
 a. God will show mercy to all who repent irrespective of their ethnic or cultural makeup.
 b. Jonah needed to go beyond a cognitive understanding of God's purpose to practical application in order to participate in God's concern for His creation.
 c. Jonah demonstrates the kind of inner conflict and tension leaders go through when God is expanding their perspective about the world.

See **Article**, *12. Jonah, First Foreign Missionary.*

8. ETHNIC PREJUDICE.[28] One of the first questions raised in the story of Jonah surrounds his reasoning for not wanting to go to Nineveh, the capital of Assyria. The answer to Jonah's resistance comes later in chapter four as he is discussing with God his reason for fleeing. He claimed that he ran because of God's nature of being gracious, merciful, slow to anger, and abundantly loving. Jonah was aware that God would not destroy the Ninevites if they repented from their wrongdoing. By implication this discourse shows that Jonah did not want God to be merciful to this ethnic group. He held a common prejudice of this time against non-Israelites.

Leadership Observations/ Principles/ Values Suggested by this concept:
 a. God does not discriminate based on ethnicity or culture.
 b. Jonah demonstrates that followers of God can easily harbor prejudice against other peoples, hoping that they would not benefit from God's mercy or grace.
 c. A paradigm shift will often be necessary to alter ethnic prejudice

---

[27] This is a logical inference. How else could Jonah have had such a powerful ministry in Nineveh? He had no positional power. He was an outsider. I believe it was his testimony of his experience with God—disobedience, God's miraculous deliverance, the fish's depositing of Jonah in Assyria—which was part of the convincing that God was indeed speaking through Jonah. See **Article**, 29. *Spiritual Authority Defined—Six Characteristics.*

[28] This is dealt with more fully, or at least exposed to us more clearly in the N.T. in the long term paradigm shift that Peter and Jesus followers went through (Samaritan woman incident; Peter's vision and experience with Cornelius; Barnabas and Paul's experience Antioch and the sending out to the Gentiles; Paul's confrontation of Peter in Galatians, etc.).

Jonah

CLINTON'S BIBLICAL LEADERSHIP COMMENTARY SERIES

Seeing God's Perspective—
A Crucial Paradigm Shift

Verse By Verse Commentary

Jonah 1:1-4

I. (ch1:1-17) Jonah's Disobedience and Discipline

Chapter 1
1 Now the word of the LORD[1] came to Jonah the son of Amittai,[2] saying, 2 "Go to Nineveh,[3] that great city, and proclaim my message there; I know how wicked they are."[4] 3 But instead Jonah planned to go to Spain[5] away from the presence of the LORD. He went down to the seaport Joppa, and found a ship going to Spain. He paid the fare, and boarded the ship to go to Spain away from the presence of the LORD.

4 But the LORD sent out a great wind on the sea causing a bad storm.[6] The ship was in danger of breaking

---

[1] Jehovah (SRN 03068), the existing one. This phrase "the word of the LORD came" is the Old Testament functional notation for a revelatory word from God, often used with a prophet. Its New Testament equivalent is *rhema (SRN 4487)*. We do not know how the word came, just that it came. We do know that leaders are people who must be able to discern God's speaking. A leader is a person with God-given capacity and God-given responsibility and who is influencing specific groups of people toward God's purposes. To influence toward God's purposes requires that ability to know God's purposes, that is, to hear from God. Jonah heard from God.

[2] I am assuming that the Jonah mentioned in 2 Kings 14:25 is the same as the Jonah of this book. Other scholars do not necessarily hold this. In that passage Jonah is spoken of as having prophesied to Jereboam II (giving us some information as to the time of Jonah's ministry) and having seen the prophecy come true. Thus Jonah is a true prophet come from God. See **Article**, 8. *Jonah, Biographical Sketch*.

[3] Nineveh was the capital of the Assyrian empire, a nation of cruel and violent warfare. Jonah was aware of this empire and its threat against the Israel. He was hoping God would bring judgment on Nineveh (seen later, Jon 4:2). See **Article**, 24. *Nineveh*.

[4] The point of this phrase is that God was going to bring judgment for their wickedness. It is not as if God had just found out about their sins. What this does show us is that God patiently deals with a people over time but there comes a time when judgment will fall.

[5] Tarshish is the location in the KJV and other texts. Several modern translations use Spain. The point being that Jonah was going in the opposite direction from where he was supposed to go. Someone has aply said, "If you want to run away from God, there will be a boat ready—implying that Satan can also engender circumstances." One can not trust in circumstances alone for guidance. Could he get away from an omnipresent God? David didn't think so (see Psa 139). And as it turned out, Jonah couldn't. This is a clear willful disobedience based on a misperceived notion of God and non-Jewish people. Jonah needs a paradigm shift concerning God's purposes for non-Jewish people and His purposes to use Jewish people to bless these non-Jewish people. See *Negative Testing Pattern*, **Glossary**. See **Articles**, 16. *Jonah, Sovereign Guidance;* 25. *Paradigms and Paradigm Shifts;* 30. *Testing Patterns;* 17. *Jonah, Obedience Testing*.

[6] The book of Jonah repeatedly emphasizes God's providential work: Here (1:4) God causes the storm; (1:7) the lot picks Jonah; (1:16) The storm ceases; (1:17) prepared the great fish to be there to swallow Jonah; (2:10) So the LORD spoke to the fish, and it vomited Jonah onto dry land; (4:6) . 6 And the LORD God prepared a plant; (4:7) God prepared a worm; (4:8) God prepared a vehement east wind. A leader must recognize that God does providentially work to shape that leader. God works providentially as well as sovereignly in the events and activities that shape a leader. See *providential, sovereign,* **Glossary**.

Jonah 1:5-14

up. 5 The sailors were desperately afraid. Everyone of them cried out to his god.[7] They lightened the ship by throwing cargo overboard. But Jonah was below soundly sleeping while all this was going on.
6 So the captain came to him, and said to him, "What are you doing sleeping at a time like this? Get up and call on your God. Perhaps your God will have mercy on us, and spare our lives."[8]

7 And the sailors said to one another, "Come, let us cast lots, that we may know for whose cause this trouble has come upon us." So they cast lots, and the lot fell on Jonah.[9] 8 Then they said to him, "Please tell us! Why has this happened to us?   What is your occupation? Where do you come from? What is your country? And of what people are you?"[10]

9 So he said to them, "I am a Hebrew; and I fear the LORD, the God[11] of heaven, who made the sea and the dry land." 10 Then the men became even more afraid. They said to him, "Why have you done this?" For the men knew that he fled from the presence of the LORD, because he had told them.

11 Then they asked him, "What can we do to you that the sea may be calm for us?" --for the sea was getting worse.[12] 12 And he said to them, "Pick me up and throw me into the sea. Then the sea will become calm for you. For I know that this tremendous storm is because of me."[13] 13 Nevertheless the men rowed hard to return to land, but they could not, for the storm continued to worsen.[14] 14 Therefore they cried out

---

[7] This is a life crisis situation. These sailors, experienced mariners, recognize the imminent danger. In times of crises folks often are driven to the supernatural for help. Such was the case with these sailors. Notice the contrast when Jonah is awakened.

[8] Jonah does not call upon God to save the ship. He knows that his disobedience is the reason for the trouble the ship is in. He is running away from God. But the captain is desperate. Perhaps Jonah's God will answer prayer. The prayers of the sailors are not working.

[9] *Cast lots* was a methodology for supernaturally determining something. Pieces of wood or stone were used to find out how and when to do something. In this case it would show who the guilty person was. Notice in Acts 1:23-26 this method is used by the eleven apostles to choose Matthias. Note the world view implicit in this. The sailors assume that the storm has come as punishment for something. Why? Did they assume that any storm had some reason behind it? Or was this a special sense—perhaps God's providential working again. Jonah is picked via the lots. Note this is again an implicit providential working of God.

[10] Having determined that Jonah is guilty and is the reason for the storm, the sailors now want to know why. They ply Jonah with questions to find out why the punishment of the storm.

[11] LORD, (Jehovah SRN 03068); God (Elohim 0430). When Jonah mentions God, the creator of earth and seas, the sailors know they are on the right track. Jonah is the cause of their trouble. Jonah admits he is running away from God. They want to know why.

[12] Since God is the creator of the earth and seas, the sailors assume He can stop the storm. Perhaps they were expecting an answer like sacrifice to Him. They do recognize God as having the power to stop the storm.

[13] How did Jonah know that throwing himself overboard would solve the situation? Again perhaps some implicit providental working, a sensing of God's will, is going on here.

[14] The sailors were fearful that if they threw Jonah overboard, Jonah's God would consider it murder and perhaps sink the ship. Therefore they try even harder to row the ship toward land.

Jonah 1:15-2:5

to the LORD and said, "We pray, O LORD, please do not let us perish for this man's life, and do not charge us with innocent blood; for You, O LORD, have done as it pleased You."[15] 15 So they picked up Jonah and threw him into the sea, and the storm ceased. 16 Then the men feared the LORD exceedingly, and offered a sacrifice to the LORD and made promises.[16] 17 Now the LORD had prepared[17] a great fish to swallow Jonah. And Jonah was in the belly of the fish three days and three nights.

II. (ch 2:1-10) Jonah's Deliverance

Chapter 2[18]
1 Then Jonah prayed to the LORD his God from the fish's belly.

2 And he said:
"I cried out to the LORD because I was in trouble,[19]
And He answered me.
"Out of the belly of Sheol I cried,[20]
And You heard my voice.[21]

3 For You threw me into the deep,[22] Into the heart of the seas,
And the waves churned all around me;
All Your sea billows and Your waves passed over me.
4 Then I said,
`I have been cast out of Your sight;
Yet I will look again toward Your holy temple.'[23]
 5 The waters surrounded me, [even] to my soul;
The deep closed around me;
Sea weeds were wrapped around my head.

---

[15] LORD, (Jehovah SRN 03068). The sailors pray to the LORD, the self-existent one and ask for forgiveness for throwing Jonah overboard before they throw him. They recognize God's sovereign and providential working. "You have done as it pleased you."

[16] The storm stops. The sailors know that God has stopped it. They offer sacrifices to God for delivering them. One would like to know what promises were made. And did they keep them. This crisis situation is typical of "fox hole" promises. Whatever the case these men know they have been delivered by God.

[17] Another providential reminder. God is at work.

[18] Chapter 2 verses 1-9 are in Hebrew Poetry. . A number of English Bibles translate in part or whole using poetic format. This is a reflective and transparent recollection of a critical time in the shaping of a prophet. It is significant that this portion of Jonah is in Hebrew Poetic format. Poetry is the language of the heart. Jonah was deeply affected, emotionally, by his crisis situation. And finally he closes by worshipfully singing his poetic response to God. See *celebration*, **Glossary**. See **Articles**, 14. Jonah, *Hebrew Poetry*; *Habakkuk, Celebration—A Leadership Function*; *2. Bible Translations and Hebrew Poetry*; *31. Transparency With God*.

[19] This is a typical crisis response of a person who knows God. A desperate situation requires desperate praying. See **Article**, 11. *Jonah, Desperate Praying*.

[20] Sheol, the place of the dead. Jonah sees himself as good as dead.

[21] Jonah sees God as the one who answered his desperate prayer for help.

[22] Jonah knows that God has worked providentially through the storm and the sailors. It is a sovereign God who is shaping him.

[23] Perhaps a case of the idiom, the prophetic past. See *prophetic past*, **Glossary**. See **Article**, 4. *Figures and Idioms in the Bible*.

6 I went down to the base of the underwater sea mountains;
I thought I was imprisoned there forever;
Yet You have rescued me from that pit, O LORD, my God.
7 "When my life was slipping away, I remembered the LORD;
And my prayer reached You, in Your holy temple.
8 "Those who worship worthless idols miss your mercy.[24]
9 But I will sacrifice to You
With the voice of thanksgiving;
I will pay what I have vowed.
Salvation comes from the LORD."[25]

10 So the LORD spoke to the fish, and it vomited Jonah onto dry land.[26]

III. (ch 3:1-10) Jonah's Obedience

Chapter 3
1 Now the word of the LORD came to Jonah the second time,[27] saying, 2 "Go to Nineveh, that great city, and preach to it the message that I tell you."[28] 3 So Jonah arose and went to Nineveh. This time he obeyed the word of the LORD. Now Nineveh was a large city. It took three days to walk through it.[29] 4 Jonah began to enter the city on the first day's walk. Then he cried out and said, "In forty days Nineveh will be destroyed!"[30]

---

[24] Jonah gives God the credit for answering his prayer and saving him from his hopeless situation. He then contrasts his answered prayer with those who worship idols and do not know God and can't get God's mercy. This reinforces the notion of Jonah's worldview that saw God as exclusively for Israel and not for the Assyrians. This is the paradigm that God will change in chapter 4.

[25] This Hebrew Poetry stanza climaxes with a worshipful recognition of God's deliverance. One wonders what vows Jonah made--Willingness to go to Nineveh?

[26] Again the providential working of God is deliberately pointed out.

[27] We are not sure how much time has elapsed. Most likely Jonah has made his way back to Jerusalem and worshipped God in the temple. He has fulfilled his prophetic utterance of worshipping God there. This would be an apt time for God to challenge again.

[28] Pusey notes that the original call was to speak *against the city*. Pusey contrasts that with this call to speak *unto the city*. Pusey's observation seems to be the first call was to announce judgment. But this call had in it the note of conditional judgment. That is, there is the possibility of repentance and alleviation of the judgment. I have translated the two calls by *proclaim my message* and *preach to it the message I tell you*. The first does imply judgment because of the qualifying phrase describing God's awareness of their wickedness. The second is more open ended. See (Pusey 1907:123,124).

[29] Modern scholarship doubts the size of this city. But some ancient cities did in deed put walls around large land masses including arable land, to withstand long sieges.

[30] This is a summary of Jonah's speaking. Why did they listen to him? He was a foreigner. He was probably speaking through an interpreter. I think it was because he shared his testimony about his disobedience concerning the boat, the fish, and God's intervention. I believe they saw spiritual authority. And too, they knew they were guilty of wickedness and excessive cruelty and violence. This in my mind is the real miracle of the book. The Ninevites recognized God in this message and they heed it. See *spiritual authority*, **Glossary**. See **Article**, *29. Spiritual Authority Defined—Six Characteristics*.

Jonah 3:5-4:2   page 17

5 So the people of Nineveh believed God. They proclaimed a fast. They put on sackcloth as a sign of repentance, from the greatest to the least of them.[31] 6 Then word came to the king of Nineveh. He arose from his throne and laid aside his robe, covered himself with sackcloth and sat in ashes. 7 He and his nobles proclaimed a decree widely throughout Nineveh, saying, "Let neither man nor beast, herd nor flock, taste anything. Do not let them eat, or drink water. 8 But let man and beast be covered with sackcloth, and cry mightily to God. Yes, let every one turn from evil ways and from violence.[32] 9 Who can tell if God will turn from His fierce anger and have mercy on us, so that we may not perish?"[33] 10 Then God saw that they turned from their evil way.[34] And God relented from the disaster that He had said He would bring upon them, and He did not do it.[35]

IV. (ch 4:1-11) Jonah's Reaction

Chapter 4
1 But Jonah was really upset about this turn of events. He became angry.[36] 2 So he prayed to the LORD, and said, "LORD, was not this what I said when I was still in my country? That is why I previously ran to Spain.[37] For I knew that You are a gracious and merciful God, slow to anger and abundant in

---

[31] This is a widespread movement. All of the common people are involved. Notice the indications that they had genuinely repented. Fasting was done in times of sadness or sorrow. Sackcloth was a rough, dark-colored cloth made from goat or camel hair. They dressed this way, fasted and sat in dust to indicate their extreme sorrow for what they had done. See also Job 2:8; La 2:10; Mt 12:41; Lk 11:32 for other indications of this sort of activity. The Matthew and Luke quotes are words from Jesus confirming the genuine repentance of the Ninevites. For Jesus, this was a real historical account involving a real Jonah.

[32] Violence is singled out as the special sin of Nineveh. Whether or not restitution occurred remains to be seen. It is interesting to note that Habakkuk, when talking about God's judgment on Babylon also singles out violence. Babylon was the eventual conqueror of Assyria.

[33] The movement included both the leadership of Nineveh as well as the common folk. The King along with his council (shows leadership structures in Nineveh) proclaim an edict affirming what was popularly happening. There was recognition that public praying to God and repentance might avert the disaster that had been preached by Jonah.

[34] The repentance is genuine. It is not the fasting that does it. It is not just the prayer that does it. It is, that they turned from their evil ways. How long it lasted is not known. But God did honor that genuine repentance. See **Article**, *24. Nineveh*.

[35] This not bringing the judgment upon Nineveh is what upsets Jonah so. See the next several verses.

[36] Jonah, like Habakkuk, is honest with God. He is angry. And he takes his anger right to God. He is looking for some answer from God to quell his anger. To justify this action of God in not punishing Assyria. They deserve the punishment. And too, Jonah's patriotism shows out. He knows these same Assyrians may well destroy Israel. See **Article**, *31. Transparency With God*.

[37] Here we find the background to Jonah's running away in chapter 1. It was not explicitly stated there but is given here. Jonah knew that God might well spare Nineveh. He was actually afraid that his ministry might be successful and God would spare Nineveh. His patriotism shows out.

Jonah 4:5-11

lovingkindness, One who relents from doing harm.[38] 3 Therefore now, O LORD, please take my life from me, for it is better for me to die than to live!"[39] 4 Then the LORD said, "Is it right for you to be angry?"[40]

5 So Jonah went out of the city and sat on the east side of the city. There he made himself a shelter and sat under it in the shade, till he might see what would become of the city.[41] 6 And the LORD God prepared a plant and made it come up over Jonah, that it might be shade for his head to deliver him from his misery. So Jonah was very grateful for the plant.[42] 7 But as morning dawned the next day God prepared a worm.[43] The worm so damaged the plant that it withered. 8 And it happened, when the sun arose, that God prepared a vehement east wind;[44] and the sun beat on Jonah's head, so that he grew faint. Then he wished death for himself, and said, "It is better for me to die than to live." 9 Then God said to Jonah, "Is it right for you to be angry about the plant?" And he said, "Yes, I am angry enough to die!"[45] 10 But the LORD said, "You are concerned for a vine that you did not plant nor make it grow. It grew in a night and perished in a night. 11 "And should I not be concerned for Nineveh, that great city? There are more than one hundred and twenty thousand persons who cannot discern between their right hand and their left--and much livestock?"[46]

---

[38] Jonah has probably remained in the city for the 40 days that was warned about in his judgment message. And God has not brought judgment.

[39] Like Elijah, successful ministry has brought with it a problem. Jonah actually wanted judgement to fall. His message of repentance has been heeded. He now despairs, knowing probably that Assyrian will destroy Israel in the future. Like Elijah, he is upset with the situation and wants to die. He is actually blaming God for his success in ministry.

[40] This is probably a rhetorical question. Interpreted—You have no right to be angry!" God will now demonstrate why. See *rhetorical question*, **Glossary**. See **Article**, 4. *Figures and Idioms in the Bible*.

[41] Like Habakkuk, who isolated himself in the field on a watchtower to hear from God, Jonah does likewise. He moves outside the city to see if God perchance might bring judgment.

[42] Jonah likely built a bower of tree branches or the like. God covered it with a vine (kikayon SRN 07021) which had broad leaves such as a castor bean or cucumber plant. Again we have the providential working of God explicitly pointed out. God is going to use the action of the plant and its removal to answer the rhetorical question already asked.

[43] Again explicit providential working of God is pointed out. God prepared the worm.

[44] Again explicit providential working of God is pointed out. God prepared the wind.

[45] Having committed himself to being angry over the plant and hot desert wind, Jonah is now ready to hear God's explanation of this little experiential learning experiment. See *affect, experiential* in **Glossary**.

[46] The whole point of the book is now given by God. God is the maker of all nations and is concerned about them. He will show mercy to those who repent. Israel, represented by Jonah, were to have been God's means for reaching the nations. Jonah got this message. He indeed went through a paradigm shift on how God viewed the nations (typified in Assyria) and how God viewed Israel's role in reaching those nations. See paradigm shift, **Glossary**. See **Article**, *13. Jonah, God's Shaping Activities; 25. Paradigms and Paradigm Shifts*.

For Further Leadership Study
1. Notice the repeated pattern, *the way up is down* which is often how God must lead in order to get a person where He wants him/her (location wise, attitude wise, and guidance wise--see Joseph, Moses and others).
2. Recognize the problem of inflexibility [47] in most strong leaders. One of their strengths is convictions and a strong will. The other side of the coin of this strength is inflexibility. Paradigm shifts are a major way God breaks through inflexibility to take a leader own in development. Study Jonah to learn vicariously about inflexibility in your own life. Ask, if God were to come into my own life with a Jonah-like experience, what is the inflexibility that He would deal with? If you can't answer this, get some of your followers or peers to help you see some of your inflexible ways and thinking that God may want to deal with.

Special Comments
Key verses 3:10 and 4:1-3. From a leadership standpoint the illustration of how a paradigm shift takes place is very instructive since much of leadership influence is doing that, bringing about major perspective changes in people's thinking.

---

[47] Inflexible leaders: 1. have a tendency to plateau, 2. tend not to be life-long learners, 3. tend to be naive realists, 4. do not perceive paradigm shifts very easily, 5. tend not to finish well. God frequently uses brokenness experiences to take them through paradigm shifts, which overcome these tendencies.

For Further Study

Jonah

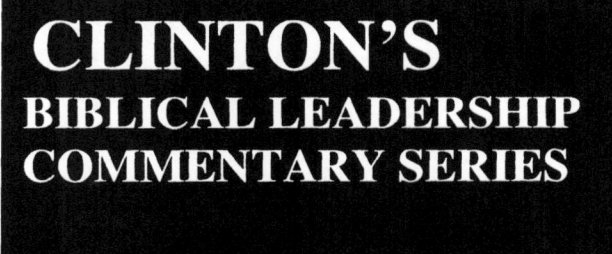
CLINTON'S BIBLICAL LEADERSHIP COMMENTARY SERIES

Seeing God's Perspective—
A Crucial Paradigm Shift

Commentary Articles

Leadership Articles[1] (bold faced articles appear in other commentaries as well).

1. Biblical Framework—The Redemptive Drama
2. Bible Translations and Hebrew Poetry;
3. Biographical Study in the Bible, How To Do
4. Figures and Idioms in the Bible
5. Getting God's Perspective, A Leader's Necessity—Jonah's Dilemma
6. God's Shaping Processes with Leaders
7. Isolation Processing —Learning Deep Lessons from
8. Jonah, Biographical Sketch
9. Jonah, Brokenness
10. Jonah, Contextual Flow—Seeing the Flow
11. Jonah, Desperate Praying
12. Jonah, First Foreign Missionary?
13. Jonah, God's Shaping Activities
14. Jonah, Hebrew Poetry
15. Jonah, Eight Important Ideas to Communicate
16. Jonah, Sovereign Guidance
17. Jonah, Obedience Testing
18. Learning Vicariously From Other Leaders' Lives. (Heb 13:7,8)
19. Leadership Eras In The Bible, Six Identified
20. Leadership Genre—7 Types)
21. Left Hand of God, The
22. Macro Lessons—Defined
23. Macro Lessons: List of 41 Across Six Leadership Eras
24. Nineveh
25. Paradigms And Paradigm Shifts—Illustrated in Habakkuk and Jonah
26. Pivotal Points
27. Prophetic Crises, 3 Major Biblical Times
28. Six Biblical Leadership Eras, Approaching the Bible with Leadership Eyes
29. Spiritual Authority Defined—Six Characteristics
30. Testing Patterns
31. Transparency With God (modify Habakkuk to fit Jonah)

In addition to these numbered articles, which are included in the Jonah commentary, I mention other articles, which occur in other commentaries. Those will be unnumbered. All numbered articles, those relating to Jonah specifically, are included in this commentary.

---

[1] Articles listed with numbers are included with this commentary. Some articles, without numbers occur in other commentaries.

Article 1

1. Biblical Framework—The Redemptive Drama

Introduction

In each of the overviews on the various individual books in the leadership commentary series I have a section called **Where It Fits**. In that section, I try to deal with the application of my first general hermeneutical principle,[2]

Language Principle 1 Book and Books
In The Spirit, Prayerfully Study The Book As A Whole In Terms Of Its Relationship To Other Books In The Bible (i.e. the Bible as a whole) **TO INCLUDE**:
   a. its place in the progress of redemption (both as to the progress of revelation, what God has said, and also the notion of what God has done in redemptive history)
   b. its overall contribution to the whole or Bible literature (i.e. *its purposes —why is it in the Bible?*) and
   c. its abiding contribution to present time.

I seek to find **Where It Fits** using two basic overall frameworks:

1. *The Unfolding Drama of Redemption*—that is, telling the story of what God has said and done in the Bible.[3]

2. *The Leadership Framework*. Since this is a leadership commentary series, I want to trace the contribution of a book to leadership. The leadership era it fits in helps inform us as to how to interpret its leadership findings.

This article is concerned with the first of these two frameworks: *The Unfolding Drama of Redemption*. I have previously dealt with the second framework in several articles.[4]

I will first introduce the overall framework with a diagram. Then I will give a brief synopsis for each chapter of the redemptive drama. Finally, I will list the Bible books in terms of the chapters of the redemptive drama.

---

[2] See Appendix G in **Having A Ministry That Lasts** for the whole hermeneutical system I use.

[3] I am deeply indebted to a teaching mentor of mine, James M. (Buck) hatch who introduced me to this framework in his course, Progress of Redemption, given at Columbia Bible College. I have used his teaching and adapted it in my own study of each book in the Bible in terms of the Bible story as a whole. I have also written in depth on this in my handbook, **The Bible and Leadership Values**. This article is a condensed version of that larger explanation.

[4] See **Articles**, *28. Six Biblical Leadership Eras; 22. Macro Lesson Defined; 23. Macro Lessons--List of 41 Across Six Leadership Eras.*

1. Biblical Framework—The Redemptive Drama   page 25

Overall Framework—Redemptive Drama Pictured

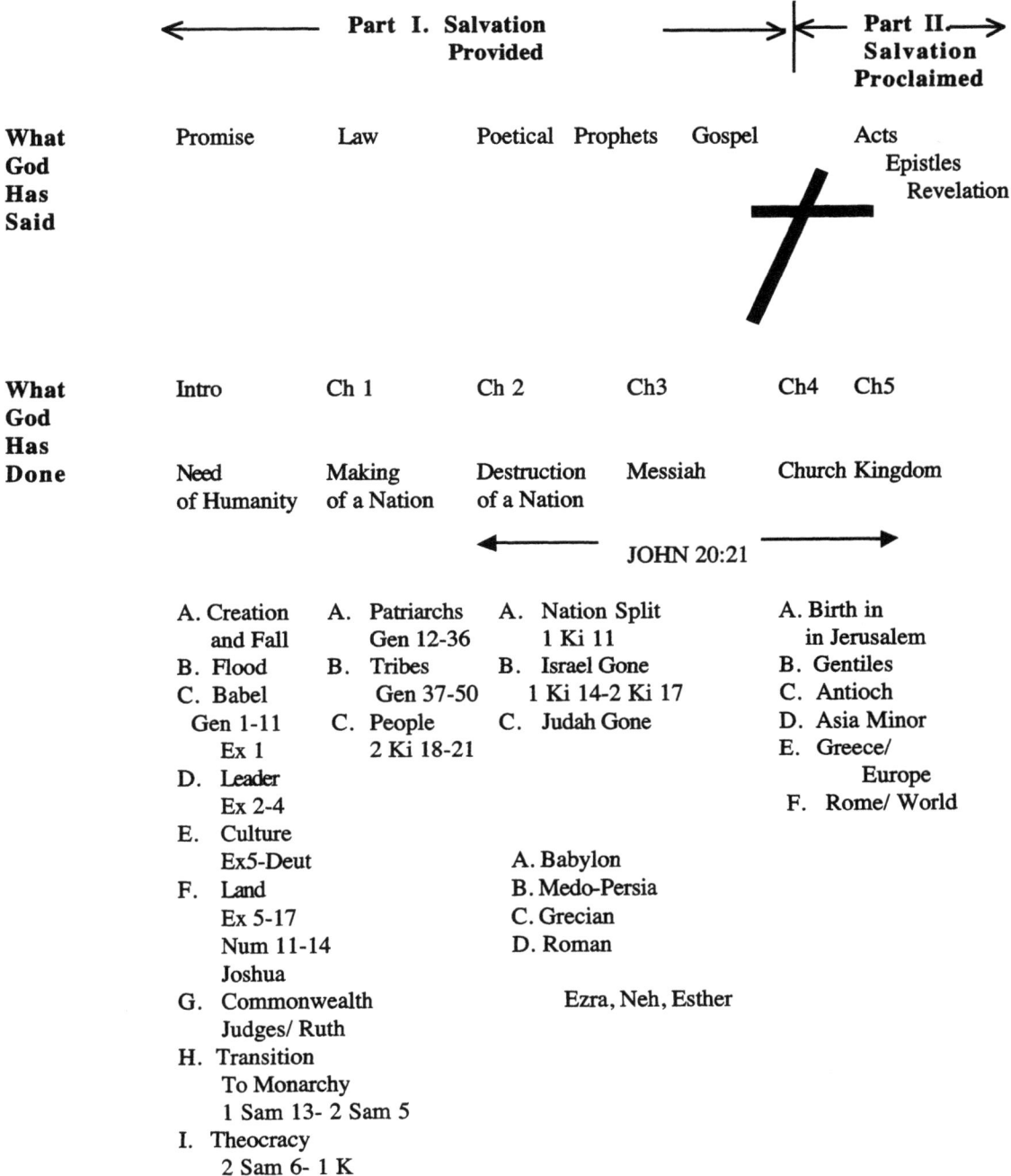

Figure Jnh 1-1. Overview of Redemptive Drama Time Line

The **Time-Line of the Redemptive Story** contains six sections,
>   Introduction,
>   Chapter 1. The Making of A Nation,
>   Chapter 2. The Destruction of A Nation,
>   Chapter 3. Messiah,
>   Chapter 4. The Church, and
>   Chapter 5. The Kingdom.

1. Biblical Framework—The Redemptive Drama

This story is briefly explained in a Running Capsule of the Redemptive Story. The story traces **what God does** and **what He says** throughout the Bible. And it shows that there is a progressive revelation of God throughout the whole drama. The Bible is unified around this salvation history. Once this is recognized then the notion of intentional selection becomes important. Each book in the Bible is there for a purpose and contributes something to this salvation story.

It is this framework, which provides the macro context for studying each book of the Bible. Where is the book in the progress of redemption time-line? What does it contribute to it? Why is it there? What would we miss if it were left out? Understanding each book in terms of its own purpose is a preliminary first step that must be done before we can interpret it for leadership findings.

The Running Capsule for the Redemptive Story

I will first give an overview and then give more detail from each part of the redemptive drama.

Overall

At the center of the Biblical revelation is the concept of a God who has intervened in human history. He created the human race. He has revealed himself to that race. That race rebelled against His desires. In its fallen state it continually rebels against His wishes and desires and for the potential that it could accomplish.

So He started again and selected specifically a people through whom He could reveal Himself to the world. God moves unswervingly toward His purpose which is to redeem people and relate to them. He moves toward His purposes whether or not the people He has chosen follow them or not. They can willingly be a part in which they enjoy the blessings of God or they can be by-passed and He will find other ways to accomplish His purposes. He patiently works with them to include them in His purposes. But when all is said and done He moves on with or without them.

All the time He is increasingly revealing more of Himself and His purposes to His people. They come to know Him as a mighty God, all powerful and controlling, yet allowing human beings their choices. He is a holy God, that is, a being of perfection. He reveals His purposes as that of having a Holy people following Him. People who are becoming Holy as He is holy. They learn that to fall short of His demands or standards is to sin against Him and is deserving of retribution if justice is to be satisfied.

Part I of the redemption drama, **SALVATION PROVIDED**, is His selection of a people, which will prove foundational to accomplishing His purposes. Out of that people will come one who is central in the decrees of God. Not an afterthought but mysteriously beyond our thinking, known to God. Look at Revelation 13:8, the Lamb slain before the foundation of the world. In terms of what we know of God today, we see this Part I as revealing to us, God the Father, that is, the God who is source of all that we are and to whom we relate, infinite, eternal, powerful, a spirit.

God protects that line through which He will come over a period of many years and in times of failure on their part to know Him and obey Him as they should.

His incarnation into the world begins Part II of the Redemptive Drama, **SALVATION PROCLAIMED**. Galatians 4:4, in God's time. That incarnate God, manifest in the flesh, to communicate directly with the human race, to be a part of it, to share in its joys and sorrows, finally pays the supreme price of rejection, by a world who wanted to call its

1. Biblical Framework—The Redemptive Drama

own shots, the death of the Cross, perfection paying the perfect price to satisfy God's Holy just demands. The great dilemma was solved, how God could be absolutely just and yet lovingly receive to Himself, those for whom justice demanded the harsh penalty of death. That time in which Jesus lived and walked and taught and did so many things to reveal God to us is the time, as we now know it of God the Son, God revealed to a human race as one of that race. Having accomplished the first portion of His work, the Cross, He ascended to heaven and will yet come again. Having ascended, He sent the Holy Spirit into the world, the intimation of what is to come, the Spirit who indwells those people He has chosen.

In the meantime while we wait we are involved in Part II **Salvation Proclaimed**, which shows that this message was more than just for the Jews but for a whole world. And that is what we are about today, the proclamation of that reconciling message, that God has provided a way in which sinful human beings can be rightly related to Him and progress to live a satisfying and fruitful life, in harmony with His purposes. And as they live this purposeful life, demonstrating the power and presence of God in their time on earth, they know that God is going to make all things right someday—there is a justice coming; the Lord Jesus, now a risen Savior, a life-giving Spirit will return to claim His own. There will be a time of His reigning on earth and then there will be eternity. And we who have been called out, as a people to His name, will reign with Him for all eternity. In terms of what we know today, this is the Age of God, the Spirit.

<u>Introduction</u>

Genesis tells us of many beginnings. It tells of the beginning of the creation, the human race, of sin in the world, of the spread of the race, of judgment on the race and a new beginning for the race. It does not satisfy all our questions. We would ask more and want more. But it does give us the backdrop for the salvation story. Humanity is in need. It can not get along with itself. It has alienated itself from God. Left to itself it will be destructive at best. There is a need. And the salvation story, which begins in Genesis chapter 12 will give God's response to meet that need.

<u>Chapter 1. The Making of a Nation</u>

God's basic plan is to choose a people and to reveal Himself and His plans for reconciling the world to Himself through that nation. Chapter 1 tells of the story of God's building of the nation.

If I were to pick out the most important events in the making of a nation, Chapter 1 of the redemptive drama I would say the following would certainly be a part of it.

1. The call of Abraham—the Abrahamic Promise
2. The renewal of the covenant with Isaac
3. The renewal of the covenant with Jacob
4. The deliverance of Jacob and sons through Joseph
5. The call of Moses
6. The power encounters in Egypt and the Exodus
7. The Red Sea deliverance
8. The Spies in the Land/corporate failure of a faith check
9. The Giving of the 10 Commandments/covenant
10. Moses' failure—striking the rock
11. Moses' outstanding leadership in the desert years with a rebellious followership and his transition of Joshua into leadership
12. Crossing of Jordan
13. Circumcision at Gilgal
14. Joshua meets the Captain of the Hosts
15. Capture of Jericho
16. Failure at Ai

1. Biblical Framework—The Redemptive Drama

17. Success at Ai
18. Gibeonite deception
19. Capture of Land (lack of total obedience)
20. Repetitive Failure—moving from dependence to independence. The Cycle of the Judges (need for centralized influence)
21. Samuel's unifying influence
22. Saul's anointing and failure
23. David's anointing and success
24. David's failure and discipline
25. David's preparation for building the temple

Lets examine some of the Bible books, which present these events.

From Genesis

From the introduction we know that humanity is not in good shape and is in need of intervention by God. And God has a plan thought out in eternity past.

God chooses one man, Abraham, and Promises (*The First Great Revelation—The Promise*) to make of him a great nation and to give them land and to bless the world through his offspring. (Gen 12:1-3, 7; 15:4,18, et al) Now God plans to use the nation He will bring forth to be a channel of redemption and revelation of Himself. So He begins to build a nation. For a nation you need people (including numbers) a coherent culture, a land, and a leader.

God begins to work on these things—the people first (the land has people on it who will be judged eventually when they are too evil to be redeemed). From this one man, who exemplifies faith in God's promise, comes a son, Isaac. Isaac has two sons, one of whom, Jacob, becomes the successor of the family line through which God will work—the 12 heads of the tribes: Reuben, Simeon, Levi, Judah, Zebulun, Issachar, Dan, Gad, Asher, Naphtali, Joseph, Benjamin.

Joseph, a son of Jacob's old age and his favorite, is sold into slavery by his jealous brothers (Acts 7:9). Because the patriarchs were jealous of Joseph they sold him as a slave into Egypt. But God was with him and rescued him from all his troubles. He gave Joseph wisdom and enabled him to gain the goodwill of Pharaoh king of Egypt; so he made him ruler over Egypt and all his palace.) Joseph, a person of proven integrity, rises to power through a series of providential appointments in which he shows wisdom from God upon several occasions. God gives some dreams to Pharaoh, the ruler of Egypt, which predict some good years followed by famine years. Joseph gives a wise plan to Pharaoh on how to prepare for it. He is put in charge and is right on target to protect his own family when the famine hits. The family comes to Egypt and rides through the famine years. It stays and expands in the land. Joseph, never losing sight of God's promise, exacts a promise from his brothers and fellow Israelites that they will take him back into the land when God takes them back. That is how Genesis ends.

From Exodus

Exodus opens many years later. There are many Israelite descendants, so many in fact, that the Egyptian King is fearful of them so he subjugates them. They are slaves and being ill-treated. Persecution takes the form of enforced labor and attempts to cut down the population (executing the boy babies).

God, having fulfilled the first part of his plan, getting a people, now works on the second part—getting a leader. Moses, an Israelite baby is preserved providentially and

1. Biblical Framework—The Redemptive Drama

taken into the palace and educated as an Egyptian royal class person. As he reaches adulthood he recognizes that his people by blood relationship are in great bondage. So he wants to free them. His first attempt to help them is a disaster. He kills an Egyptian and has to flee Egypt. He goes to Midian, settles down, marries a Midianite woman, and has a family. After forty years, God selects him via a miraculous revelation, to go back to Egypt to lead God's people out of Egypt and into the promised land. Moses goes back and after 10 major confrontations with the Egyptian ruler (in which God-given power is seen—Moses certainly has spiritual authority) the people are freed to leave. But on the way the Egyptian ruler has second thoughts and pursues with his military. The military should overtake the Israelites who will be trapped by the Red Sea. God miraculously intervenes and they escape across the Red Sea on dry ground. The sea moves back as the military forces start to cross and they are wiped out. This is the heart of *the Exodus*.

From Exodus and Leviticus

God next begins to build the people culturally into what He will need. He gives them the LAW, the second great revelation and reveals more of Himself, His standards, and His purposes. The tabernacle, which He gives the plans for reveals more of who God is in terms of access and revelation. The rest of EXODUS is given to that, revealing who God is as is the whole of LEVITICUS. It is especially in Leviticus that the holiness of God is developed—an understanding of sin and its implications; what atonement is (that is, being made right with God by making up for wrong against Him).

From Numbers

After disobedience and a lack of faith prevent the people from going in to the land (see NUMBERS) they wander for 40 years in the Sinai desert until the older rebellious people die off. During the desert years they learn to trust in God's provision. God reveals Himself primarily through his leader Moses. Near the end of the 40 years they are again ready to go into the land. God has a people, a culture, a leader, Moses, and a leader to take his place, Joshua. Moses prepares them for that push into the land by giving them a series of addresses (DEUTERONOMY—second law). These messages, his final words to them, reflect warnings drawn from their desert experience, remind them of standards of obedience which reflects what they have learned of God, and gives encouragement in the form of expectations as they enter the land. He closes his final words to them with songs of warning and blessing that portend the future. And thus we are ready for the third part of God's plan to build Himself a people—getting them into the land.

From Joshua

Joshua transitions into leadership with some sterling miraculous interventions by God, which give him the spiritual authority he will need to follow Moses (a hard act to follow) as leader. Joshua seizes Jericho, after following a supernaturally revealed plan for its capture. He proceeds after an unexpected failure, which teaches an important corporate lesson on obedience, to the people, to split the land in two militarily and then begins to mop up in the north and south. The land is allotted. Each tribe has a portion, just as Moses had planned. They decentralize and begin to settle into their spots—with much trouble. After having been so long in a centralized authoritarian mode, they enjoy being decentralized and having autonomy. But this decentralization eventually leads to spiritual deterioration. This brings us up into the times of the judges.

From Judges

For a long period of time, longer than we in the United States have been a nation, the twelve tribes live scattered. There is frequent civil war in specific locales and much fighting with various surrounding nations and peoples who were not totally destroyed when the land was taken.

1. Biblical Framework—The Redemptive Drama page 30

In short there is an oft repeated cycle: the people deteriorate spiritually getting far from God, God brings judgment upon them, they finally recognize that their problem is relationship with God—they repent and cry out for God's help. He sends along leaders, very charismatic who usually lead a volunteer army to defeat their enemies. There are at least 13 of these including: Othniel, Ehud, Shamgar, Deborah (Barak), Gideon, Abimelech, Tola, Jair, Jephthah, Ibzan, Elon, Abdon, and Samson. Some of these are more well known than others. Gideon and Samson for example. These are evil times and few there are who follow God.

In a section of the Judges (Judges 2:7) the writer sums it up well, "After Joshua had dismissed the Israelites, they went to take possession of the land, each to his own inheritance. The people served the Lord through out the lifetime of Joshua and of the elders who outlived him and who had seen all the great things the Lord had done for Israel." And then again in the closing portion a repeated phrase haunts us—Judges 21:25, "In those days Israel had no king; everyone did as he saw fit." These are the pre-kingdom years. Corporately the people are negatively prepared for the kingdom, which will come.

From Ruth

There is a spark of life during those dreadful times. Ruth introduces us to that life by showing that there were some people of integrity who honored the Lord. This little romantic book shows how God provides and also allows us to see how the line through which the redeemer will later arise progresses.

The Judges and Ruth are pre-kingdom times. They prepared the Israelites to want a centralized structure after so much independence and autonomy. The Israelites were dependent upon voluntary armies raised up in times of crisis. Many times, other of the tribes than the one threatened, were not interested in their local squabbles and would not fight for them. Thus the entire commonwealth of tribes comes to the place where it needs, wants, and will accept a kingdom. Again God steps in and provides a transition leader—Samuel.

From 1 Samuel

The first thirteen chapters show how Samuel was providentially raised up as a leader. His ministry as judge was not just a momentary deliverance but a continual one. He visited the different tribes and judged them—that is, established law and justice for them. Samuel paves the way for a centralized kingdom. Crises around the people spur the need; Samuel's own sons are not able to replace him. The people demand a king—showing their need for one but also showing that they basically did not trust the unseen King. God gives them one king, Saul, who outwardly is what they would expect. But he fails repeatedly to follow God. His kingdom is spiritually bankrupt. God replaces him with David, whom God describes as *a man after my own heart*. The last part of 1 Samuel describes Saul's fall and David's early pre-kingdom years, in which David is gaining military expertise as a guerrilla warfare leader with a para-military band.

From 2 Samuel and 1 Chronicles and the Psalms

2 Samuel and 1 Chronicles give David's story—one written earlier to it and one written later. David is a long time in getting the kingdom as Saul's descendants try to hold on to the kingdom. After seven years of civil war, David is ruling a smaller part of Israel, the kingdom is united. God gives a covenant to David concerning his descendants. The poetical literature, particularly the Psalms, emerge more solidly from this era. David is an artistic person who spends time alone with God in worship. Many of the Psalms come out of those times alone with God, many spurred on by crises in David's kingdom. The kingdom is established under David and expands. In mid-life David has a major sin which

1. Biblical Framework—The Redemptive Drama   page 31

tarnishes his lifetime. He has one of his military leaders killed in order that he might take his wife for himself. It and failure to manage his family well lead to a rebellion by one of his sons Absalom. David is deposed briefly but comes back winning a strategic battle. He is reinstated. Most of the rest of his kingdom is downhill. David's son, Solomon, after some manipulation and political intrigue succeeds David.

A number of the Psalms are ascribed to David. They reveal something of the personal touch—what that great leader was feeling during some of the more important times of his kingdom. They particularly show his need for God and why God calls him a "man after my own heart."

From Proverbs and Ecclesiastes

Solomon has the best start of any king in all the history of Israel. There is peace in the land. The borders have expanded almost to the full extent of God's promise. There is money and resources in the kingdom as well as a good military. Times are stable. Solomon builds the temple for God—a symbol of the centralized importance of religious worship in the capital. Solomon's early years are characterized by splendor. Most likely during the early and middle part of his reign many of the Proverbs were collected. These sayings embody truth that has been learned over the years (times of the Judges, times of the kingdom) about how to live harmoniously with others. Toward the end of his reign, he slips and falls away from following God. In this latter part of his reign, he writes Ecclesiastes which sums up much that he has learned over his lifetime. Its cynical tone shows need for an intimate relationship with God that is missing.

The nation is there. There are people. They know of God and his desires for them. There is a land. But they continually fail to live up to what God wants. During the reigns of David and Solomon the kingdom reaches its zenith. And thus ends Chapter 1, the making of a nation. In it all, God is seen to weave His purpose all around a people who frequently rebel against Him. They freely choose to live as they do, whether following after God or not. But even so He manages to move unswervingly forward to His purposes.

Chapter 2. The Destruction of a Nation

The story-line of chapter 2 hinges around the following major events:
1. Solomon goes away from the Lord, great warning—had the best start of any king yet did not finish well.
2. Rehoboam (1 Kings 12) makes unwise decision to increase taxes and demands on people—kingdom splits as prophecy said. 10 tribes go with the northern kingdom, Judah with the southern.
3. The northern kingdom under Jereboam quickly departs from God. Jereboam is used as the model of an evil king to whom all evil kings are likened; He had a good start also—God would have blessed him.
4. The southern kingdom generally is bad with an occasional good Kings and partially good kings: Asa, Jehoshaphat, Joash, Amaziah, Uzziah, Jotham, Hezekiah, Josiah. But the trend was always downward. The extended length of life of the southern kingdom, more than the northern kingdom, is directly attributed to the spiritual life of the better kings. Spiritual leadership does make a difference.
5. During both the northern and southern kingdoms God sent prophets to try and correct them—first the oral prophets (many—but the two most noted were Elijah and Elisha) and then the prophets who wrote.

Now in order to understand this long period of history you should know several things:
1. The History books that give background information about the times.

1. Biblical Framework—The Redemptive Drama

2. The Bible Time-Line, need to know when the books were written.
3. Need to know the writing prophets: northern or southern kingdom, which crisis, direct or special.

The History Books

The history books covering the time of the destruction of a nation include 1, 2 Samuel, 1,2 Kings, and 1,2 Chronicles. The following chart helps identify the focus of each of these books as to major content.

Chart Jnh 1-1 The History Books—Major Content

1 Samuel	2 Samuel 1 Chronicles	1,2 Kings 2 Chronicles
Samuel, Saul, David	David	1,2 Kings: Solomon to Zedekiah 2 Chronicles exclusively on line of Judah

There are four categories of prophetical books. Prophetical books deal with three major crises: the Assyrian crisis which wiped out the northern kingdom; the Bablonian crisis, which wiped out the southern kingdom; the return to the land after being exiled. There are also prophetical books not specifically dealing with these crises but associated with the time of them. The prophetical books dealing with these issues are:

A. Northern—Assyrian Crisis
   Jonah, Amos, Hosea, Nahum, Micah
B. Southern—Babylonian Crisis
   Joel, Isaiah, Micah, Zephaniah, Jeremiah, Lamentations, Habakkuk, Obadiah
C. In Exile
   Ezekiel, Daniel, Esther
D. Return From Exile
   Nehemiah, Ezra, Haggai, Zechariah, Malachi

In addition, to knowing the crises you must know that prophets wrote:

A. Direct to the Issue of the Crisis either Assyrian, Babylonian, or Return To The Land
   Amos, Hosea, Joel, Micah, Isaiah, Jeremiah, Ezekiel, Haggai, Zechariah, Malachi
B. Special
   Jonah, Nahum, Habakkuk, Obadiah, Zephaniah, Daniel.

The special prophets, though usually associated with one of the crisis times, wrote to deal with unique issues not necessarily related directly to the crisis. The following list gives the special prophets and their main thrust.

1. Jonah—a paradigm shift, pointing out God's desire for the nation to be missionary minded and reach out to surrounding nations.
2. Nahum—vindicate God, judgment on Assyria.
3. Habakkuk—faith crisis for Habakkuk, vindicate God, judgment on Babylon.
4. Obadiah—vindicate God, judgment on Edom for treatment of Judah.
5. Zephaniah—show about judgment, the Day of the Lord.

1. Biblical Framework—The Redemptive Drama   page 33

6. Daniel—give hope, show that God is indeed ruling even in the times of the exile and beyond, gives God's plan for the ages.

<u>The Destruction of A Nation—The Return From Exile</u> (see page 32)

Several Bible books are associated with the return to the land from the exile. After a period of about 70 years (during which time Daniel ministered) Cyrus made a decree which allowed some Jews (those that wanted to) to return to the land. Some went back under Zerrubabel, a political ruler like a governor. A priest, Joshua, also provided religious leadership to the first group that went back. This group of people started to rebuild the temple but became discouraged due to opposition and lack of resources. They stopped building the temple. Two prophets, after several years, 10-15, addressed the situation. These two, Haggai and Zechariah, were able to encourage the leadership and the people to finish the temple.

Another thirty or forty years goes by and then we have the events of the book of Esther, back in the land. Her book describes the attempt to eradicate the Jewish exiles—a plot which failed due to God's sovereign intervention via Esther, the queen of the land and a Jewish descendant going incognito, and her relative Mordecai.

Still another period of time passes, 20 or so years and a priest, Ezra, directs another group to return to the land. The spiritual situation has deteriorated. He brings renewal.

Another kind of leader arrives on the scene some 10-15 years later. Nehemiah, a lay leader, and one adept at organizing and moving to accomplish a task, rebuilds the wall around Jerusalem. He too has to instigate renewal.

Finally, after another period of 30 or so years we have the book of Malachi, which again speaks to renewal of the people. The Old Testament closes with this final book.

A recurring emphasis occurs during the period of the return. People are motivated to accomplish a task for God. They start out, become discouraged, and stop. They must be renewed. God raises up leadership to bring renewal.

<u>Preparation for the Coming of Messiah—The Inter-Testamental Period</u>

I do not deal with this in detail, that is, in terms of the various historical eras.[5] Some 400+ years elapse between the close of the Old Testament and the Beginning of the New Testament. There are significant differences in the Promised Land. The following chart highlights these differences.[6]

Chart Jnh 1-2 Differences in Palestine—Close of O.T., Beginning of N.T.

The End of the Old Testament	The Beginning of the New Testament
1. Palestine was part of a Persian satrapy, since Persian, an eastern nation was the greatest governmental power in the world at the time.	1. Palestine was a Roman province, since the entire world had come under the sway of the western Nation of Rome.
2. The population was sparse.	2. One of the most dense parts of the Roman empire.
3. The cities of Palestine as a whole were	3. There was general prosperity throughout

---

[5] In **Leadership Perspectives**, I do deal more in a detailed way with the various historical sub-phases of this period of history. A number of books in the Catholic canon occur during this period of time.
[6] These notes are adapted from material studied with Frank Sells at Columbia Bible College in his Old Testament survey course.

heaps of rubbish.	Palestine.
4. The temple of Zerubbabel was a significant structure.	4. The temple of Herod the Great was a magnificent building.
5. There were no Pharisees or Sadducees, although the tendencies from which they developed were present.	5. The Pharisees and Sadducees were much in evidence and strong in power.
6. There were no synagogues in Palestine.	6. Synagogues were located everywhere in the Holy Land. There was no hamlet or village so small or destitute as to lack a synagogue.
7. There was little extra-biblical tradition among the Jews.	7. There was a great mass of tradition, among both the Jews of Palestine and those of the dispersion.
8. The Jews were guilty of much intermarriage with the surrounding nations.	8. There was almost no intermarriage between Jews and non-Jews.
9. Palestine was under the rule of a Hebrew.	9. Palestine was under the rule of an Edomite vice-king, Herod the Great.
10. The Hebrew governor was regarded by the Jews as their spiritual leader.	10. The scribes and priest were regarded by the Jews as their spiritual leaders.

In addition to differences, there were some similarities between end of O.T. times and beginning of N.T. times.

1. **Freedom from idolatry**. God had used the Babylonian Captivity to free His people from their oft-repeated tendency to idolatry.
2. **Israel in two great divisions**, the Jews of the Homeland (Isolation) and the Jews of the Dispersion (who were scattered throughout the world). In the time of Malachi a relatively small proportion of God's chosen people was located in Palestine, while by far the larger part was still in exile. Although Palestine was much more thickly populated in the time of Christ than in the time of Malachi, the same general situation prevailed as to the two-fold division of Israel into Palestinian Jews and Jews of the Diaspora (Dispersion), with a far greater number in exile than in the land of Canaan.
3. **Externalism and dead orthodoxy**. A comparison of Malachi (the last prophetical book of the Old Testament) and Nehemiah (the last historical book of the Old Testament) with the Gospels indicates that the outward conformity of the Pharisees to the law which they inwardly revolted from, was but an advanced step of the hypocritical conformity which had marked many Israelites at the end of Old Testament days.

It was during the inter-testamental period that these changes occurred. Daniel had foretold of the various empires that would emerge after Babylon: the Medo-Persian, the Grecian, and the Roman. Each of these were used by God to prepare the way for the coming of Messiah, the next chapter in the redemptive drama.

Galatians 4:4 states that Messiah came at the "fullness of time." That is, the time was ready. Some have suggested a fivefold preparation for Christ's Coming.

1. Religious Preparation—both negative and positive
2. Political Preparation—world at peace

1. Biblical Framework—The Redemptive Drama   page 35

   3. Cultural Preparation—lack of meaning; cultural vehicle through which to spread the Gospel
   4. The Social Preparation—great needs; life under bondage
   5. The Moral Preparation

Chapter 3. Messiah

At the right moment in time—Jesus was born. His miraculous birth attested to his uniqueness.

He was the fulfillment of the Old Testament as to many of its prophecies, types, symbols. He was the seed of the woman who dealt a fatal blow to the seed of the serpent (Genesis 3:15); he was the tabernacle who lived among us (Exodus 25-40); he was the arch type of the brazen serpent, lifted up that people might look, see and be healed (Numbers 21); he was the arch types of the Levitical offerings, the perfect sacrifice (Leviticus 1-5); he was that prophet like unto Moses (Deuteronomy 18); he was the ultimate fulfillment of the Davidic covenant (2 Samuel 7); he was the Messianic Sufferer (Psalm 22); he was the one who was anointed to preach good news to the poor, to proclaim freedom for the captives, and release from darkness those who are prisoners, to proclaim the year of the Lord's favor (Isaiah 61:1ff) and the Suffering Servant (Isaiah 53); he was the righteous branch from David's line (Jeremiah 23); he was the one shepherd, the servant David, the prince of Ezekiel (Ezekiel 37); he was the one greater than Jonah, the sign after three days he arose (Jonah 21); he was the proper leader coming out of obscure Bethlehem (Micah 5:2); and we could go on.

Matthew showed he was the Messiah King, rejected. Mark showed him to be vested with divine power, a person of action and authority. Luke showed him to be the perfect representative of the human race: one of courage, ability, social interests, sympathy, broad acceptance. And John showed him to be Immanuel, God with us, revealing God to us and acting to demonstrate grace and truth, the heartbeat of the divine ministry philosophy.

The bottom line of the story line is given in a quote taken from John, "He was in the world, and though the world was made through him, the world did not recognize him. He came unto his own, but his own did not receive him. Yet to all who received him, to those who believed in his name, he gave the right to become children of God, children born not of natural descent, nor of human source but born of God. The Word became flesh and made his dwelling among us. We have seen his glory, the glory of the One and Only, who came from the Father, full of grace and truth." (John 1:10-14).

The story of this chapter of the redemptive drama ends abruptly. But there is a postscript. Each of the Gospel stories and the Acts tell us of Jesus Christ's resurrection. After His death He arose and was seen for a period of about 40 days upon various occasions. During those days He gave the marching orders for the movement He had begun. The great commissions repeated five times, Matthew 28:19,20, Luke 24:46,47, Mark 16:15, John 20:21, and Acts 1:8. Each of these carry the main thrust which is to go into the world and tell the Good News of salvation, that people can be reconciled to God. Each also carries some special connotation. It is these marching orders, which set the stage for Chapter 4, The Church, in the redemptive story.

Chapter 4. The Church

The essence of the story line of chapter 4, is contained in the book of Acts. Its central thematic message is the essence of the story line.

1. Biblical Framework—The Redemptive Drama

Theme: **The Growth Of The Church**
- which spreads from Jerusalem to Judea to Samaria and the uttermost parts of the earth,
- is seen to be of God,
- takes place as Spirit directed people present a salvation centered in Jesus Christ, and
- occurs among all peoples, Jews and Gentiles.

This basic phenomenon reoccurs as the Gospel spreads across cultural barriers throughout the world. Though the message of the book of Acts covers only up through the first two thirds of the first century its basic essence reoccurs throughout the church age until the present time in which we live.

About half of the book of Acts tells of the formation of the church in Jerusalem and its early expansion to Jews, Samaritans, and finally to Gentiles. The latter half of the book traces the breakout of the Gospel to Gentiles in Asia and Europe. The structure of the book highlighted by the linguistic discourse markers (the Word of the Lord grew) carries the notion of a God-given church expanding.

Structure: There are seven divisions in Acts each concluding with a summary verse. The summary verses: 2:47b, 6:7, 9:31, 12:24, 16:5, 19:20, 28:30,31

I.	(ch 1-2:47)	The Birth of the Church in Jerusalem
II.	(ch 3-6:7)	The Infancy of the Church in Jerusalem
III.	(ch 6:8-9:31)	The Spread of the Church into Judea, Galilee, Samaria
IV.	(ch 9:32-12:24)	The Church Doors Open to the Gentiles
V.	(ch 13-16:5)	The Church Spreads to Asia Minor
VI.	(ch 16:6-19:20)	The Church Gains a Foothold in Europe
VII.	(ch 19:21-28)	The Travels of the Church's First Missionary To Rome (The Church on Trial in its Representative Paul)

As to details there are many important pivotal events in the Acts, many of which have similarly reoccurred in the expansion of the Gospel around the world and throughout church history. Acts begins with Jesus' post resurrection ministry to the disciples and his Ascension to heaven. Then the disciples are gathered at Jerusalem praying when the Pentecost event, the giving of the Holy Spirit to the church, as promised in Luke's version of the Great Commission, happens and Peter gives a great public sermon which launches the church.

Early church life is described. Peter and John imbued with power heal a lame man at the temple gate and are put in prison. They are threatened and released. An incident with Ananias and Sapphira shows the power and presence of the Holy Spirit.

Stephen an early church servant has a strong witness and is martyred for it. General persecution on the church breaks out. The believers are scattered and preach the gospel where ever they go. Phillip, another early church servant leads an Ethiopian palace administrator to Christ and has ministry in Samaria.

Saul, the persecutor of Christians, is saved on the road to Damascus. Peter demonstrates Godly power in several miraculous events. Peter is divinely chosen to preach the Gospel to a Gentile, Cornelius. Herod kills James and imprisons Peter. Peter is miraculously delivered.

1. Biblical Framework—The Redemptive Drama

The story line now switches to follow the missionary efforts of Barnabas and Paul (formerly Saul) to Cyprus and Asian minor. It then goes on to follow Paul's efforts which go further into Asia minor and Greece. Paul makes a return visit to Jerusalem where he is accused by the Jewish opposition in Jerusalem. Eventually after several delays and hearings he is ordered to Rome. The book ends with the exciting journey to Rome, including a shipwreck.

The books of the New Testament were written to various groups during the church chapter. Many were written by Paul. These generally were letters to the various churches which had resulted from his missionary efforts. Each was contextually specific—written at a certain time, written at a certain stage of Paul's own development as a leader, and dealing with a specific situation—either an individual in a church or to a corporate group, some church at a location or in a general region.

Other New Testament books were not written by Paul. The book of Hebrews, author uncertain, John's three letters, Jude's one letter and Peter's two letters all are of a general nature. With the exception of possibly 2nd and 3rd John, these letters were written to believer's in general in scattered regions—probably Asia minor.

All of these, Paul's letters, and the general books, deal with the church. They give us insights into church problems, church situations at that time, and the essence of what the church is and how Christians ought to live. These New Testament books are filled with leadership information. Each of them represents a major leadership act of a leader seeking to influence followers of Christ. Many of them have actual details that reflect leadership values, leadership problem solving, and leadership issues. All of them have important modeling data.

We would have an unfinished story if we were left only with *just these* New Testament books. We would have a task. And men and women would be out and about the world attempting to fulfill that task. But where is it leading. What about those Old Testament prophecies yet to be fulfilled about *that day*. Our story is incomplete. We need to know how this redemptive drama is going to end. And so the Revelation.

Chapter 5. The Kingdom

The final book of the Bible is aptly named. The Revelation (unveiling, revealing, making clear) of Jesus Christ (the unveiling of Jesus Christ) brings closure to the redemptive drama. This final book in the Bible has among others these purposes:

1. to reveal future purposes of Jesus Christ and graphically show the power He will unleash in accomplishing His purposes, which include bringing about justice and bringing in His reign,
2. to show those purposes and power to be in harmony with His divine attributes, and
3. to bring a fitting climax to the redemptive story developed throughout Scripture.

The theme statement of the book of Revelation highlights the fitting climax of the redemptive drama.

1. Biblical Framework — The Redemptive Drama

Theme: **God's Ultimate Purposes For His Redemptive Program**
- center in the Person of His Son,
- involve His churches,
- will take place in a context of persecution and struggle — as described cryptically by many visions,
- will focus on the triumph of Jesus and his judgment of all things in harmony with his divine attributes, and
- will be realized in final victory for His people and ultimate justice accomplished in the world.

God's intent from the first of Genesis on has been to bless His people with His eternal presence. Ezekiel closes his book with that thought in mind. Numerous of the prophets point to a future day in which things would be made right and God would dwell with His people. The plan has had many twists and turns but through it all God has sovereignly moved on to His purpose.

Some have followed hard after God and were included in His purposes. Others refused to follow God. They were cast aside. God moved on.

In the New Testament God prepares a way where He can reveal Himself in justice and love and reconcile all people unto Himself. The Cross climaxes all of God's preparation to bless the world. The message of the Cross is seen to be for all. The church goes out into all the world. It has its problems. But always it seeks to be part of God's future purposes looking forward to Christ's return. Were there no Revelation, the Redemptive Story would be incomplete. The Revelation brings to a fitting climax all of God's working to bless the world. There is an ultimate purpose in history! Justice is meted out! And then a final blessing — God's eternal presence of with His people.

Suggested Chronological Writing of New Testament Books

When we study a given book of the bible we should know where it occurs in the redemptive drama. We should be familiar with what God has revealed to that point in time and what God has done redemptively up to that time. Table Jnh 1-1 below list each book of the Bible in terms of the Chapter in the redemptive story in which it falls. I have attempted to list each book in chronological order though there is not scholarly consensus on when some of these books were written.

Table Jnh 1- 1. Bible Books Related To Chapters of the Redemptive Drama

The Bible Books: Chapter 1. The Making of a Nation

Exodus	Joshua	2 Samuel	Ecclesiastes
Leviticus	Judges	1 Chronicles	Song of Songs
Numbers	Ruth	Psalms	
Deuteronomy	1 Samuel	Proverbs	

The Bible Books: Chapter 2. The Destruction of a Nation

1,2 Kings	Hosea	Zephaniah	Daniel	Nehemiah
2 Chronicles	Micah	Jeremiah	Haggai	Malachi
Jonah	Isaiah	Lamentations	Zechariah	
Joel	Nahum	Obadiah	Esther	
Amos	Habakkuk	Ezekiel	Ezra	

The Bible Books: Chapter 3. Messiah

Matthew	Mark	Luke	John

1. Biblical Framework—The Redemptive Drama   page 39

The Bible Books: Chapter 4. The Church

James	2 Corinthians	Colossians	Titus	2 John
Acts	Galatians	Philemon	2 Timothy	3 John
1 Thessalonians	Romans	1 Peter	Hebrews	
2 Thessalonians	Ephesians	2 Peter	Jude	
1 Corinthians	Philippians	1 Timothy	1 John	

The Bible Book   Chapter 5. Kingdom
Revelation

Article 2

2. Bible Translations And Hebrew Poetic Format

Introduction

In another article[7] I have mentioned that more than 1/3 of the Old Testament is in *Hebrew Poetic* format. Some Bibles, particularly some of the later versions, have recognized the importance of showing the *Hebrew Poetry* as poetry. They have attempted to display phrases, couplets, and stanzas of Hebrew Poetry so that the English reader is made aware of it.

Comparison of Bibles and Indications of Hebrew Poetry Format

In the study of Hebrew Poetry, the first step is to recognize it. Then one must identify and label lines. And finally there is the analysis of relationships between lines. A good start on this procedure is to get a Bible, which already has identified Hebrew Poetry and printed it so you can recognize it.[8] Table Jnh 2-1 lists a number of Bibles and comparatively displays how (or how not) they picture **Hebrew Poetry**.

Table Jnh 2-1. Bibles and Poetic Format

None	Some	All
KJV	ASV (Job, Psa, Prov, SOS, Lam, few others)	RSV
LB	NBV (Psa, SOS, Lam, Joel, few others)	NRSV
AB	PB (Job, Psa, Prov, Ecc, Isa, Jer, Lam, Eze, some Dan, Hos, Joel, Amos, Obad, Mic, Nah, Hab, Zeph, Hag, Zech, Mal)	NEB
	GNB (almost all passages, just a few scattered minor passages; Proverbs is not poetic format)	TLB[9]

---

[7] See **Article**, *14. Jonah, Hebrew Poetry* included in this commentary.

[8] Sometimes even though the Bible prints in poetic format, you will find yourself disagreeing with the identification of lines. The poetic formats of the different Bible versions do not necessarily agree with each other. Nor will you.

[9] **The Learning Bible—Contemporary English Version**, prints all Hebrew Poetry in poetic format. However, be warned it will also do reduction statements of couplets, so that frequently you don't have all the lines of the stanza. Instead you have the meaning of the couplet(s) given in a reduction statement.

2. Bible Translations And Hebrew Poetic Format

Key To Abbreviations Used in Table Hab 3-1

KJV = King James Version
LB = Living Bible
AB = Amplified Bible
ASV = American Standard Version
NBV = New Berkley Version
PB = Paragraph Bible
GNB = Good New Bible (Today's English Version)
RSV = Revised Standard Version
NRSV = New Revised Standard Version
NEB = New English Bible
TLB = The Learning Bible (Contemporary English Version)

There are perhaps other versions, which also print in poetic format. These given represent the Bibles, which I regularly use in my own personal study of Hebrew Poetry.

Some Help In Noting Parallelism in Printed Poetic format

Most Bibles use some basic scheme to standardize their printing format. Some capitalize the first word of a phrase. Some capitalize only the first word of the phrase of an extended unit. Some indent to indicate the second line of a couplet. Some give spaces between stanzas. It is helpful to recognize some of these methods. The following table relates what I have found concerning printed formats. The RSV and NRSV has been the most helpful in this regard. Unfortunately none of these Bibles actually gives a key to their own printing of Hebrew Poetry format.

Table Jnh 2-2. Some Help In Noting Parallelism In Printed Poetic Format

Bible	Phrases	Couplets	Extended Parallelism	Stanzas
RSV (NRSV)	Begins a new phrase of couplet at left margin. 2nd phrase of couplet is indented. Any related phrase beyond couplet is also indented. Continuations of a phrase are indented more than a new phrase	First phrase always begins at far left. 2nd phrase is indented about 3 spaces.	1st word of phrase of a series of related parallel phrases is capitalized. Each succeeding phrase is lower case and indented 3 spaces. These sub-units almost always yield a major idea for the entire unit.	Spaces (also in prophets, it gives some titles summarizing the unit)
GNB	Like RSV	Like RSV	Like RSV	Like RSV
ASV	Starts each phrase with a capital letter at left margin	Usually terminates with a period or its equivalent	None	None
PB	Like ASV	Like ASV	Not clear	Spaces or indents

Table Jnh 2-2 continued

NEB	Each line is a phrase	Simple couplets done like ASV	Not clear; do some indenting	Spaces
NBV	Like RSV except 2nd line not indented	1st phrase of couplet is capitalized	Like RSV except succeeding lines not indented	Spaces and indents 1st line of stanza
TLB	Like RSV	Like RSV; 1st word of 2nd phrase of couplet is also capitalized	Not clear.	Spaces between stanzas; also some topic headings at beginning of stanza

Conclusion

From a comparative study of Bibles, which print in Hebrew Poetry format, you will see that identification of lines and phrases is not an exact thing. You will frequently have to modify that given in one of these Bibles to show what you are seeing in lines and relationships between the lines.

Here is how I have identified the poetic section of Jonah.

Chapter 2[10]
 1 Then Jonah prayed to the LORD his God from the fish's belly.

2 And he said:
"I cried out to the LORD because I was in trouble,
And He answered me.
"Out of the belly of Sheol I cried,
And You heard my voice.

 3 For You threw me into the deep, Into the heart of the seas,
And the waves churned all around me;
All Your sea billows and Your waves passed over me.
4 Then I said,
`I have been cast out of Your sight;
Yet I will look again toward Your holy temple.'
 5 The waters surrounded me, [even] to my soul;
The deep closed around me;
Sea weeds were wrapped around my head.

 6 I went down to the base of the underwater sea mountains;
I thought I was imprisoned there forever;

---

[10] Chapter 2 verses 1-9 are in Hebrew Poetry. This is a reflective and transparent recollection of a critical time in the shaping of a prophet. It is significant that this portion of Jonah is in Hebrew Poetic format. Poetry is the language of the heart. Jonah was deeply affected, emotionally, by his crisis situation. See **Article,** *14. Jonah, Hebrew Poetry.*

2. Bible Translations And Hebrew Poetic Format

Yet You have rescued me from that pit, O LORD, my God.
7 "When my life was slipping away, I remembered the LORD;
And my prayer reached You, in Your holy temple.
8 "Those who worship worthless idols miss your mercy.
9 But I will sacrifice to You
With the voice of thanksgiving;
I will pay what I have vowed.
Salvation comes from the LORD."

10 So the LORD spoke to the fish, and it vomited Jonah onto dry land.

Article 3

3. Biographical Study in the Bible, How To Do

Introduction

Biographical data represents the single most important leadership source in the Scriptures. There is much biographical information.

Definition   <u>Biographical</u> data refers to that large amount of information in the Scriptures which is made up of small narrative slices of life about a person.

These narrative slices or vignettes give information about Bible characters, which allows us to perceive processing, pivotal points, leadership acts or other such interpretations from this source material. The more slices there are the more we can build to a more complete biography.

Sometimes God allows us a glimpse into the inner life of His servants as he develops them. Some books in the Bible are given dominantly just for that purpose. Some do that but have another more important or at least as important other message.

Three such glimpses into God's shaping processes with leaders include Job, Habakkuk, and Jonah. In fact, the major reason for inclusion of these books in the Scriptures is to give us God's ways of working with leaders. Consider the main leadership insights from these three.

1. Job	Isolation processing—most comprehensive treatment of it in the Scriptures; theological delving into the nature of suffering. A paradigm shift concerning the nature of suffering.
2. Habakkuk	Doubting the nature and activities of God. A faith challenge. A paradigm shift about God and his activities.
3. Jonah	Major paradigm shift—how God views others; obedience.

These three books illustrate one of the four types of biographical information in the Scriptures—the critical incident type.

Four Types of Biographical Information

There are four major categories. There is some overlap in these at the borders between them. Table Jnh 2-1 describes these four sources.

3. Biographical Study in the Bible, How To Do

Table Jnh 3-1. Four Types of Biographical Sources

Type	Explanation
1. **Critical Incident Source.**	A single incident or series of incidents taking place in a very short time. There may actually be a large amount of information but all focused on a short time-interval. The information can be interpreted for processing or for a leadership act or other such findings. *example: Job, Habakkuk, Jonah*
2. **Mini-Sources.**	Multiple incidents over a period of time which allows the creation of an abbreviated time-line and the possibility to see some patterns over time. *example: Asa, Jehoshaphat, Hezekiah*
3. **Midi-Sources.**	Multiple incidents over the whole lifetime, which allow not only the creation of an abbreviated time-line but some processing from the various time periods. *example: Barnabas, Joseph, Daniel, Joshua, Peter, Jeremiah*
4. **Maxi-Sources.**	There is much information in the Scripture on the character. *example: Moses, David, Jesus, Paul, Jeremiah*

Biblical Leaders To Study

I list here those Biblical leaders who should be studied because they will give information essential or very helpful for leadership. Some of these lessons will be positive encouragement. Some will present warnings. There are four groupings that should be studied. I have not listed all that I could. You may want to add to these different lists.

Jnh List 3-1 All Who Finished Well (Mini, Midi, Maxi Types)

1. Abraham
2. Joseph
3. Moses
4. Joshua
5. Caleb
6. Samuel
7. Elijah
8. Elisha
9. Daniel
10. Jeremiah
11. Jesus
12. Paul
13. Peter
14. John
15. Jacob
16. Isaac

By finished well I mean that at the end of their lifetime they:
1. were enjoying intimacy with God,
2. were still growing, had a learning posture,
3. left behind a legacy—achieved things for God that contributed to his on-going redemptive plan,
4. realized potential, achieved their destiny: a. fully; b. limited; c. somewhat,
5. had Godly character,
6. had lived out convictions about God's truth and promises and demonstrate them to be real.

Jnh List 3-2. Some—Not Sure About Their Finish (Mini, Midi, Maxi Types)
1. Nehemiah
2. Jephthah

Jnh List 3-3. Some Who Did Not Finish Well (Mini, Midi, Maxi Types)
1. Gideon
2. Saul
3. David
4. Solomon
5. Uzziah
6. Hezekiah
7. Asa
8. Jehoshaphat
9. Josiah
11. Samson
12. Others—you add them on:

3. Biographical Study in the Bible, How To Do

Jnh List 3-4. Critical Incident Types
1. Job
2. Habakkuk
3. Jonah
4. Ezra
5. Esther
6. Abigail
7. Mordecai
8. Isaiah
9. Ezekiel
10. Hosea
11. Deborah
12. Barak
13. Timothy
14. Titus

The basic approach to the study of Biblical leaders includes 12 steps. But depending on which type you are studying you may or may not be able to use all the steps. Such is the case especially with the first three types of biographies. The commentaries on Habakkuk and Jonah illustrate the benefit of studying critical incidents.

12 Steps For Studying Bible Leaders
The following outline gives a basic approach to biographical study in the Bible. Not all 12 steps can be done with each leader but they provide the ideal framework that should be attempted. Do as many of the 12 steps as you can, depending on the material available for a leader.

<u>Step 1</u>. **Identify All The Passages That Refer To The Leader.**
   a. Use an exhaustive concordance to help you identify all such passages.
   b. There are two kinds of passages:
     (1) *Direct,* which refers to actual historical vignettes—a short literary sketch of a given slice of life, which gives raw data about the person and his/her actions. This is data that can be interpreted for leadership findings.
     (2) *Indirect*, not actual vignettes but references to the leader or accomplishments usually in retrospect such as summary passages, intentional selection which groups several important names, etc.
   c. For the *Direct*—actual historical vignettes—Number and label each vignette separately for reference.
   d. For the *Indirect*—note the commentary on the leader. What was said? Why important? Why remembered? Why selected? Ultimate contribution? Some trait or characteristic?
   e. Books written by the leader or prophecies made by the leader.

<u>Step 2</u>. **Seek To Order The Vignettes Or Other Passages In A Time Sequence.**
   a. Bible dictionaries or encyclopedias usually have articles on most Bible characters. These articles usually help in establishing time of events in the life. Actual vignettes as given in the Bible may be out of chronological order (e.g. Jeremiah).
   b. Remember the time period in the progress of redemption in which the leader is acting. Put the leadership in the broader time framework.
   c. Remember the leadership era in which the leader is acting. Remember what is expected of a leader in that era. Remember the kind of leader he or she is and the basic thrust of leadership for that kind of leader at that time.
   d. Note how the leader fits those stereotypes or doesn't.
   e. Notice if the leader is breaking new ground.

<u>Step 3</u>. **Construct A Time-Line If You Can. At Least Tentatively Identify Major Development Phases.**
   a. See **Article**, *Time Line Defined for Biblical Leaders*. See also examples of time-lines. See Joseph, Barnabas, and Joshua for examples.
   b. Sometimes not enough information is given to fill out the time-line completely. You can tentatively construct to fill in gaps as long as you know it is only suggestive.

3. Biographical Study in the Bible, How To Do

    c. Be especially alert to how the leader finished.
    d. Check for the six major barriers to finishing well: sex, family, money, pride, power, plateauing and locate along the time-line.
    e. Check for any of the five major enhancements to finishing well: life time perspective, renewal experiences, guarding of the inner life with God—spiritual disciplines, mentoring, learning posture. Locate along the time-line.
    f. See if the person's life illustrates or sheds light on any of the seven major leadership lessons: lifetime perspective, power base, ministry philosophy, learning posture, leadership emergence, relational empowerment, sense of destiny.

Step 4. Look For Process Items (Critical Events, People, Happenings) In The Life.
    a. **The Making of A Leader** by Clinton or **Leadership Emergence Theory** defines process items in-depth, that is, shaping activities used by God. Usually a critical incident can be viewed through several process item grids. *See process item definitions*, **Glossary**.
    b. But even if you do not know the names of processes you can analyze what happened in some critical situation.

Step 5. Identify Pivotal Points From The Major Process Items.
    a. Seek to identify the kind of pivotal point it is. See *pivotal point*, **Glossary**.
    b. Seek to determine what might have happened or the after effects of the pivotal point. Various kinds of lessons can be learned from this analysis.
    c. How can knowing about this pivotal point be of aid to other leaders or emerging leaders?

Step 6. Seek To Determine Any Lessons You Can From A Study Of These Process Items And Pivotal Points. Use The Certainty Continuum To Help You Identify The Level Of Authority For Using The Lessons You Find. See **Article**, *Principles of Truth*.
    a. Seek to identify specific lessons first (use wording of the specific situation, time, place, and person concerned).
    b. Seek to abstract the specific lessons into wording that could apply more broadly.
    c. Assess the level of authority for application of the lesson. See **Article**, *Principles of Truth*.

Step 7. Identify Any Response Patterns (or unique patterns).
    a. The **Leadership Emergence Theory** Manual identifies 23 patterns. The *Destiny Pattern* is especially helpful. Use the patterns to help you see ideas and lessons in the leader's life. See *patterns; destiny processing; destiny patterns, Four Types*; **Glossary**. See **Article**, *Destiny Pattern*.
    b. Look for unique patterns that only fit the leader's life.

Step 8. Study Any Individual Leadership Acts In The Life. Use The Approach Demonstrated In This Chapter. See *leadership act*, **Glossary**.
    a. Identify leadership style(s).
    b. Identify the situation—look for any dynamics, micro or macro that shed light on the situation.
    c. Study the followership. See **Article**, *Followership—10 Commandments*.

3. Biographical Study in the Bible, How To Do

<u>Step 9</u>. **Use The Overall Leadership Tree Diagram To Help Suggest Leadership Issues To Look For.** See **Article**, *Leadership Tree Diagram*.
   a. Use the basal elements to suggest things to look for.
   b. Use the influence means (individual) to help you suggest things to look for, i.e. look at the leader in terms of leadership style theory.
   c. Use the influence means (spiritual power) to help you suggest things to look for.
   d. Use the influence means (corporate) to analyze the power situations wrapped up in institutions, or tradition, or cultural family patterns.
   e. Use the value bases to help you identify values—philosophical or cultural or theological that are worth noting.

<u>Step 10</u>. **Use The List Of Major Functions (Task Functions, Relationship Functions And Inspirational Functions) To Help Suggest Insights. Which Were Done, Which Not.** See **Article**, *Leadership Functions*.
   a. Were there relational functions in view?
   b. Were there task functions in view?
   c. Were there inspirational functions in view? Usually you will always have something on this function.

<u>Step 11</u>. **Observe Any N.T. Passages Or Commentary** (indirect source—anywhere in Bible) **On The Leader. Especially Be On The Lookout For** *Bent Of Life* **Evaluation.**
   a. For example, Ezekiel refers to Daniel three times. This is actually a contemporary evaluation of Daniel. See Eze 14:14,20; 28:3. Three names are listed in the first two: Noah, Daniel, and Job. These are intentionally selected—the focus is righteousness. The third commends Daniel's wisdom. This is bent-of-life testimony. This is what stands out as an important thing to be remembered about the character. These kinds of hints can then lead you back to the direct data for focused study. That is, now go back and study these three characters for ideas on righteousness. Study Daniel for ideas about wisdom in a leader.
   b. The N.T. references are usually bent of life types. See Ro 4:20,21 about Abraham and his faith. See Ac 7 for Stephen's comments. All of these indirect type of references give us focuses with which to go back and search the direct data.

<u>Step 12</u>. **Use The Presentation Format For Organizing Your Display Of Findings For Steps 1-11.**
   a. The presentation format is a technical layout for presenting the highlights of your data. The order of presentation is logically arranged.
   b. This standardized approach to presenting findings is used by me and by all that I teach in workshops, seminars, and classes. It makes for ease of referencing material.
   c. For popular consumption (articles, booklets, books, public preaching, etc.) you would not use this technical format but take out of it that which you want to use.

Presentation Format—Findings On Bible Leaders

The following is a logical order of presenting data. It is standardized for reference purposes. When doing an actual study, the information available on the character and the nature of the findings will actually determine which of these categories are actually filled. Attempt to do them all.

3. Biographical Study in the Bible, How To Do

1. *Biblical Name(s)* — Primary: Other:

2. *Biblical Data*:
   Here list the direct contextual material on the leader studied, the indirect references to the leader, and note especially any summary passages on the leader (if an O.T. leader look especially for N.T. references or assessment on that leadership).

3. *Abbreviated Time-Line*:
   Construct a time-line with development phases—as much as possible from the data given. Recognize that the time-line is incomplete (if more data were given—more phases or sub-phases probably could be distinguished).

4. *Giftedness Indications*:
   If O.T., then list areas of natural abilities, acquired skills or special anointings seen in the leader's life. If N.T., attempt to identify gift-mix or gift-cluster.

5. *Sphere of Influence*:
   Here give the followership being influenced. If possible note direct, indirect or organizational categories.

6. *Major Contributions*
   Assess the leader's achievements in God's on-going redemptive program in the Bible.

7. *Biblical Context*
   Here use the overview of Biblical Leadership Time-line. You want to place this leader, contextually, in terms of kind of leadership expected during that time period.

8. *Capsule*
   Give a narrative overview of the leader's life in paragraph format based on a linear time organization of Bible vignettes or data. This narration should follow the time-line and give information that allows one to put the major findings in context.

9. *Major Lessons*
   A. Pivotal Points
   B. Major Processing
   C. Barriers to finishing Well
   D. Here include lessons learned from leadership acts —Give actual analysis in an Appendix attached to the presentation.
   E. General/ Other
   F. Major Lessons Stated

10. *Ultimate Contribution Set*
    Here use the categories from the ultimate contribution explanation to assess the long term achievement of this leader. See *ultimate contribution set*, **Glossary**. See **Article**, *Leaving Behind a Legacy*.

11. *Appendices*:
    Here you would include any leadership acts analyzed or any other pertinent information such as family tree diagrams, etc.

Conclusion

You will not have enough time in your lifetime to learn all you can about leadership through your direct experience or even observation of it around you. You will need to learn vicariously, that is, study and learn from the lives of others. The Bible is probably one of the richest sources for leadership study. And biographical information is the largest single leadership genre. Make the most of it.

Article 4

4. Figures and Idioms In The Bible

Introduction to Figures

All language is governed by law—that is, it has normal patterns that are followed. But in order to increase the power of a word or the force of expression, these patterns are deliberately departed from, and words and sentences are thrown into and used in unusual forms or patterns which we call figures. A figure then is a use of language in a special way for the purpose of giving additional force, more life, intensified feeling and greater emphasis. A figure of speech is the author's way of underlining. He/She is saying, "Hey, take note! This is important enough for me to use a special form of language to emphasize it!" And when we remember the fact that the Holy Spirit has inspired this product we have—the Bible—we are not far wrong in saying figures are the Holy Spirit's own underlining in our Bibles. We certainly need to be sensitive to figurative language.

Definition   A <u>figure</u> is the unusual use of a word or words differing from the normal use in order to draw special attention to some point of interest.

For a figure, the unusual use itself follows a set pattern. The pattern can be identified and used to interpret the figure in normal language. Here are some examples from the Bible. I will make you fishers of people. Go tell that fox. Quench not the Holy Spirit. I came not to send peace but a sword. As students of the Bible we need to be sensitive to figures and know how to interpret and catch their emphatic meaning.

Definition   A figure or idiom is said to be <u>captured</u> when one can display the intended emphatic meaning in non-figurative simple words.

One of the most familiar figures in the Bible is Psalm 23:1. The Lord is my shepherd. I shall not lack. *Captured*: God personally provides for my every need.

E.W. Bullinger, an expert on figurative language, lists over 400 different kinds of figures. he lists over 8000 references in the Bible containing figures. In Romans alone, Bullinger lists 253 passages containing figurative language. However, we do not need to know all of those figures for the most commonly occurring figures number much less than 400. Figure Jnh 3-1, below, lists the 11 most common figures occurring in the Bible. If we know them we are well on our way to becoming better interpreters of the Scripture. In fact, you can group these 11 figures under three main sub-categories, which simplifies learning about them.

4. Figures and Idioms In The Bible

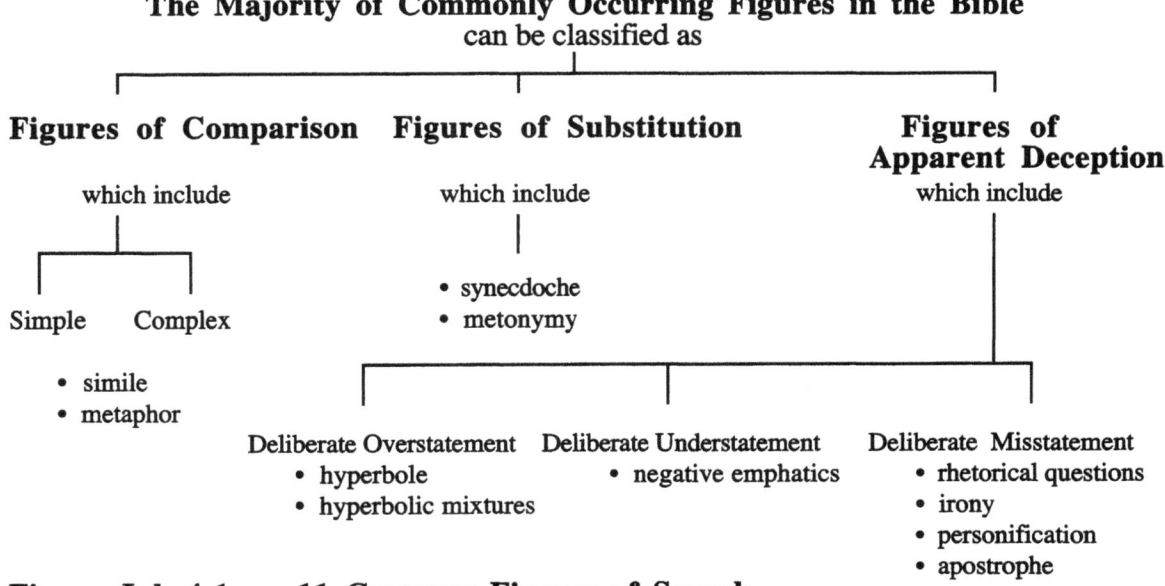

Figure Jnh 4-1.   11 Common Figures of Speech

Table Jnh 3-1 below gives these 11 figures of speech, a Scriptural reference containing the figure, and the basic definition of each of these figures.

Table Jnh 4-1. 11 Figures in the Bible Defined

Category/ Figure	Scriptural Example	Definition
Figures of Comparison: 1. Simile 2. Metaphor	simile—Isa 53:6 metaphor—Ps 23:1	A <u>simile</u> is a stated comparison of two unlike items (one called the real item and the other the picture item) in order to display one graphic point of comparison. A <u>metaphor</u> is an implied comparison in which two unlike items (a real item and a picture item) are equated to point out one point of resemblance.
Figures of Substitution 3. Metonymy 4. Synecdoche	metonymy—Ac 15:21 Moses for what he wrote synecdoche—Mt 8:8 roof for the whole house.	A <u>metonymy</u> is a figure of speech in which (usually) one word is substituted for another word to which it is closely related in order to emphasize something indicated by the relationship. A <u>synecdoche</u> is a special case of metonymy in which (again usually) one word is substituted for another to which it is related as, a part to a whole or a whole to a part.
Figures of Apparent Deception— Deliberate Overstatement: 5. Hyperbole 6. Hyperbolic mixtures	hyperbole—1 Co 4:14-16 ten thousand instructors hyperbolic mixture—2 Sa 1:23 swifter	A <u>hyperbole</u> is the use of conscious exaggeration (an overstatement of truth) in order to emphasize or strikingly excite interest in the truth. Hyperbole is sometimes combined with other figures such as comparison and substitution. When such is the case it is called a <u>hyperbolic mixture</u> figure.

4. Figures and Idioms In The Bible

	than eagles, stronger than lions	
Figures of Apparent Deception— Deliberate understatement: 7. Negative emphatics	negative emphatics—Mk 12:34 not far = very near	A figure of <u>negative emphasis</u> represents the deliberate use of words to diminish a concept and thus call attention to it or the negating of a concept to call attention to the opposite positive concept (I have deliberately merged two figures, litotes and tapenosis into one because of the basic sameness of negative emphasis).
Figures of Apparent Deception— Deliberate Misstatement: 8. Rhetorical questions 9. Irony 10. Personification 11. Apostrophe	rhetorical question—1Ti 3:5 irony—2Co 12:13 personification —Heb 4:12 apostrophe—1 Co 15:55	A <u>rhetorical question</u> is a figure of speech in which a question is not used to obtain information but is used to indirectly communicate, (1) an affirmative or negative statement, or (2) the importance of some thought by focusing attention on it, or (3) one's own feeling or attitudes about something. <u>Irony</u> is the use of words by a speaker in which his/her intended meaning is the opposite of (or in disharmony with) the literal use of the words. <u>Personification</u> is the use of words to speak of animals, ideas, abstractions, and inanimate objects as if they had human form, character, or intelligence in order to vividly portray truth. <u>Apostrophe</u> is a special case of personification in which the speaker addresses the thing personified as if it were alive and listening.

I have developed in-depth explanations for all of the above figures. I have developed study sheets to aid one in analysis of them. Further I have actually identified many of these in the Scriptures and captured a number of them.[11]

Introduction to Idioms

Idioms are much more complicated that figures of speech.

Definition   An <u>idiom</u> is a group of words, which have a corporate meaning that can not be deduced from a compilation of the meanings of the individual words making up the idiom.

What makes idioms difficult is that some of them follow patterns while others do not. For the patterned idioms, like figures, you basically reverse the pattern and capture the idiom. Table Jnh 3- 2 lists the patterned idioms I have identified in the Bible.

Table Jnh 4-2.   13 Patterned Idioms

Idiom	Example	Definitive principle/ Description
Three Certainty Idioms: 1. Double certainty (pos/neg) 2. Fulfilled (promised/proposed)	double certainty— 1Ki 18:36 fulfilled— Ge 15:18 prophetic past—Jn	<u>double certainty</u>—a negative and positive statement (in either order) are often used to express or imply certainty. <u>fulfillment</u>—in the fulfillment idiom things are spoken of as given, done, or possessed, which are only promised or proposed. <u>prophetic past</u>—in the prophetic past idiom the

---

[11] See my self-study manual, **Interpreting the Scriptures: Figures and Idioms**.

4. Figures and Idioms In The Bible — page 53

3. Prophetic past	13:31	past tense is used to describe or express the certainty of future action.
4. Superlative (repetitive superlative)	Ge 9:25 servant of servants Isa 26:3 peace, peace = perfect peace 2Ti 4:7	The <u>Hebrew superlative</u> is often shown by the repetition of the word. Paul uses a variation of this by often using the noun form and a verb form of the same word either back to back or in close proximity. (the good struggle I have struggled).
5. Emphatic comparisons	1Pe 3:3,4	This takes three forms: <u>absolute for relative</u>: one thing (importance or focus item) is emphasized as being much more important in comparison with the other thing (the denial item). The form not A but B really means A is less important than B. <u>relative for absolute</u>: One thing is positively compared to another when in effect it is meant to be taken absolutely and the other denied altogether. <u>abbreviated emphatic comparisons</u>: Half of the comparison is not given (either the focus item or denial items). Half of the statement is given. The half missing is an example of ellipsis and is to be supplied by the reader.
6. Climactic arrangement	Pr 6:16-19 Ro 3:10-18	To emphasize a particular item it is sometimes <u>placed at the bottom of a list</u> of other items and is thus stressed in the given context as being the most important item being considered.
7. Broadened kinship	Ge 29:5	Sometimes the terms son of, daughter of, mother of, father of, brother of, sister of, or begat, which in English imply a close relationship have a much wider connotation in the Bible. Brother and sister could include various male and female relatives such as cousins; mother and father could include relatives such as grandparents or great-great-grandparents, in the direct family line; begat may simply mean was directly in the family line of ancestors.
8. Imitator	Ge 6:2, 11:5	to indicate that people or things are governed by or are characterized by some quality, they are called <u>children of</u> or a <u>son of</u>. or <u>daughter of</u> that quality.
9. Linked noun	Lk 21:15	Occasionally two nouns are linked together with a conjunction in which the second noun is really to be used <u>like an adjective</u> modifying the first noun.
Indicator Idioms: 10. City indicator 11. List indicator 12. Strength Indicator	city indicator La 1:16, daughter of Zion list indicator Pr 6:16, these 6 yea	<u>city indicator</u>—idiomatic words, daughter of or virgin of or mother of. <u>list indicator</u>—2 consecutive numbers—designates an incomplete list of items of which the ones on the list are representative; other like items could be included. <u>strength indicator</u>—a horn denotes aggressive strength or power or authority.

4. Figures and Idioms In The Bible

	7 Strength indicator 1Sa 2:1,10	
13. Anthropomorphism	Lk 11:20	In order to convey concepts of God, <u>human passions, or actions, or attributes are used to describe God.</u>

In addition, to the patterned idioms there are a number of miscellaneous idioms, which either occur infrequently or have no discernible pattern. I have labeled 32. Their meaning must be learned from context, from other original language sources, or from language experts' comments, etc.

Table Jnh 4-3. 15 Body Language Idioms

Name	Word, Phrase, Usually Seen	Example	Meaning or Concept Involved
1. Foot gesture	shake off the dust	Mt 10:14, Lk 9:5 et al	have nothing more to do with them
2. Mouth gesture	gnash on them with teeth; gnashing of teeth	Ps 35:16; 37:12 Ac 7:54 et al	indicates angry and cursing words given with deep emotion and feeling
3. Invitation	I have stretched forth my hand(s)	Ro 10:21; Pr 1:24; Is 49:22	indicates to invite, or to receive or welcome or call for mercy
4. New desire	enlighten my eyes, lighten my eyes	Ps 13:3; 19:8; 1Sa 14:29; Ezr 9:8	to give renewed desire to live; sometimes physical problem, sometimes motivational inward attitude problem
5. Judgment	to stretch forth the hand; to put forth the hand	Ex 7:5; Ps 138:7; Job 1:11	to send judgment upon; to inflict with providential punishment
6. Fear	to shake the hand, to not find the hand, knees tremble	Is 19:16; Ps 76:8	to be afraid; to be paralyzed with fear and incapable of action.
7. Increase punishment	to make the hand heavy	Ps 32:4	to make the punishment more severe
8. Decreased punishment	to make the hands light	1Sa 6:5	to make punishment less severe
9. Remove punishment	to withdraw the hands	Eze 20:22	to stop punishment
10. Repeat punishment	to turn the hand upon	Is 1:25	to repeat again some punishment which was not previously heeded
11.	to open the	Ps 104:28;	to generously give or bestow

4. Figures and Idioms In The Bible   page 55

Generosity	hand	145:16	
12. Anger	to clap the hands together	Eze 21;17; 22:13	to show anger; to express derision
13. Oath	to lift up the hand	Ex 6:8; 17:16; De 32:40; Eze 20:5,6	to swear in a solemn way; take an oath; an indicator of one's integrity to consider worthy to be accepted; to accept someone or be accepted by someone
14. Promise	to strike with the hands (with someone else)	Pr 6:1; Job 17:3	become a co-signer on a loan; to conclude a bargain
15. Accept	to lift up the face	Nu 6:26; Ezr 9:6; Job 22:26	to consider worthy to be accepted; to accept someone or be accepted by someone

Table Jnh 4-4.   14 Miscellaneous Idioms

Name	Word, Phrase, Usually Seen	Example	Meaning or Concept Involved
1. Success	tree of life	Pr 3:18; 11:30; 13:12; 15:4	idea of success, guarantee of success, source of motivation to successful life
2. Speech cue	answered and said	Mt 11:25; 13:2 and many others	indicates manner of speaking denoted by context; e.g. responded prayed, asked, addressed, etc.
3. Notice	verily, verily	Many times in Jn	I am revealing absolute and important truth; give close attention (this is a form of the superlative idiom)
4. Time	___ days and ___ nights	Jn 1:17; Mt 12:40; 1Sa 30:11; Est 4:16	any portion of time of a day is indicated by or represented by the entire day
5. Lifetime	forever and ever	Ps 48;14 and many others	does not mean eternal life as we commonly use it but means all through my life; as long as I live
6. Separation	what have I to do with you	Jn 2:4; Jdg 11;12; 2Sa 16:10; 1Ki 17:18; 2Ki 3;13; Mt 8:29; Mk 5:7; Lk 8:28	an expression of indignation or contempt between two parties having a difference or more specifically not having something in common; usually infers that some action about to take place should not take place
7. Reaction	heap coals of fire	Ro 12:20; Pr 25:21	to incur God's favor by reacting positively to a situation in which revenge would be normal
8. Orate	open the mouth	Job 3:1	to speak at great length with great liberty or freedom

4. Figures and Idioms In The Bible

9. Claim	you say	Mt 26:25,63,64	means it is your opinion
10. Excellency	living, lively	Jn 4:10,11 Ac 7:38; Heb 10:20; 1Pe 2:4,5; Rev 1:17	used to express the excellency of perfection of that to which it refers
11. Abundance	riches	Ro 2:4; Eph 1:7; 3:8; Col 1:27; 2:2	used to describe abundance of or a great supply
12. Preeminence	firstborn	Ps 89:27; Ro 8:29; Col 1;15, 18; Heb 12:23	special place of preeminence; first place among many others
13. Freedom	enlarge my feet; enlarge	2Sa 22:37; Ps 4:1; 18:36	freed me; brought me into a situation that has taken the pressure off, taken on to bigger and better things
14. Reverential respect for	fear and trembling	Ps 55:5; Mk 5:33; Lk 8:47; 1Co 2:3; 2 Co 7:15; Eph 6:5, Php 2:12	describes an attitude of appropriate respect for something. The something could be God, could a person, or could be a combination including some process. Sometimes indicates confronting a difficult situation or thing with a strong awareness of it and possible consequences

Again I would recommend you refer to my manual **Figures and Idioms** to see the approach for capturing the patterned idioms.

Figures and Idioms should be appreciated, understood, and should be interpreted with emphasis. Hardly any passage, which is any one of the seven leadership genre, will be without some figure or idiom.

Closure
This article is included in the Jonah commentary for two reasons. One, you need to be aware of the importance of figures and idioms when studying the Bible and this article gives a rather complete source (relatively, that is,) for help in that direction. Two, the book of Jonah contains several metonymies, some metaphorical language, an instance of the prophetical past idiom and a rhetorical question.

Article 5

5. Getting God's Perspective, A Leader's Necessity—Jonah's Dilemma

Introduction

The difference between leaders and followers is perspective. The difference between effective leaders and other leaders is better perspective. One issue highlighted in the book of Jonah stresses the importance of a leader getting perspective from God. An important leadership lesson illustrated by God's providential and sovereign work with Jonah could be stated this way.

> **Frequently, where strong leaders are concerned, God must often take the leader through a paradigm shift in order for the leader to get God's perspective.**

This is the case with three great Old Testament leaders: Job, Habakkuk, and Jonah.

In Job's case, especially, and somewhat in Jonah's God not only takes the leader through a paradigm shift but also a brokenness experience.

Definition   Brokenness is a state of mind in which a person recognizes that he/she is helpless in a situation or life process unless God alone works.

It is a state of mind in which a person acknowledges a deep dependence upon God and is open for God to break through in new ways, thoughts, directions, and revelation of Himself that was not the case before the brokenness experience. Job, for sure, went through brokenness. Jonah did too, at least somewhat.

Someone has said all real leaders of God "walk with a limp." That, of course, is a reference to the Jacob all-night experience in which he wrestled with God. This all-night experience demonstrated Jacob's deep need for God in a crisis situation. Total dependence upon God was at the root of the need. Leaders almost always accomplish more lasting results for God when they have been deeply processed in terms of character and essential relationship to God. This kind of processing includes sometimes some very negative things such as conflict, crises—general and life threatening, leadership backlash, and isolation. It results in a leader who is stripped of the wrong kind of self-reliance and in its place knows utter dependence upon God. The experience of going through this high learning curve full of darkness is called brokenness. An understanding of brokenness allows for vicarious learning as well as responsiveness to God's purposes in it. I am suggesting then, that Jonah's runaway experience including his near death crisis and his reflective after-ministry time under the sun was a brokenness experience that forever altered his view of God and God's concern for others.

5. Getting God's Perspective—Jonah's Dilemma

Because leaders are usually strong willed people, like Jonah, God will of necessity take them through paradigm shifts and even brokenness experiences which will allow them to know more of God and see His perspectives on things. We are leaders who can learn vicariously from other leader's lives, particularly Bible leaders who experienced paradigm shifts and brokenness. Or perhaps we will have to learn these lessons first hand. A major leadership lesson is in view here.

Effective Leaders Maintain A Learning Posture Throughout Life.[12]

We do well to maintain a learning posture, so that we can go through paradigm shifts as part of a natural learning curve process.

Jonah's Dilemma

Read the text from chapter 4 of Jonah given below. The people of Nineveh have repented and God has not brought judgment on Nineveh.

> Chapter 4
> 1 But Jonah was really upset about this turn of events. He became angry.[13]
> 2 So he prayed to the LORD, and said, "LORD, was not this what I said when I was still in my country? That is why I previously ran to Spain.[14] For I knew that You are a gracious and merciful God, slow to anger and abundant in lovingkindness, One who relents from doing harm.[15]

Jonah believed that Assyria would probably attack and destroy his own country sometime in the near future. Certainly the threat was there. Jonah hoped for God's judgment to fall. And on top of that, he like the Jewish nation, as a whole, saw God as exclusively for the Jewish people. So, he wanted God's judgment to fall. When it didn't, and God showed mercy, Jonah was upset. God's dealing with Jonah showed God's heart for others. This was a theological problem for Jonah as well as a practical one involving survival of his nation.

---

[12] This is one of seven major leadership lessons that have emerged in my studies of leadership over the past 21 years. They are: (1) Effective Leaders View Present Ministry in Terms Of A Life Time Perspective. (2) Effective Leaders Maintain A Learning Posture Throughout Life. (3) Effective Leaders Value Spiritual Authority As A Primary Power Base. (4) Effective Leaders Who Are Productive Over A Lifetime Have A Dynamic Ministry Philosophy. (5) Effective Leaders View Leadership Selection And Development As A Priority Function In Their Ministry. (6) Effective Leaders See Relational Empowerment As Both A Means And A Goal Of Ministry. (7) Effective Leaders Evince A Growing Awareness Of Their Sense Of Destiny. It is the second one I am referring to in this suggested idea. See **Article**, *Leadership Lessons—Seven Major Lessons Identified*.

[13] Jonah, like Habakkuk, is honest with God. He is angry. And he takes his anger right to God. He is looking for some answer from God to quell his anger. To justify this action of God in not punishing Assyria. They deserve the punishment. And too, Jonah's patriotism shows out. He knows these same Assyrians may well destroy Israel. See **Article**, 31. *Transparency With God*.

[14] Here we find the background to Jonah's running away in chapter 1. It was not explicitly stated there but is given here. Jonah knew that God might well spare Nineveh. He was actually afraid that his ministry might be successful and God would spare Nineveh. His patriotism shows out.

[15] Jonah has probably remained in the city for the 40 days that was warned about in his judgment message. And God has not brought judgment.

5. *Getting God's Perspective* — *Jonah's Dilemma*

Macro Lessons Being Emphasized

Let me suggest the important perspective macro lesson[16] that is a major focus of the book.

> **24. Perspective**
> **Leaders must know the value of perspective and interpret present happenings in terms of God's broader purposes.**

Both Habakkuk and Jonah needed to learn this major leadership lesson. And they did. When God tells Habakkuk emphatically to carefully observe (1:5) what is going on up north with the Babylonian empire and to see it through God's eyes, Habakkuk is being introduced to the broader purposes of God. Babylon will be used of God but also will later be punished. God is working out justice in a complex world.

God orders Jonah to go to Nineveh, another nation like Babylon, that will be used to discipline God's people. Jonah does not want to go. He actually fears that the Ninevites will repent and God will extend mercy instead of judgment to them. But Jonah is missing two perspectives: 1. God extends the possibility of repentance to all peoples (Jews included) till the people refuse to repent. 2. God wants to reach all peoples, not just be the God of the Jewish people.

Table Jnh 5-1 lists several other macros that we, from a distance and with great hindsight can see. Jonah most likely did not see them. But from our present understanding of the redemptive program of God and standing in the church leadership era we can see them.

Table Jnh 5-1. Other Macros Seen in Jonah

Macro Lesson Number	Name	When Seen	Statement of Lesson/ Explanation
21	Recrudescence	Kingdom Leadership Era	God will attempt to bring renewal to His people until they no longer respond to Him./ This was true of the northern kingdom to whom Jonah ministered as a prophet. And God shows here that the same is true of other nations.
22	By-pass	Kingdom Leadership Era	God will by-pass leadership and structures that do not respond to Him and will institute new leadership and structures./ Jonah could not see this. In fact, the only reference to his prophetic ministry is a positive one. God blessed the northern kingdom for a short time as predicted by Jonah. But the kings of the northern kingdom to a man failed to follow God. There was no renewal whatsoever in the northern kingdom.

---

[16] A <u>macro-lesson</u> is a high level generalization of a leadership observation (suggestion, guideline, requirement), stated as a lesson, which repeatedly occurs throughout different leadership eras, and thus has potential as a leadership absolute. See **Articles**, *22. Macro Lessons — Defined; 23. Macro Lessons — List of 41 Across Six Leadership eras.*

5. Getting God's Perspective—Jonah's Dilemma

			And God demolished it. A great warning to us all.

Closure

Three valuable lessons that we should see from a study of Jonah are simple ones.

Lesson 1.
Much perspective can be gained by leaders by the study of the Bible using leadership eyes.

Lesson 2.
God is concerned that peoples around the world be given a chance to know Him and respond to Him.[17]

Lesson 3.
We can seek God's perspectives and with a positive learning posture and change our ways and perspectives to follow hard after God.

Let me emphasize in closing, the first lesson. Suppose you agree with what I say, that much perspective can be gained by studying the Bible using leadership eyes. What should you do? I suggest for follow-up work on this that you do the following. All of these are materials that I have developed.

1. Study **Leadership Perspectives**—which will give you the leadership paradigms through which to see leadership in the Bible as well as methodology for studying each of the seven leadership genre.

2. Study **The Bible and Leadership Values**—which will give you insights into leadership topics seen in all the books of the Bible.

3. **Having A Ministry That Lasts—By Becoming a Bible Centered Leader.** This book will give frameworks that will help you move toward becoming a Bible Centered Leader—one of the goals of studying leadership in the Bible.

4. Study of all of the Biblical Leadership Commentary series will also greatly aid you in seeing leadership things in the Bible. At the writing of this article there are the following leadership commentaries: **Clinton Leadership Commentary** (containing: 1,2 Timothy; 1,2 Corinthians; Php; Phe; Jn; Da) and the following individual commentaries: Titus; Haggai; Habbakuk; Jonah.

But whatever you do don't forget, as a leader you need better and better perspectives that will inform your leadership. Jonah learned this lesson. You must too.

---

[17] Jonah fought God on this one. Do we? Are we part of the great movement in our day to reach out to the nations?

Article 6

6. God's Shaping Processes with Leaders

Introduction

One major leadership lesson derived from comparative study of effective leaders states,

Effective leaders see present ministry in light of a life time perspective.[18]

This article deals with God's shaping processes with a leader.[19] It gives important aspects of perspective that all leaders need. Six observations of God's shaping processes with leaders include the following.

1. God first works in a leader and then through that leader.
2. God intends to develop a leader to reach the maximum potential and accomplish those things for which the leader has been gifted.
3. God shapes or develops a leader over an entire lifetime.
4. A time perspective provides many keys. When using a time perspective, the life can be seen in terms of several time periods, each yielding valuable informative lessons. Each leader has a unique time-line describing his/her development.[20]
5. Shaping processes can be identified, labeled, and analyzed to contribute long lasting lessons.[21]
6. An awareness of God's shaping processes can enhance a leader's response to these processes.

Figure Jnh 6-1. Describes a generalized time line and some of the processes used by God over a lifetime.

---

[18] I have identified seven which repeatedly occur in effective leaders: 1. Life Time Perspective—Effective Leaders View Present Ministry In Terms Of A Life Time Perspective. 2. Learning Posture—Effective Leaders Maintain A Learning Posture Throughout Life. 3. Spiritual Authority—Effective Leaders Value Spiritual Authority As A Primary Power Base. 4. Dynamic Ministry Philosophy—Effective Leaders Who Are Productive Over A Lifetime Have A Dynamic Ministry Philosophy Which Is Made Up Of An Unchanging Core And A Changing Periphery Which Expands Due To A Growing Discovery Of Giftedness, Changing Leadership Situations, And Greater Understanding Of The Scriptures. 5. Leadership Selection And Development—Effective Leaders View Leadership Selection And Development As A Priority Function In Their Ministry. 6. Relational Empowerment—Effective Leaders See Relational Empowerment As Both A Means And A Goal Of Ministry. 7. Sense Of Destiny—Effective Leaders Evince A Growing Awareness Of Their Sense Of Destiny. See the **Article**, *Leadership Lessons—Seven Major Identified*.

[19] See also the **Article**, *Leadership Selection*, which gives an overview across time of the major benchmarks of God's development of a leader.

[20] See **Article**, *Time-Lines: Defined for Biblical Leaders*.

[21] See **For Further Study Bibliography**, Clinton's **Leadership Emergence Theory**, a self-study manual which gives detailed findings from research on God's shaping processes with leaders. This manual describes 50 shaping processes in detail. This article touches on only a few of these shaping processes.

6. God's Shaping Processes with Leaders

I. Ministry Foundations	II. Early Ministry	III. Middle Ministry	IV. Latter Ministry	V. Finishing Well
• character shaping	• leadership committal • authority insights • giftedness discovery • guidance	• ministry insights • conflict • paradigm shifts • leadership backlash • challenges	• spiritual warfare • deep processing • power processes	• destiny fulfillment

Figure Jnh 6-1. Some Major Shaping Processes Across The Time-Line

Shaping in Early Ministry —In and Then Through

Most younger emerging leaders in their initial exuberance for ministry feel they are accomplishing much. But in fact, God is doing much more in them than through them. The first years in ministry are tremendous learning years for a young leader who is sensitive to God's working in his/her life. God works on character first, even before a leader moves into full time leadership. Table Jnh 6-1 lists four major shaping processes dealing with character and four major shaping processes dealing with early ministry.

Table Jnh 6-1. Early Shaping Processes Identified and Defined

Type	Name	Explanation/ Biblical Example
Character	Integrity Check	A shaping process to test heart intent and consistency of inner beliefs and outward practice./ Daniel 1:3,4.
Character	Obedience Check	A shaping process to test a leader's will for obedience to God. /See Abraham, Ge 22.
Character	Word Check	A shaping process to test a leader's ability to hear from God./ See Samuel ch 3.
Character	Ministry Task	A shaping process to test a leader's faithfulness in performing ministry./ See Titus, Corinth trip (references in both 1,2Co).
Foundational Ministry	Leadership Committal	A shaping process, part of Guidance, to recruit a leader into ministry and to continue to engage that leader along the ministry path destined for him/her. /See Paul, Ac 9,22,26.
Foundational Ministry	Authority Insights	A shaping process to help leaders learn how to deal with leaders over them and folks under them./ See Ac 13 Barnabas and Paul.
Foundational Ministry	Giftedness Discovery	A shaping process in which a leader learns about natural abilities, acquired skills, and spiritual gifts that God wants to use through that leader./ See Phillip, Ac 8.
Long Term Ministry	Guidance	A shaping process in which God intervenes in the life of a leader at critical points to direct that leader along the ministry path destined for him/her./ See Paul, Ac 16.

6. God's Shaping Processes with Leaders

Shaping in Middle Ministry —Efficient Ministry[22]

During middle ministry the leader now sees God working through as much as in the leader. Leaders identify giftedness. They learn how to influence; they are learning to lead. They gain many perspectives that channel their ministry toward effectiveness. Table Jnh 6-2 lists some of the more important shaping processes that happen during this developmental phase.

Table Jnh 6-2. Middle Ministry Shaping Processes—Identified, Defined

Type	Name	Explanation/ Biblical Example
Character/ Ministry	Conflict	A shaping process in which a leader learns perseverance, surfaces defects in character, gets new perspective on issues, and learns how to influence in less than ideal conditions./ See Paul, Ac 19 Ephesus.
Breakthroughs in Ministry	Paradigm Shifts	A shaping process in which God gives breakthrough insights that allow a broadening of perspective so as to propel the leader forward in ministry. /See Paul, Ac 9.
Character/ Ministry	Leadership Backlash	A shaping process in which a leader learns about follower reactions and about perseverance, hearing from God, and inspirational leadership./ See Moses, Ex 5.
Renewal/ Long Term	Challenges	A shaping process in which a leader is induced along the lines of new ministry; a part of the guidance process to take a leader along the life path. /See Paul and Barnabas, Ac 13.

Latter Ministry And Finishing Well—Effective Ministry

The essential difference between middle ministry and latter ministry has to do with focus.[23] In middle ministry the leader learns to be efficient in ministry—that is, to do things well. In latter ministry and the finishing well time the leader learns to be effective—that is, to do the right things well. There is a further deepening of character which enhances the leader's spiritual authority. There is a growing awareness of spiritual warfare. The leader learns to minister with power. Table Jnh 6-3 lists some of the shaping processes that take place in the latter part of a leader's lifetime.

Table Jnh 6-3. Latter Ministry Shaping Processes—Identified and Defined

Type	Name	Explanation/ Biblical Example
Deep Processing	Crises	A shaping process in which a leader's person or ministry is threatened with discontinuation; an overwhelming time in which the leader feels intense issues which could torpedo his/her whole ministry./ See Paul, 2Co.
Deep Processing	Isolation	A shaping process in which a leader is set aside from ministry and goes through a searching time about identity and a deepening trust of God./ See Paul, Php.
Long Term Guidance	Negative Preparation	A shaping process in which an accumulative effect of a number of negative things in the life and ministry of a leader is used by God to release that leader from some previous ministry and give freedom to enter another ministry./ See

---

[22] We surmise, but not with certainty, that the incidents described in Jonah take place in the latter part of his middle ministry. We do not have enough information to say for sure. But a young leader would not be listened to by the Ninevites. The type of deep processing suggests the latter time of middle or early part of latter ministry.

[23] See **Article**, *Focused Life*.

6. God's Shaping Processes with Leaders

		Paul, 2Co.
Long Term Guidance	Divine Contacts	A shaping process in which God uses some person in a timely fashion to intervene in a leader's life to give perspective—could be directed toward personhood, ministry, or long term guidance./ See Paul and Barnabas, Ac 9:27.
Long Term Guidance	Double Confirmation	A shaping process in which God gives clear guidance by inward conviction and by external conviction (unsought)./ See Paul and Ananias, Ac 9.
Effective Ministry	Power Issues	A group of shaping processes including power encounters, gifted power, networking power and prayer power. The leader learns balance between own effort and God's enabling through him/her. The leader learns to minister effectively with God's power./ See Elijah, 1Ki 18 et al.

Conclusion

Awareness of these shaping processes allows a leader to combat the usually overwhelming attitude of *why me?* By seeing that these shaping processes occur in many leaders lives, leaders are affirmed that they are not way off base. It is part of God's way of developing a leader. A leader who understands what is happening in his/her life stands a better chance of responding to the processes and learning the lessons of God in them than one who is blindsided by these processes.

Notice that Jonah's story contains the following process items: ministry task (usually happens in early ministry but sometimes in middle ministry); obedience check (usually early ministry but sometimes in the case of a boundary time, could occur in middle ministry); crises (usually middle ministry or latter ministry); isolation (middle and latter ministry) and paradigm shift (can occur early, middle or latter but is often necessary in middle or latter in order to move a leader into focused ministry). Jonah's pivotal point probably occurred in the latter part of his middle ministry.

See *Integrity Check; Obedience Check; Word Check; Ministry Task; Leadership Committal; Authority Insights; Giftedness Discovery; Guidance; Conflict; Paradigm Shifts; Leadership Backlash; Faith Challenge; Leadership Challenge; Crises; Isolation; Negative Preparation; Divine Contacts; Double Confirmation; Power Encounters; Prayer Power; Gifted Power; Networking Power;* **Glossary**. See **Articles**, *Sovereign Mindset; Isolation Processing—Learning Deep Lessons from God; 29. Spiritual Authority—Defined, Six Characteristics*. See **For Further Study Bibliography—The Making of A Leader; Leadership Emergence Theory;** The Life Cycle of a Leader.

> **Article 7**

7. Isolation Processing—Learning Deep Lessons from God

Introduction

Leaders get set aside from ministry. Isolation[24] is the term used to describe this process. Sometimes the leader is directly set aside by God, sometimes by others, sometimes by self. In Jonah's case and Habakkuk's case, these leaders got aside, away from ministry, in order to hear from God. Both desperately needed isolated time alone to hear from God.

Whatever the case, whether self-initiated or God-initiated, isolation results in deep processing in the life of a leader. More than 90% of leaders will face one or more important isolation times in their lives. Most do not negotiate these times very well. Knowing about them and what God can accomplish in them can be a great help to a leader who then faces isolation.

Defining and Describing Isolation

What is isolation?

Definition Isolation processing refers to the setting aside of a leader from normal ministry or leadership involvement due to involuntary causes, partially self-caused or voluntary causes for a period of time sufficient enough to cause and/or allow serious evaluation of life and ministry.

Some notable Biblical examples include Job, Joseph, Moses, Jonah, Elijah, Habakkuk, Jesus, Paul.

Usually this means the leader is away from his/her natural context usually for an extended time in order to experience God in a new or deeper way. Sometimes isolation can occur in the ministry context itself.

Isolation experiences can be short—like intensive time spent away in solitude to meet God. Both Jonah and Habakkuk were of this nature. Or it can last up to several months and occasionally more than a year. Figure Jnh 7-1 describes isolation in terms of three major categories.

---

[24] See also Trebesch, **Isolation—A Place of Transformation in the Life of A Leader.**

7. Isolation Processing—Learning Deep Lessons from God

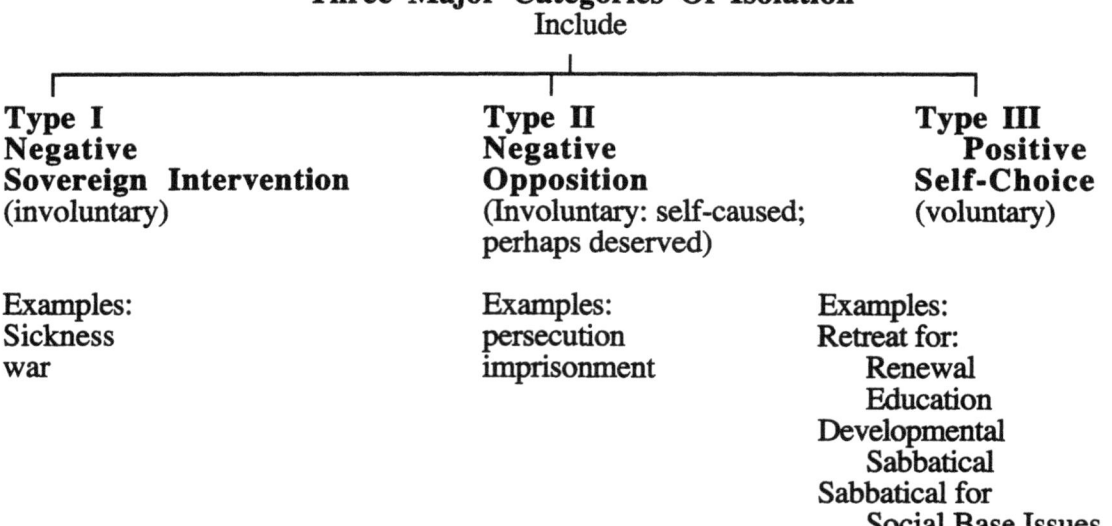

Figure Jnh 7-1. Three Types of Isolations

These isolation experiences can be viewed in terms of perceived intervention of God in them. Figure Jnh 7-2 gives a continuum correlating the isolation experiences to a leader's understanding of God's place in them.

Clear—Divine Intervention		Less clear—Providential
TYPE I	**TYPE II**	**TYPE III**
• sickness	• personality conflicts	• self-choice renewal (Jonah)
	• prison	• organizational issues
	• persecution	• self-choice development
		• ministry issues (Jonah)
		• artificial, short intensive (Jonah)
		• self-choice for social base

Figure Jnh 7-2. Isolation Sovereignty Continuum

Table Jnh 7-1 gives results observed in comparative studies of leaders in isolation.

Table Jnh 7-1. Isolation Results

Isolation Type	Results or Uses of Isolation
I. Negative/ Sovereign Intervention	lessons of brokenness; learning about supernatural healing; lessons about prayer; deepening of inner life; an intensified sense of urgency to accomplish; developing of mental facilities; submission to God; dependence upon God.
II. Negative/ Opposition	lessons of brokenness; submission to spiritual authority; value of other perspectives; dependence upon God

7. Isolation Processing—Learning Deep Lessons from God

III. Positive/ Self-choice	new perspective on self and ministry (Jonah); rekindling of sense of destiny; guidance; oneself to change; upon wider body of Christ

Overlapping Features in Many Isolation Experiences

Table Jnh 7-2 lists some common things that happen to leaders in isolation.

Table Jnh 7-2. Common Happenings in Isolation

Isolation	Some Happenings
I or II	1. Sense of Rejection
I or II	2. Sense of stripping away--getting down to core issues
I, II or III	3. Eventually a deep need for God
I, II or III	4. Searching for God
I, II, or III	5. Submission to God (Jonah)
I, II, or III	6. Dependence upon God (Jonah)
I, II, or III	7. Rekindling of desire to serve God in a deeper way (probably Jonah)

Bible Characters and Isolation Lessons From Their Lives

Job, Moses, Elijah, Jonah, Habakkuk, and Paul provide some important isolation lessons. See the Tables, which follow listing each of these Bible Characters and observations about isolation.

Job

Job faced sickness, loss of life, loss of wealth, loss of friends, and loss of status as an important person. Table Jnh 7-3 suggests some things that can be learned from Job's Type I isolation experience.

Table Jnh 7-3. Job and Type I Isolation

Step	Explanation
1.	**Begin With The End In Mind** (need a framework/ perspective). In isolation, deep-seated ideas are challenged in such a way as to capture our attention and force us to come to essential values. Maybe it is only in isolation that they could be challenged. But know that isolation will end and God will teach lessons even about deep-seated ideas.
2.	**Analyze From The Known To The Unknown.** Apart from unusual revelation, we can only search out answers in terms of what we know. That is, the first step in the isolation process— search out what is happening in terms of what you do know (e.g. paradigms).
3.	**Recognize That The Unknown Can Serve Two Functions.** When anomalies arise we must recognize that they may not really be anomalies and will be cleared up in the end (in which case it is a matter of faith and waiting), or they are real and will force us into new paradigms.
4.	**Expect God's Intervention. God may give insight if a new paradigm is needed or may require a faith response.**
5.	**Believe In God's On-Going Answer.** The book of Job shows us that God is in charge of our individual processing—no matter how or through whom it may come, even including Satanic origin. We do not have all the answers. He does. We must trust Him in them.

Moses

In Ex 2:11-15, there is an incident in which Moses kills an Egyptian and then flees (He 11:23-28 and Ac 7:23 give an interpretation of this). Then in Ex 3:7 and following, God calls Moses to a major task, the very one he had tried on his own and given up. There is a major difference in the Moses of Ex 2 and the Moses of Ex 3. Nu 12:3 describes it. Something happened. I want to suggest that it was a brokenness[25] experience. And that brokenness experience was part of isolation processing for Moses.

Moses experienced this Type II isolation processing. It included aspects of geographical and cultural isolation. Three characteristics of geographic and cultural isolation include: 1. It is more powerful in its early effects; wears off with time and as assimilation occurs. (This is seen also in the life of Daniel.) 2. In Geographic/ cultural isolation there is a loss of self-esteem. The things you were and value in the old culture are usually not so respected and valued in the new. 3. There is often a loss of momentum and vision.

Table Jnh 7-4. Moses and Type II Isolation

Lesson	Explanation/ Generalized
1	**Look for leadership committal processing as a means toward ending isolation.** Often isolation involves and may terminate with God's renewal of call. See *progressive calling;* **Glossary**.
2	**God has to sometimes take a vision away in order to later accomplish that vision in his way.** Keep an open hand to plans, visions, future work.
3	**Humility is often the fruit of isolation processing--an unhealthy egotism is broken.** God can unleash great power through a broken/ humble leader without fear of that leader abusing the power.

Elijah

Elijah had two impactful isolation experiences. The first was a Type I, clearly God directed. The second was a Type II. I do not think Elijah ever fully recovered from the second experience. Table Jnh 7-5 gives some observations about the Type I experience. Table Jnh 7-6 gives the Type II isolation experience which arose due to persecution.

Table Jnh 7-5. Elijah's Type I Isolation Experience, 1Ki 17:1-6 — Some Observations

Observation	Explained
1	Isolation was God-directed (vs 2,3)
2	Success brings problems (vs 7 brook dries up--he prayed for no rain)
3	God will provide in isolation (vs 4, 9, 14)
4	God protects in isolation (I Kings 18:10).

Elijah's Type II isolation experience was the fallout from one of the most successful ministry events recorded in the O. T. He has just seen God move mightily in a power encounter[26] with the prophets of

---

[25] See *brokenness*, **Glossary**.

[26] This is the classic power encounter which defines others. The steps of a *Power Encounter* include:
1. There is a confrontation between God and Evil. 2. The forces are recognized for that--the issues are who is more powerful and thus deserving of allegiance. 3. There is a public demonstration so that both forces can be seen by all as to who is more powerful. 4. God demonstrates publicly His power and defeats the evil forces so that there can be no doubt about to whom allegiance should be given. 5. Aftermath--God is glorified, evil forces are punished; there may be a response toward God. See *power encounter*, **Glossary**.

7. Isolation Processing—Learning Deep Lessons from God

Baal on top of Mount Carmel—a true mountain top experience. When he flees from persecution he moves into an isolation experience—again a mountain top experience—this time, Mount Sinai. Note that again as with the first experience, success brings with it problems.

Table Jnh 7-6. Elijah's Type II Isolation Experience, 1Ki 19 —Persecution— Running For His Life

Observation	Explained

1. The Situation	Vs4 Desert Isolation—
	   1. Hope gone; despair; take my life, (vs 4,5)
	   2. Angel touches him--provision (vs 5,7)
	   3. Horeb--Mountain of God--40 days/ 40 nights); cave
	What are you doing? God shows up.

2. Notice the Steps	Step 1. The feelings: I alone/ stood up for God/ persecution Step 2. Presence of God—the antidote to the feelings. Step 3. God answers--not you alone (vs11), 7000 who have not bowed the knee
3. The Price To Pay	Power encounters can be costly--they drain away energy—After mountain-experiences expect attacks from Satan, evil forces; you may well crash hard in the valley. Elijah never again has a major ministry success?
4. Rejection/ God's Affirmation	In isolation there is a sense of personal rejection and a need for divine affirmation. Notice how God does this. **Small Still Voice**. Not the spectacular like you might expect or hope for.
5. Leadership Selection	Elijah imparted power and authority to Elisha--one who was faithful, tenacious, wanted what Elijah had. He carried on Elijah's ministry with more power than Elijah. Elijah's isolation experiences brought spiritual authority. Emerging leaders are drawn to leaders with spiritual authority.

One of the most important things to see from Elijah's isolation experiences is that isolation is frequently accompanied by a sense of personal rejection. It is divine affirmation that we need. God will meet us--maybe not in the way we expect.

Table Jnh 7-6. Jonah's Type III Isolation Experience—Need for Perspective

Observation	Explained
1	Jonah needs God's perspective. He wanted God to bring judgment on the Assyrians. He is angry with God.
2	Jonah goes through deep processing, again a near death experience in the sun in order to hear God's perspective. Even though this was self-initiated, Jonah goes through deep processing.
3	Jonah goes through the paradigm shift and sees God's concerns for the nations. Frequently, a new paradigm is needed when a leader seeks isolation.

Table Jnh 7-6. Habakkuk's Type III Isolation Experience—Need for Perspective

Observation	Explained
1	Habakkuk has heard from God concerning his situation. God has given an answer which is difficult for him to agree with. He wants God's clarification.

7. Isolation Processing—Learning Deep Lessons from God   page 70

2	In isolation, Habakkuk hears God's explanation. He processes it reflectively.
3	Habakkuk goes through the paradigm shift and sees that God's ultimate justice will be accomplished and that God will be gloried in this. for the nations. Frequently, a new paradigm is needed when a leader seeks isolation.

Paul

Paul had numerous isolation experiences. It is from his life that the concept of repeated isolation experiences occurring in a leader's life emerged. Five are worth noting—1) his short days in Damascus with Ananias, Ac 9; 2; 2) His 2 to 3 years in Arabia mentioned in Gal; 3) His short prison experience in Philippi seen in Ac 16:23; 4) His four years in Rome (during which Eph, Col, Phm, Php were written); 5) His short few months in Rome just before his death. Table Jnh 7-7 suggests nine observations drawn from a comparative study of Paul's isolation experiences.

Table Jnh 7-7. Nine Observations from Paul's Isolation Experiences

Isolation Experience	Description and Observations
1. Galatian Isolation Reflection	Paul's Galatian/Arabia--Pre-Ministry isolation was a Type III self-choice isolation. It was a time of Reflection in which he worked out his Christology. Basic Principle: **Reflection is a major goal and means of processing during isolation.** Reflection will happen in isolation. Depending on the kind of isolation there will be questions. A seeking after something—time for thinking. (2Ti is especially filled with reflection; a looking back on a lifetime given to the Gospel.)
2. Prison Isolation; Response Attitude	A. In general, the following principle makes the difference in whether the isolation is profitable or not. **A sovereign mindset in processing makes the difference in immediate response and in long lasting results.** Attitude is everything. Notice Paul's attitude as reflected in: Eph 3:1; 4:1; Col 4:3,9,10; Phm 1; Php 1:12; 4:22. Paul saw a God-ordained purpose behind isolation. What does it mean to have a *sovereign mindset* in processing? It means to recognize that however the isolation may have come about—unjust determination, terrible circumstances, or whatever—you must recognize that God has an ultimate purposes in it: 1) to demonstrate the sufficiency of the supply of the Spirit of Christ, 2) to do specific things fitting the immediate situation, 3) to open up new thinking that could not have been possible, 4) to bring long-range productivity out of it (spiritual authority).
3. Intense Focus	**Critical issues come into focus during isolation processing.** Isolation forces one to focus usually first on why, causes of it, and then later on the purposes of it. And finally with a powerful concentration that allows for problem solving, new revelation to meet situations, and insights that could only come because of the situation.
4. Evaluation—	**Divine evaluation of character, leadership commitment, and perspective is in focus in isolation processing.**

7. Isolation Processing—Learning Deep Lessons from God

Divine Perspective	Frequently, what happens is a recognition that God is allowing you to search your life and ministry and evaluate it in light of the situation and often with resulting paradigm shifts that will affect your ministry philosophy and the rest of your life.
5. Deepened Relationship	**A deepened relationship with god is always a major goal of isolation processing.** Philippians, the last of the first set of prison epistles and the most positive upbeat of all of Paul's letter culminates four years of isolation which have been filled with crises. It is filled with the importance of union with Christ. Its message points out what can happen in isolation processing—a grasping of the sufficiency of Christ for life.
6. Basis for Long Range Productivity	**Long lasting productivity is often rooted in isolation processing.** The prison epistles may never have been written had Paul been on the go. But set aside, reflection time produced thinking in regard to his own personal sanctification intimacy with Christians (Php), church problems (Col), the nature of the church (Eph), the solving of a problematic social institution (Phm). But not just products, attitudes and ideas are born in isolation which may come to fruition down road. 1. Specific things—people touched, saved, advise given, etc. 2. Modeling—an intangible product 3. written achievements—one product of isolation.
7. The importance of praise	**Praise is a major weapon in isolation processing.** In external isolation you probably feel less like praising than almost anything else, yet it is at that juncture that praise is probably the most important faith challenge. See Php jail experience, Ac 16, and the tone of praise in all the prison epistles--most of the opening prayers carry that note of praise. Praise will release power, new perspective in isolation.
8. Short Isolation	**Life changing and ministry changing revelation may come even in a short isolation experience.** Moses, 40 days of isolation by self-choice (divine drawing); Paul in two different times (Ac 9, Ananias, Ac 16 Philippian jail experience)
9. Intensified Prayer	**Isolation processing often presses a person into intensified prayer burdens and efforts.**

Let me summarize what we can see in Paul's isolation experiences. Such experiences will tell a leader whether or not that leader has a sovereign mindset. They will also force reflection and evaluation of one's self in relation to: God, truth, a ministry, the past, the future. Critical issues come into focus. Peripheral issues are seen for what they are. In normal times we worry about a lot of things--many peripheral and non-essential. But in isolation times we get down to basic issues: who we are, what we really know, where we are going, who God really is, what He wants from us, etc. A leader will deepen his/her relationship with God—because that is what really matters--more than our ministry, more than the problems around us. A leader may discover the importance of praise or see an intensified outpouring of prayer, or the roots for long range productivity in our lives.

Knowing these things, so what? How can observing these principles in the life of Paul help us as we life schedule or as we work through a present isolation experience? How can we be proactive? Here are some suggestions:

1. **Reflection**—If you are not a thinker or if you are a thinker but are confused in isolation, because you know that reflection is important, you should get with someone in the body of Christ who has either natural abilities of analytical skills, discernment, or

7. Isolation Processing—Learning Deep Lessons from God

spiritual gifts of exhortation, teaching, word of wisdom, word of knowledge and ask for help on getting an overall perspective on what the intent of God is in the isolation. In terms of mentor types, you need to get with a spiritual guide or mentor counselor.

2. **Response Attitude**—Acknowledge that God is in this isolation. By faith accept this and then move with a learning posture through it. I am going to learn great things from God. Others may be to blame but God is in it.

3. **Intense Focus**—Recognize that critical issues will be pointed out in the isolation processing.

4. **Divine Perspective Evaluation**—Do self-evaluation of your life and ministry. Some suggestions as to how to do this: Be alert to values. Expect new revelation. Know that paradigm shifts often occur in isolation.

5. **Deepened Relationship**—Spend time in intimacy disciplines with God; extended times of silence, solitude, prayer, Bible study, fasting.

Conclusion
Here are some final warnings and assurances about isolation.

1. **Expect it**. About 90% of leaders go through an isolation experience of Type I or II.
2. **Recognize that there will be a sense of rejection in it.** Because of this it is helpful to keep a log of your divine affirmation and ministry affirmation items. Review them alone with God and feel anew His acceptance.
3. **Determine beforehand to go deep with God**. He will take you into a place of more dependence, perhaps a place of intimacy that you could not have without this kind of processing.
4. **Know that God will indeed meet you in isolation** though at first He may appear remote. Do not try to move out of isolation on your own until God has met you. Otherwise, you may go through a repeated isolation experience.
5. **Know the uses of isolation** and seek to see and sense which of these God is working into your life.
6. For a Type III isolation experience **set goals** for personal growth that include dependence, intimacy, and a deeper walk with God.
7. **Talk to other Christians who have gone through deep processing**. They will give you perspective with a proper empathy.
8. If the isolation is self-initiated, be transparent with God as you seek His perspective on your situation. Expect God to probably take you through a paradigm shift. He did for Job, Jonah and Habakkuk. He can well do this for you, if that is the need.

As a leader you will face isolation. Will you meet God in it and see His purposes in it fulfilled? Remember, isolation processing comes to almost all leaders. Expect repeated isolation processing. It is needed throughout a lifetime. Don't forget, attitude is crucial. Perspective can make the difference—knowing what isolation does, that it does end, that it will accomplish many important things. If you sense you are plateauing then self-initiate an extended time of isolation—get help from mentor counselors and mentor spiritual guides.

Article 8

8. Jonah, Biographical Sketch

Introduction

Jonah is a type 1 biographical source. This type is called a Critical Incident Source.[27]

Definition   A type 1 biographical source of leadership information is labeled a <u>Critical Incident Source,</u> when its source material is comprised of a single incident or series of incidents taking place in a very short time.

There may actually be a large amount of information but all focused on a short time-interval. The information can be interpreted for processing or for a leadership act or other such findings. Other examples besides Jonah include Job and Habakkuk. Though information is minimal in critical incident sources, valuable lessons can be learned.

What is Known About Jonah

Jonah is mentioned 24 times in the Scriptures. Table Jnh 8-1 gives the basics about these references.

Table Jnh 8-1. References to Jonah in the Scripture

Reference	What is Seen About Jonah
2 Ki 14:25	He is the son of Amittai. He was from Gathhepher in Zebulun in Galilee. He prophesied in the time of Jereboam II in the northern kingdom. His prophecy was a positive one which came true. He is called God's servant.

18 times in book of Jonah: 1:1,3,5,7,15, 17 (twice) 2:1,10 3:1,3,4 4:1,5,6 (twice),8,9	Jonah is the son of Amittai, hence connecting him to the Jonah who prophesied in Jereboam II's kingdom.
	Lots of information about Jonah is given in the book:
	  He hears from God.
	  He is strong willed.
	  He disobeys God because he does not want the Ninevites to repent and God show this mercy.
	  He is picked out by lots (supernatural identification) as being the cause of the storm.
	  He was in the belly of the great fish for three days and nights.
	  He is a poet. He describes the near death crisis incident in poetic language.
	  He prays for deliverance from the crisis.
	  He had spiritual authority that was recognized by the Ninevites. They repented at his strong preaching.

---

[27] 3. **Article**, *Biographical Study In The Bible, How to Do* which gives 4 categories of biographical source material.

8. Jonah, Biographical Sketch

	He is not afraid to show his emotions. He is honest with God. He tells God how he feels and why he feels the way he does. He goes through a paradigm shift. We have the book. No one would be this open and transparent about this experience unless he had come to see God's viewpoint about it.
Mt 12:39	Jesus accepts the Jonah story in the Bible.
Mt 12:40	Jesus uses the Jonah time in the whale to illustrate his own coming death and resurrection.
Mt 12:41	Jesus indicates degrees of judgment. He applauds the Ninevites repentance and condemns his own hearers for lack of repentance at his prophetic words.
Mt 16:4	Jesus accepts the Jonah story in the Bible. Again he uses it to illustrate what will happen to him.
Lk 11:29	Jonah again used as a sign.
Lk 11:30	Jesus compares his ministry to Jonah's ministry.
Lk 11:32	Jesus compares response to Jonah's ministry and lack of response to his own ministry.

What Can We Surmise About Jonah

Jonah was most likely a strong leader who typically viewed God as exclusively for the Jewish people. Because he was strong willed he made a decision to knowingly disobey God. And he followed through on his decision. He had an artistic temperament. His reflection on the crisis experience in the belly of the great fish was done in Hebrew Poetry. He had spiritual authority. For some reason his message was heeded when he spoke to the Ninevites. He was transparent with God just as Habakkuk was. He was humble enough to write up his testimony for others to see. Obviously his intent was that others should see how God does care for other peoples beside the Jewish people.

Other articles analyze the shaping incidents which happened to Jonah: a ministry task, obedience check, crisis experience, and isolation. Most likely Jonah was in the latter stages of his ministry time-line. One, these kind of shaping incidents frequently occur then. Two, his message was heeded. A message from a young leader would probably not carry weight.

Jesus authenticates Jonah's ministry as being real.

What Can We Learn from Jonah

Biographical study is important. Books like Job, Habakkuk, and Jonah are included in the canon of Scripture. That they are there is important. There are lessons to be found in them. As leaders, we can learn vicariously leadership lessons from such study. Let me briefly suggest two lessons that leaders need to know about God, which are seen in Jonah. Then I will discuss 7 general observations.

8. Jonah, Biographical Sketch — page 75

Lesson 1. God sovereignly (or providentially) intervenes in human affairs to accomplish His purpose. This sovereign power can be manifested:
- in circumstances (vs 3 found a ship)
- in control of nature (vs 4 the great wind and violent storm)
- in decision making (vs 7 the lots)
- in the animal kingdom (vs 17 a great fish, timing) Note the fish does not destroy him—even goes from Tarshish to Nineveh
- in nature (supenatural overriding—provided vine, vs 7 east hot wind (Santa Anas), worm to destroy the vine, then used the whole thing as an object lesson

Lesson 2. God is concerned about individuals (Jonah, the sailors, the Ninevites, animals, and life). He is concerned enough to send messengers to reveal what they need to hear.

There are seven observations about leaders and God's dealings with them that are worth noting:

Observation 1.
God processes individuals so that they can learn about him (Jonah).

Observation 2.
Humankind can choose to go against God's purposes (Both Jonah and the Ninevites illustrate this).

Observation 3.
God may after initial failure reprocess an individual toward his purposes (Jonah illustrates this).

Observation 4.
Crises experiences are God's call to know him deeply and to pursue His purposes (Jonah and the Ninevites illustrate this).

Observation 5.
Fasting is a sign of serious intent before God and can be a means of intensifying prayer effort (the Ninevites illustrate this).

Observation 6.
God's guidance is clear guidance (at least when seen in retrospect). He,
- a. can use normal human means (lots)
- b. can use circumstances (boat ready)
- c. can use nature (great fish; shrub)
- d. can speak to us (to Ninevites through Jonah; to Jonah directly).

Observation 7.
A leader's testimony can carry great impact (Jonah gives us his story).

Closure
As leaders, we can learn directly via our own experience or indirectly, that is, vicariously from the lives of others. Jonah is a leader whose legacy goes on today because he was not afraid to tell his story. And because he told his story, we can benefit today in our leadership. Jonah is one who fits the leadership mandate.

8. Jonah, Biographical Sketch

> Remember your former leaders. Imitate those qualities and achievements that were God-Honoring, for their source of leadership still lives—Jesus! He, too, can inspire and enable your own leadership today.
> Hebrews 13:7,8 Clinton Interpretive Paraphrase

He is worthy to be imitated, especially in his honest relationship with God.

Article 9

9. Jonah, Brokenness

Introduction

Someone has said all real leaders of God "walk with a limp." That, of course, is a reference to the Jacob all-night experience in which he wrestled with God. This all-night experience demonstrated Jacob's deep need for God in a crisis situation. Total dependence upon God was at the root of the need. Leaders almost always accomplish more lasting results for God when they have been deeply processed in terms of character and essential relationship to God. This kind of processing includes sometimes some very negative things such as conflict, crises—general and life threatening—leadership backlash, and isolation. It results in a leader who is stripped of the wrong kind of self-reliance and in its place knows utter dependence upon God. The experience of going through this high learning curve full of darkness is called brokenness. An understanding of brokenness allows for vicarious learning as well as responsiveness to God's purposes in it.

It is interesting to observe that in the three unique Old Testament biographical books dealing primarily with God's shaping of leaders, that two of the three involve brokenness. Both Job and Jonah went through personal real brokenness. Habakkuk vicariously went through brokenness. All three went through important paradigm shifts, learning of God's perspective in their situation.

Brokenness Described

When I say Jonah and Job went through a brokenness experience, what do I mean? Here is how I define the concept.

Definition <u>Brokenness</u> is a state of mind in which a person recognizes that he/she is helpless in a situation or life process unless God alone works.

It is a state of mind in which a person acknowledges a deep dependence upon God and is open for God to break through in new ways, thoughts, directions, and revelation of Himself that was not the case before the brokenness experience. Table Jnh 9-1 gives some examples of brokenness.

Table Jnh 9-1 Biblical Examples of Brokenness

Person	Description
Hagar	Hagar's persecution and dismissal by Sarah broke her before God and caused her to despair of any hope at all. She knows total **rejection**. It was God who became her only hope. Genesis 21.
Jacob	Jacob in Genesis 32 faced a **life threatening situation** in which he was forced to desperately depend upon God.
Joseph	Joseph in Genesis 37 was faced with **loss of life**. This was the first of

9. Jonah, Brokenness

	numerous brokenness experiences that shaped Joseph for a great work for God.
Job	Job is broken **physically**. He **loses family and finances** and almost loses his friends. But in his brokenness he gets new perspective on God and suffering.
Moses	Moses' attempt to save the Israelites in his own way was a shattering experience that broke him. See Exodus 2 for this **loss of vision.** Exodus 3, occurring many years later, is God's restoration of the vision. It is clear that dependence upon God was a major difference.
Hannah	Hannah's **inability to have a child** and the daily **torment** she received from Peninnah about it brought her to the end of herself. She was driven to pray in desperation for her situation. See 1 Sa 1,2.
David	David's experience with sin unchecked in his life and his eventual confrontation by Nathan along with his **repentant response** to God illustrates brokenness. 2 Samuel 12; Psalm 51 (see especially verse 17).
Jonah	Jonah goes through a **near death experience**, which is clearly providential and as a result learns dependence upon God for life itself. Later he goes through a paradigm shift and sees God's perspective on the Ninevites.
Isaiah	Isaiah's **awesome experience** in seeing a holy God allowed him to see himself in a new light and as unworthy to serve. See Isa 6.
Elijah	After a powerful mountain top experience, Elijah **runs for his life.** Elijah is isolated, depressed, and broken. He goes through a paradigm shift in which God lovingly cares for him shows him he is not alone in standing for God.
Jeremiah	A number of times in the book Jeremiah is threatened with **loss of life** and actually **imprisoned** and nearly **starves to death**. He several times throughout the book shows that he is at rock bottom in his ministry. God meets him over and over again in his brokenness experiences accompanying his **rejected prophetic ministry**.
Peter	Peter's 3 denial experiences shattered his **self-confidence.** Jesus' restoration completed the process. Luke 22:54-62; John 21.
Paul	Paul's experience on the road to Damascus was an awesome experience that broke through a mis-directed **perspective** of serving God. Acts 9.

Means God Uses in Bringing Brokenness and Purposes

God uses crises—general and life threatening, sickness, persecution, conflict, isolation, awesome revelations of Himself, conviction of sin, and the like to accomplish the brokenness. The happenings may be stretched out over an extended period of time or concentrated . What does God accomplish with this brokenness process? Brokenness can accomplish any or several of the following :

- **new perspective**--paradigm shifts allowing us to see dependence upon God and to see things we could not see before,
- a **release of the Spirit,**
- new awareness of the **inner life**,
- **maturity** in character,
- **spiritual authority** in our leadership,
- more **effective ministry.**
- a healthy respect for **sinfulness**

In Jonah's case of brokenness, at least the following were involved.

9. Jonah, Brokenness

- √ **new perspective**—paradigm shifts allowing us to see dependence upon God and to see things we could not see before. Jonah was utterly cast upon God to deliver him. And this near death experience drove Jonah to depend upon God. Eventually it led him to seeing God's perspective on the Ninevites.
- √ a **release of the Spirit**—this is implied in the powerful ministry Jonah had when he preached in Nineveh.
- √ new awareness of the **inner life**—certainly implied in the transparent dialog between God and Jonah.
- √ **maturity** in character—Jonah has a much broader understanding of other peoples and God's concern from them. A very mature perspective, especially when compared with his fellow Jews who viewed God as exclusively for Israel and not concerned with other nations.
- √ **spiritual authority** in our leadership. Jonah had spiritual authority has implied by the Ninevites response to his ministry.
- √ more **effective ministry.** Jonah certainly had an effective ministry. Too effective as far as he was concerned.
- a healthy respect for **sinfulness**; not sure about this one.

Some Encouragement About Brokenness Experiences

The following are encouraging words about brokenness adapted from Charles Stanley's teaching on the subject.[28]

1. When God refines us (that is, takes us through a brokenness experience) it is because he loves us and is purifying the Gold. The Gold is never destroyed. Only the dross. Refinement is a sign of God's love for us. This is certainly Job's evaluation of brokenness while in the midst of it.
2. God limits the refining process to only those things that will accomplish His purposes. Paul comments on this in Ro 8:28,29. A major purpose is to conform us to the image of Christ.
3. There is something for us to learn in God's processing—brokenness and refinement always teach us something if we are open to learn.
4. While it may seem to the contrary, God will never desert us in the process of refining us. Elijah felt that way but learned differently as did Hagar.
5. The ultimate end of brokenness/refinement will be victory if you will sense God's working in it and persevere with God in the process. Job found this out. Paul did too (2 Ti 3:10ff).
6. God is long suffering with us and will patiently refine us even if it takes a long period of time and many separate processes. Jonah's processing took several months.
7. Brokenness will sometimes result in radical obedience which may frighten us. But remember, He is responsible for the consequences of obedience.

Jesus and a Special Kind of Brokenness

John 12:24 is the picture of brokenness and release which Jesus uses to describe himself and the impending cross. But it is also the prototype of brokenness for all believers. It is this death/life process that is involved in the brokenness process. Out of the death-like experience of brokenness comes life. A mature spirit-life, which accomplishes God's purposes.

---

[28] I listened to a very powerful series of tapes on this subject from Charles Stanley. At that time, he was the senior pastor of First Baptist Church in Atlanta. I have summarized some of his findings and changed the wording a bit but basically have learned these ideas from him.

9. Jonah, Brokenness

Closure

Jonah shows us that brokenness can lead to new perspectives about God and His ways. New perspectives on God and His ways are always needed by leaders. No one necessarily likes brokenness experiences. But seeing God's hand in them and His purposes through them make the difference in how leaders will respond to them. Many leaders, as so aptly illustrated by the Bible leaders mentioned above, will go through brokenness experiences. Forewarned is forearmed.

Article 10

10. Jonah, Contextual Flow—Seeing the Flow

Introduction
Below is the flow of the contextual statements through out the book. The larger four contextual units are printed in all capitals and use major ideas in topical form to summarize the larger unit.

For *smaller units of parallelism* (like a single verse), *I* give a simple reduction of the parallelism to its single meaningful statement. For *longer stanzas* (made up of several verses), I give the overall context statement.

The book of Jonah is highly structured. Understanding its structure will make the difference in seeing its meaning—denotation and connotation.

Jonah: Contextual Flow of Book

I. (1:1-1:17) JONAH'S DISOBEDIENCE AND DISCIPLINE

1:1-3 **Context**: Jonah resists God's commission to preach in Nineveh.

    a. 1:1   **Reduction**: Jonah is commissioned by God to preach to the Ninevites.
    b. 1:2-3   **Reduction**: Jonah flees the Lord by boarding a ship to Tarshish.

1:5-11 **Context**: The Lord uses a great storm to get Jonah's attention.
    a. 1:4   **Reduction**: The Lord governs nature
    b. 1:5-6   **Reduction**: The sailors are fighting for their lives while Jonah is sleeping
    c. 1:7-8   **Reduction**: The sailors cast lots to see why the storm was so great and Jonah is implicated.
    d. 1:9-10   **Reduction**: Jonah's testimony about God causes fear among the sailors.
    e. 1:11-16   **Context**: The sailors throw Jonah overboard and the storm ceases. This gives cause for greater fear and reverence for God among the sailors.

1:17 **Context**: The Lord's discipline gives life to Jonah.
    a. 1:17   **Reduction**: Jonah is saved from drowning and is isolated in the belly of a great fish.

10. Jonah, Contextual Flow— Seeing the Flow

II. (2:1-10) JONAH'S DELIVERANCE

2:1 **Context**: After three days Jonah prays to God.

2:2-9 **Context**: Jonah's prayer of deliverance
- a. 2:2 **Reduction**: The Lord hears Jonah's prayers
- b. 2:3-6 **Context**: Jonah experiences separation from God
- c. 2:7-9 **Reduction**: Jonah acknowledges the Lord and makes some promises

2:10 **Context**: Jonah's change of heart leads to his deliverance.

III. (3:1-10) JONAH'S OBEDIENCE

3:1-3 **Context**: Jonah obeys God's commission to preach in Nineveh
- a. 3:1-2 **Reduction**: Jonah is commissioned by God to preach to the Ninevites.
- b. 3:3 **Reduction**: Jonah obeys and heads toward Nineveh.
- c. 3:4 **Reduction**: Jonah tells the Ninevites to repent or be destroyed.

3:5-10 **Context**: Jonah's obedience saves the Ninevites from destruction
- a. 3:5 **Reduction**: The Ninevites believe Jonah and respond by repenting and fasting
- b. 3:6-8 The King of Nineveh proclaims a national fast for every citizen and animal.
- c. 3:9 The King's proclamation includes wearing sackcloth, crying out to God and repenting in hopes that God will not bring destruction to Nineveh.
- d. 3:10 In response to the Ninevites' repentance, God changes his mind and does not destroy them.

IV. (4:1-11) JONAH'S REACTION

4:1-4 **Context**: Jonah confronts God about His mercy toward the Ninevites
- a. 4:1 **Reduction**: Jonah did not want God to show mercy to the Ninevites
- b. 4:2-3 **Reduction**: Jonah gives the reason why he initially fled the commission to preach to the Ninevites.
- c. 4:4 **Reduction**: The Lord questions Jonah's reaction

4:5-11 **Context**: God persuades Jonah that He cares for His creation
- a. 4:5 **Reduction**: Jonah positions himself to watch what God will do to the city.
- b. 4:6-8 **Context**: The Lord creates and destroys a bush that brings gratitude and anger, respectfully, to Jonah
- c. 4:9-11 **Context**: Using Jonah's interest in the bush as a model, God declares His concern for all that He has created.

The single thematic statement tying the larger contextual units together is,

10. Jonah, Contextual Flow— Seeing the Flow

Subject of the Book: Jonah's Reluctant Obedience

Major idea 1	• was prefaced by initial disobedience,
Major idea 2	• was necessitated by God's discipline and
Major idea 3	• brought about timely deliverance for Nineveh and
Major idea 4	• was used by God to show His concern for non-Jewish peoples.

> Article 11

11. Jonah, Desperate Praying

Introduction

It is interesting to note that Jonah, like Habakkuk, involves praying that is honest dialog with God. Unlike Nehemiah, who made it a regular habit to shoot prayers upward to God on many occasions,[29] Jonah prays in the midst of a life crisis and then dialogs with God about the results of his ministry. Yet, both of these involve desperate praying

Definition   <u>Desperate praying</u> is prayer, which cries out to God for deliverance from an overwhelming situation.

This prayer if unanswered probably means it is all over for the ministry of the desperate prayer person.

Immediate Desperate Praying—Life Crisis Situation

Notice Jonah's desperate praying. I have boldfaced the sense of desperation, that is, the life threatening implications and Jonah's helpless dependence in the situation. Remember, the following is in Hebrew Poetry. Jonah in post-event reflection wants to heighten the sense of emotional furor he felt. This is a desperate situation deeply felt.

1 Then Jonah prayed to the LORD his God from the fish's belly.

2 And he said:
"I cried out to the LORD **because I was in trouble**,
And He answered me.
"Out of the belly of Sheol I cried,
And You heard my voice.

3 For **You threw me into the deep**, Into the heart of the seas,
And the waves churned all around me;
All Your sea billows and Your waves passed over me.
4 Then I said,
`I have been **cast out of Your sight**;

---

[29] Nehemiah's praying is often desperate also. Many of the occasions are life threatening or some other kind of crisis. But with Nehemiah we have enough information to see that he habitually prayed to God, on the spot, in many situations. With Jonah we have only these two incidents—one involving deliverance in a life crisis and the other involving need for God's answer—if Jonah is to continue in ministry. Apart from getting God's perspective on this situation in Nineveh, Jonah is finished in ministry. He will turn away from following God.

11. Jonah, Desperate Praying page 85

Yet I will look again toward Your holy temple.'[30]
5 The waters surrounded me, even to my soul;
The deep closed around me;
Sea weeds were wrapped around my head.

6 I went down to the base of the underwater sea mountains;
I thought I was **imprisoned there forever**;
Yet You have rescued me from that pit, O LORD, my God.
7 "When my life was slipping away, **I remembered the LORD**;
And my prayer reached You, in Your holy temple.
8 "Those who worship worthless idols miss your mercy.
9 **But I will sacrifice to You**
With the voice of thanksgiving;
I will pay what I have vowed.
Salvation comes from the LORD."

Dialogic Desperate Praying—Long Term Ministry Implications

Chapter 4 in Jonah again reflects desperate praying but in a different way than the life threatening crisis of chapter 2. Here, it is quiet desperation. Jonah is ready to give up on ministry because he is so angry and unhappy with God's solution to the Ninevite situation. So he isolates himself, like Habakkuk, and transparently tells God of his feelings about the ministry and God's response of forgiveness to the Ninevites. God answers this desperate prayer with, again, a different kind of life threatening processing. It gets Jonah's attention. God's perspective is seen. We get the book.

Desperate praying can be active and demanding or it can be reflective and seeking. In either case, God must meet that desperate prayer. And our Biblical cases, of which Jonah is an important illustration show that God does answer desperate prayers.

Closure

I used to belittle fox-hole[31] prayers. Because I saw that many times folks did not keep their vows made in those desperate moments. I am a little more lenient in my criticism of desperate prayers and promises. Not all will follow through. But some will. But now I recognize that desperate situations are God's call for us to call upon Him. My hope is that like Jonah, these situations will indeed drive leaders to God. And I hope that such leaders, me included, will follow-through on our cries to God. If so, I know that God will accomplish His purposes through us. Such is often the ultimate end of desperate praying.

---

[30] A fox-hole promise. See next footnote. This phrase in verse 4 and the action described in verse 9 may be incidents of the prophetic past. I have translated it as a future faith statement. See *prophetic past*, **Glossary**. See **Article**, 4. *Figures and Idioms*.

[31] By fox-hole prayers I am alluding to soldiers who on the front lines and under fire from the enemy often say, "God, if you deliver me from this I will follow you" or something like that. Such promises made under fire are usually forgotten.

Article 12

12. Jonah, First Foreign Missionary?

Introduction

Whether or not Jonah is the first foreign missionary is unimportant. However, what is important is God's concern to reach out across ethnic barriers and cross-cultural barriers to reach people. The main thrust of the book is the lesson that Jonah learns,

> **God cares about other peoples besides the Jewish race and is prepared to meet them, should they respond to Him.**

And God uses people to give the message to those peoples so that they can respond—positively or negatively. Reaching out across cultural barriers will require a whole-hearted obedience to God's call to go to peoples. God deals with obedience in Jonah's case. It is a wonderful illustration of God's providential concern to call leaders to take the message to all peoples of the world. God does care for people. He wants them to know Him and relate to Him and follow just and peaceful ways.

What Jonah Knew Going In

Most likely Jonah embraced the basic paradigm of his day that God worked exclusively on the behalf of Jewish people. He was their God. Most likely Jonah did not sense the importance of the Abrahamic mandate that God was going to bless the world through Abraham's descendants. Most likely Jonah was aware of the history of Israel and how God had worked to deliver Israel in many, many situations, proving in power encounters that He alone was God. And most likely Jonah knew that Assyria was a violent nation and was expanding its empire by destroying surrounding smaller nations. All of these perspectives colored what Jonah was hearing from God in the call to go to the Ninevites and preach to them. Jonah feared Assyria and actually wanted God to bring judgment on that violent warlike nation. By not going to preach to them, perhaps Jonah was hoping to speed up God's judgment.[32] If so, his misperceived obedience was corrected by God's several providential interventions.

What Jonah Learned

Jonah learned that God is bigger than just the Jewish nation. He is concerned about people and animals and life in general. He would that all people relate to him and repent and seek to do justice and live in peace.

What God Wants Us To Know

God is indeed concerned with the nations of the world. We have much more revelation on this in the New Testament with our five repetitive proclamations of the Great Commission. But our study of Jonah should do two things for us:

---

[32] I sometimes call this a mis-perceived obedience. Jonah was living up to the paradigms he knew.

12. Jonah, First Foreign Missionary?

1. It should heighten our awareness of just how much God wants us to obey His commands to take the Gospel around the world. Obedience to God's call is crucial if our world is going to hear the Gospel.

2. It should warn us that many followers of God, like Jonah, will not have a perspective for taking the Gospel to those peoples of the world. They will need to go through a paradigm shift to see its importance. As leaders, we must help them go through this paradigm shift.

Closure

Jonah reluctantly obeyed. Later he saw the importance of this reluctant obedience. We have his testimony. How one receives a call to participate in God's redemptive program to take the Gospel to the nations, is not clear, at least from the Jonah story. But that it is important is clearly seen in the processing of Jonah. Remember, for most people, taken up with the immediacy of surviving economically in their provincial situation, a paradigm shift will be needed to get them aware of God's concerns for getting the Gospel to our world. But God is able to break through and give paradigm shifts. As leaders, we can count on that.

Article 13

13. Jonah, God's Shaping Activities

Introduction

Although the total events of Jonah's life are underrepresented, the book of Jonah gives a glimpse of God's intervention to develop him as a leader. God is involved in shaping Jonah's attitude about the Assyrians so that it conforms to God's. What is striking about this occasion is God's persistence in developing his character through different shaping processes[33] and critical incidents.[34]

The shaping macro lesson[35] was first seen in the Patriarchal Leadership Era in God's intervention in Abraham's life and continues to be observed through the Church Leadership Era. It is a simple lesson:

God shapes leaders' lives and ministry through critical incidents.

The key shaping process is a paradigm shift. Jonah needs a change in his thinking about non-Jewish nations and his assumptions about God's concern, specifically for the Assyrians. Jonah must go through a paradigm shift in order to see that God is not exclusively for Israel. However, several other shaping processes are seen: ministry task, obedience check, isolation, and life crisis. This article will touch on all these shaping activities.

The First Two Shaping Activities in Jonah's Life

Jonah's first critical incident is the call to preach to the Ninevites. This incident illustrates two major processes that are common to God's shaping of many leaders. These two are:

---

[33] Technically, in leadership emergence theory, shaping activities are called <u>process items</u> (since God's uses these items to process or shape a person). Fifty-one common process items have been identified, defined, described and illustrated in leadership emergence theory. These were derived from comparative study of many leader's case studies. Jonah illustrates several of these. Familiarity with process items can help a leader be proactive about responding to God's shaping through them. See **Article**, 6. *God's Shaping Processes With Leaders*.

[34] A <u>critical incident</u> is a special intervention (could be a series over time) in which God gives a *major value* that will flow through the life or will give *strategic direction* to narrow the leader's life work.

[35] A <u>macro-lesson</u> is a high level generalization of a leadership observation (suggestion, guideline, requirement), stated as a lesson, which repeatedly occurs throughout different leadership eras, and thus has potential as a leadership absolute. See **Articles**, 22. *Macro Lessons—Defined*; 23. *Macro Lessons—List of 41 Across Six Leadership eras*.

13. Jonah, God's Shaping Activities

- Ministry Task
- Obedience Check

Let me define each of these and suggest some of the purposes behind them.

Definition   A <u>ministry task</u> is an assignment from God which primarily tests a person's faithfulness and obedience but often also allows use of ministry gifts in the context of a task which has closure, accountability, and evaluation.

Figure Jnh 13-1 depicts how a ministry task is used by God to shape a leader.

Figure Jnh 13-1 Ministry Task Continuum—Luke 16:10 in Action

Little   Much

|———————————————————————————————————|

Primarily for   **JONAH**   Primarily For
Person Doing   **ABOUT HERE**   Doing the Task
The Task

Luke 16:10 The Little/Big Principle
The one who is faithful in little things will be faithful in big things. The one who is unfaithful in little things will be unfaithful in bigger things.

Definition   An <u>obedience check</u> refers to that special category of process items in which God tests personal response to revealed truth in the life of a person.

There are two kinds of patterns of response to an obedience check. Table Jnh 13-1 and Figure 13-2 shows show pictorially the two patterns.

Table Jnh 13-1 Positive Testing Pattern

Stage 1. The Test	Stage 2. The Response	Stage 3. The Follow-Up
God brings the test into the life of a leader.	The leader discerns the test and positively responds to it with a God-honoring and pleasing obedient response.	God expands the leader is some way or moves the leader on to the next level of responsibility.

Table Jnh 13-2 Negative Testing Pattern

Stage 1. The Test	Stage 2. The Response	Stage 3. The Follow-Up
God brings the test into the life of a leader.	The leader either does not discern the test and fails to obey God in it or sees the challenge but does not want to obey. So the leader chooses not to obey.	God brings remedial shaping to try to correct the leader.

13. Jonah, God's Shaping Activities

It is easy to see which of these patterns was Jonah's. Obviously, it was the Negative Testing Pattern. Later on in ch 3 we will see that Jonah did discern this as a test but didn't want to obey because he feared God would be merciful to the Ninevites. And later we shall see Jonah going through the positive test pattern.

So then God uses this ministry task, which was concurrently an obedience check to begin a paradigm shift in Jonah. While other prophets in the Old Testament were asked by God to preach against other countries, Jonah is the only one who was asked to physically go to the foreign country to preach the message that God gave him. In addition to this challenge, Jonah likely holds the common view of the day that God exclusively blesses Israel. The call to preach to the Ninevites required a shift in Jonah so that he would act differently from other prophets and think differently than other Israelites.

The Third Shaping Activity in Jonah's Life

Jonah's remedial training, stage 3 of the negative testing pattern, occurs when he disobeys and runs away looking for a ship to escape on. The second critical incident that God intended for Jonah's growth was the life crisis, which came as a result of the storm and the sailors throwing Jonah overboard.

Definition   The life crisis process item refers to those special intense situations of pressure in human situations which are life threatening and are used by God to test and teach dependence and other ancillary values.

This time of life crisis in the belly of a great fish forced Jonah to reflect on his near death experience, his relationship with God and his disobedience to the call to preach in Assyria. The poem in Jonah 2:1-9 described Jonah's reckoning with his immortality. He wasn't sure he was going to survive. So it makes sense that Jonah also worshipped God for being a rescuing, merciful, and holy God. The prophet recognized God's providence in sending a fish to rescue him and His sovereignty over all that He created. Finally, there is indication in the poem that Jonah recommits himself to God. He makes a fox-hole[36] committal to God. He vows to follow through on what he has promised. Jonah emerges from the belly of the fish with greater conviction about his call and deeper gratitude for God.

The Fourth Shaping Activity—Obedience Check, Passed

The next critical incident involved in the shaping of Jonah was God's second commissioning of the prophet. Having secured Jonah's attention during his isolation processing, the Lord states his intentions a second time that he wants Jonah to "go to Nineveh, that great city, and preach to it the message that I tell you."

Jonah responds positively this time to God's call on his life. This illustrates the Positive Obedience Pattern. The third stage results of the pattern have an unusual expansion and one Jonah did not want. He has almost instant success to his preaching. The Ninevites repent and God shows them mercy. Jonah has shown greater obedience this second time around but, as we will discover later in the book, his obedience comes with some reluctance. This repeated call sets the stage for the reflection that will bring the paradigm shift that is happening for Jonah regarding how he views the Assyrians. This critical incident demonstrates God's commitment to and patience in developing leaders.

---

[36] So called because in war situations where a soldier feels death is imminent he/she often calls on God to get them out of the situation with some sort of vow or promise. Usually the promise or vow is forgotten. The question is, "Will Jonah follow through?" And we see that he does.

13. Jonah, God's Shaping Activities

A Final Shaping Time

Jonah has gone outside the city and is sitting alone waiting to see if God is going to bring judgment or not. This time of reflection along is an illustration of a process item known as isolation.

Definition   <u>Isolation processing</u>[37] refers to the setting aside of a leader from normal ministry involvement in its natural context usually for an extended time involving reflective thinking so as to experience God in a new or deeper way.

In Jonah's case it was not an extended time but concluded a long time of reflection concerning this whole ministry task to preach to the Ninevites.

This critical incident in the ministry of Jonah involved a turning point—the birth and death of the plant that shaded him from the sun. It was used by God to teach an important point. God prepared a plant to protect Jonah from the sun and subsequently prepared a worm to damage the plant. The creation of the plant brought joy to Jonah while the destruction of the plant incensed him. God used the creation and destruction of the plant as an object lesson relating to the creation and destruction of the Ninevites. The creation of the Ninevites brought joy to God while the possibility of Nineveh's destruction was a concern to God. God prefers to be gracious, merciful, slow to anger and abundant in lovingkindness to his creation and for this reason he was eager to relent from destroying the Ninevites once they repented of their wickedness. The creation and destruction of the plant is crucial in advancing the paradigm shift that Jonah goes through to embrace God's perspective toward non-Jewish nations. It is this turning point that makes the difference in the paradigm shift Jonah goes through.

Definition   A <u>paradigm shift</u>[38] is a process item, which refers to God's use of an incident or series of incidents to impress upon the leader a major new perspective (for use in ministry, for viewing things, etc.)

It is clear that Jonah went through this shift since we have the book telling about this. The book itself reflecting Jonah's negative experience and the positive experience of the non-Israelites is itself evidence that Jonah got God's perspective on this. One of the major leadership observations we have learned from comparative study of leaders lives is this,

The difference between leaders and followers is perspective. The difference between leaders and more effective leaders is better perspective.

Jonah, after the paradigm shift, is a much more effective leader. He has God's view concerning the world outside of Israel. Paradigm shifts are the major way that God breaks through a leader's worldview to give new perspective.

Some General Observations Drawn From Jonah

1. God processes individuals so that they can learn about Him. This was certainly Jonah's experience.
2. Humankind can choose to go against God's purposes. Jonah willingly chose to go against God's purposes, at least initially.

---

[37] See **Article**, *7. Isolation Processing —Learning Deep Lessons from God.*
[38] See **Article**, *25. Paradigms And Paradigm Shifts.*

13. Jonah, God's Shaping Activities

3. God may after initial failure reprocess an individual toward his purposes. Jonah received remedial training concerning obedience. The second time he responded.
4. Crises experiences are God's call to know him deeply and to pursue His purposes. Jonah went deep (no pun intended) with God in his crisis experience. And it took for him. He did follow through on his vow.
5. Fasting is a sign of serious intent before God and can be a means of intensifying prayer effort. The Ninevites certainly were serious about repenting.
6. God's guidance is clear guidance. Jonah experienced God's sovereign guidance. Looking back Jonah could say, God's guidance is clear guidance.[39] Notice, God
   a. can use normal human means (lots)
   b. can use circumstances (the boat is ready)
   c. can use nature (the storm, the fish, the vine, the hot desert wind)
   d. can speak to us (directly as he did with Jonah when He explained about the destruction of the shade and His love for all peoples and creatures).

Conclusion

God shapes leaders' lives and ministry through critical incidents. This was true for Jonah and it is true today. Awareness about shaping processes and critical incidents allows a leader to participate more fully with God during the development process. Like Jonah, most leaders will face all four processes that Jonah went through. All leaders will go through paradigm shifts in order to align with God's attitudes and perspectives. The good news is that God is committed to the development of leaders. Leaders exhibit commitment to development when they submit to and learn from God's shaping activity in their lives.

---

[39] See **Article**, *16. Jonah, Sovereign Guidance.*

Article 14

14. Jonah, Hebrew Poetry

Introduction

Perhaps your feeling concerning *Hebrew Poetry* can be expressed in these words, "Why bother?" or "Is it really necessary to study *Hebrew Poetry?*" You might think that there is little need for such knowledge. It might help you to pick up a **New English Bible** and to flip through the pages of the Old Testament. As you do, notice how much of the Old Testament is in the format of **Hebrew Poetry**. It is printed in a form so that it can be easily recognized at a glance. Unless I missed my count some 528 pages out of 1499 contain *Hebrew Poetry*. In many cases the entire page is *Hebrew Poetry*. Yes, *Hebrew Poetry* is important. And for Habakkuk it certainly is important. For the whole book is in *Hebrew Poetry*.

Understanding *Hebrew Poetry* requires some appreciation of its structure. *Hebrew Poetry* is not like *English Poetry*. To our ears there is a special beauty in *English Poetry* associated with the rhyme and rhythm of the words. The beauty in the words and rhythm help us feel emotionally the beauty described. Although *Hebrew Poetry* does have some emphasis on rhyming and rhythm, its essential beauty lies in a <u>*balance of thought*</u> rather than a balance of rhyme or rhythm. *Hebrew Poetry* contains a logical rhythm, which overshadows its metrical rhythm. PARALLELISM is the name usually given to describe the balance of thought seen in Hebrew Poetry.

Hebrew Poetry expresses one thought and then follows it with another parallel thought. The two thoughts are intimately related. Discovering the relationships between the thoughts is the key to grasping the meaning of *Hebrew Poetry*. When one begins to get used to this form of expression—parallel thought relationships—he/she soon sees a deeper beauty even than that felt in the rhyme and rhythm of *English Poetry*.

Hebrew Poetry like all poetry is the language of the heart. One must learn to become sensitive to it. Recognize that it deeply moved its author. It should move your heart as well as your mind. And remember, the author took special pains to communicate what he was feeling. Such is the case with Habakkuk. This was a crucial time in his life. His meeting with God, hearing God's answer, and responding to it were deeply moving to him. That is why he took the time to put it in *Hebrew Poetry*. He also wanted to use some of it in public worship—to be sung.

14. Jonah, Hebrew Poetry

Some Values in Hebrew Poetry

1. Clarification of meaning.
One of the parallel phrases may explain the other phrase using other words so that the meaning is seen more clearly. I have identified several Hebrew Idioms because the parallel phrase explained them.

2. Recognition of the Deep Heart Intent Being Communicated
It is not just cognitive information that is being transmitted. The author wants you to know that he is shooting for *affect impact* as well. He has taken the time to clothe his message in a passionate form meant to move the heart.

3. Overall Thematic Intent of Extended Parallelism
By using the analysis method of reduction one can rather easily identify the overall intent of a stanza or several stanzas.

4. Most Public Worship Songs Were Hebrew Poetry Put To Music
Leaders need to inspire celebration. It is amazing to me to see just how many leaders in the Bible wrote music for public celebration. *Hebrew Poetry* was the medium.

Three Kinds of Parallelism
When analyzing couplets, that is, two lines of parallelism, I use a simplified classification of three types.

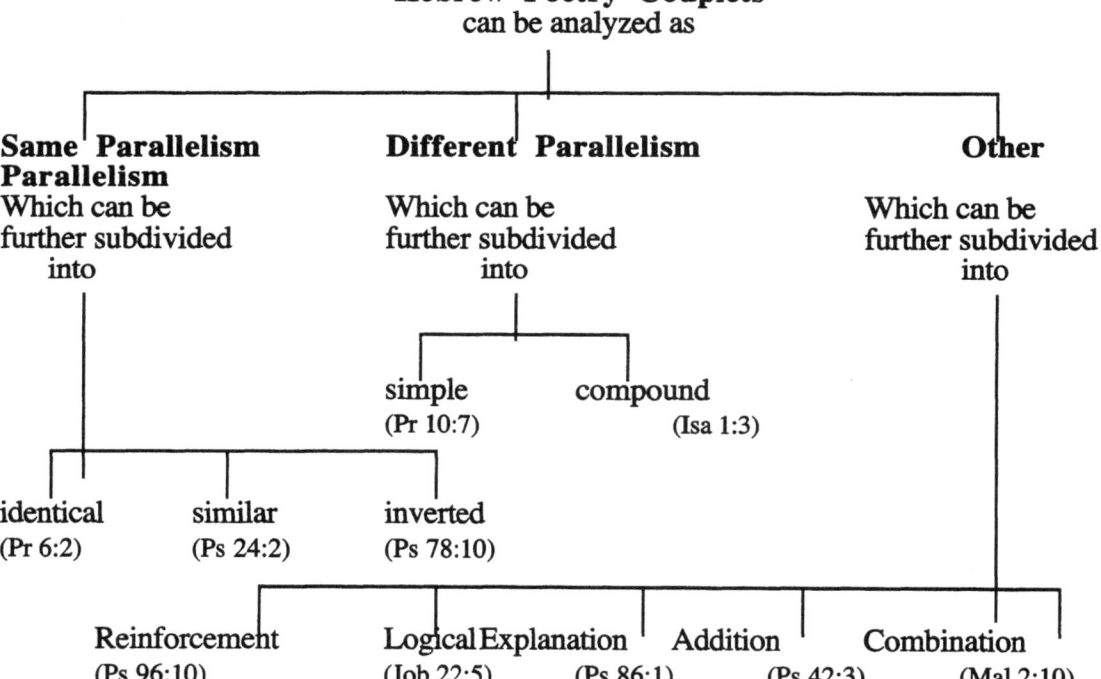

Figure Jnh 14-1 Tree Diagram Giving Overview of 3 Types of Parallelisms

14. Jonah, Hebrew Poetry

Some Basic Definitions of Hebrew Poetry[40]

The basic pattern of *Hebrew Poetry* is the placing of thoughts one right after the other in which basic relationships are expressed between the thoughts or portions of the thoughts.

Definition   Hebrew Poetry is a way of expressing relationships between parallel thoughts in an emotional language. Usually it is the repetition of phrases in which member of one phrase relate to the members of the other phrase.

Definition   Same parallelism refers to the type of *Hebrew Poetry* in which members of one phrase relate to members of the parallel phrase in basically the same way.

The technical word describing same parallelism is *synonymous parallelism*. Terry[41] identifies 3 kinds of synonymous parallelism: (1) identical (when the different members are composed of the same or nearly the same words); (2) similar (when the language and figures differ slightly but the sentiment or intent of members is the same; (3) inverted (where the members are the same in intent or thought though the order of occurrence is not the same in the parallel phrases).

Definition   Hebrew Poetry is said to be different parallelism when one or more members of one phrase is in different correspondence with its related member of the parallel.

Different is here meant to broadly include contrast, or opposite, or unlike manner. The technical name describing different parallelism is *antithetic parallelism*. Terry[42] distinguishes 2 kinds of antithetic parallelism: (1) simple, where contrast occurs in one or more members of a simple couplet); (2) compound, where two or more phrases are contrasted.

Definition   Other parallelism relates to the broad classification of *Hebrew Poetry* not specifically same or different.

The two parallel phrases relate to each other in a number of ways. This is my catch-all category. In technical language each of these is given its own name. I prefer to simply recognize all of these as one category and try to explain in my own words the relationship I see between the phrases.

Here are some of the ways that *Other Parallelism* phrases relate to one anther:

- **Reinforcement**—one phrase reinforces the other through:
  -example;
  -figurative illustration;
  -non-figurative pictorial illustration.

- **Logical**—one phrase relates to the other by:
  -answering a question;
  -posing a question;
  -giving a reason why;
  -drawing an implication;

---

[40] These definitions come from my study manual, **Interpreting The Scriptures: Hebrew Poetry**.
[41] See p. 96 Milton S. Terry, **Biblical Hermeneutics**.
[42] See p. 97 Milton S. Terry, **Biblical Hermeneutics**.

14. Jonah, Hebrew Poetry

-stating a conclusion;
-demanding an application.

- **Explanation**—one phrases clarifies the other by:
  -explaining something in particular about the entire phrase;
  -explaining what is meant in detail about one member of the phrase.

- **Addition**—one phrase introduces new thoughts:
  -adds an entire new thought—perhaps part of a buildup or progressive series of thoughts;
  -adds a new member which has no corresponding member in the other phrase.

- **Combination**—some combination of reinforcement, logical, explanation, or addition often occurs, that is, a given phrase may function in more than one way.

Jonah and Extended Parallelism—Some Basic Definitions

In Proverbs, from chapter 15 onwards, the *Hebrew Poetry* is frequently given in simple couplets. But in most of the *Hebrew Poetry* in the Old Testament, the couplets are combined into larger units. That is, couplets are grouped into stanzas. Not only is there parallelism between phrases in a couplet but there are also relationships between couplets. I call these stanza-like instances of *Hebrew Poetry*, extended parallelism. Jonah ch 2, the poetic section, is entirely made up of extended parallelism.

Definition Extended parallelism describes any unit of *Hebrew Poetry* larger than a couplet in which three or more phrases are placed in parallel. There exits the possibility of thought relationships between any of the phrases in parallel.

A helpful practice in analyzing extended parallelism is to reduce couplets to one line of emphatic meaning. Then extended relationships between lines often become more evident.

Definition A reduction statement (sometimes shortened to reduction) is a one line summary statement representing the emphatic meaning of the couplet.

To be able to state concisely yet comprehensively what a whole stanza is saying is the object of a summary. One carefully observes analysis of reductions, lines, and connectors and then condenses what is seen into a comprehensive statement.

Definition A summary statement is a condensed statement of the entire poetic unit. It consists of the subject of the unit and each major idea developed about the subject.

Definition A connector word(s) is a word(s) such as *but, and, nevertheless*, which connects two phrases or two couplets or a line with a couplet and serves to help interpret the relationships between the things connected.

Definition A connector phrase is a phrase placed between reduction statements or lines (inserted by the interpreter) to indicate the flow of thought in the extended parallelism.

Analysis Procedure

Table Jnh 14-1 gives the basic procedure for analyzing extended *Hebrew Poetry*.

Table Jnh 14-1. Basic Procedure—Analyzing Extended Hebrew Poetry

14. Jonah, Hebrew Poetry

Step	Procedure	Details
1	**REDUCTION ANALYSIS** Recognize and analyze extended parallelism.	1. Identify the stanza to be analyzed. 2. Identify and label lines. 3. Identify and label the couplets. 4. Note all correspondences. 5. Form reductions for all couplets. 6. Analyze extended relationship between reductions, lines, and sub-units. 7. Insert connector words and phrases to bring out interpretive meaning.
2	**FLOW OF THOUGHT ANALYSIS** Interpret your reduction analysis.	1. From each extended sub-unit within a stanza conclude a major idea. 2. Determine a general subject to which all major ideas relate. 3. Condense subject and major ideas into a summary statement.

Some Examples From Jonah—Chapter 2

Chapter 2

Stanza 1

Line 1   1 Then Jonah prayed to the LORD his God from the fish's belly.

Line 2   2 And he said:
Line 3   "I cried out to the LORD because I was in trouble,
Line 4   And He answered me.
Line 5   "Out of the belly of Sheol I cried,
Line 6   And You heard my voice.

Stanza 2

Line 7   3 For You threw me into the deep, Into the heart of the seas,
Line 8   And the waves churned all around me;
Line 9   All Your sea billows and Your waves passed over me.
Line 10   4 Then I said,
Line 11   `I have been cast out of Your sight;
Line 12   Yet I will look again toward Your holy temple.'
Line 13   5 The waters surrounded me, even to my soul;
Line 14   The deep closed around me;
Line 15   Sea weeds were wrapped around my head.
Line 16   6 I went down to the base of the underwater sea mountains;
Line 17   I thought I was imprisoned there forever;
Line 18   Yet You have rescued me from that pit, O LORD, my God.
Line 19   7 "When my life was slipping away, I remembered the LORD;
Line 20   And my prayer reached You, in Your holy temple.

Stanza 3

Line 21   8 "Those who worship worthless idols miss your mercy.
Line 22   9 But I will sacrifice to You
Line 23   With the voice of thanksgiving;
Line 24   I will pay what I have vowed.
Line 25   Salvation comes from the LORD."

Line 1 is preliminary, introducing the prayer, which is written in poetic format.

14. Jonah, Hebrew Poetry

Stanza 1 made up of lines 2-6 has some unusual parallelism. Line 2 and 4 are in other parallel relationship. Jonah spoke and God answered. Lines 3 and 5 are in other parallel relationship. Line 3 tells why Jonah was praying to God. Line 4 tells in figurative language where Jonah is speaking from. The great fish is spoken metaphorically as sheol, the place of the departed dead. The implication is that Jonah was as good as dead when in desperation he cried out to God. Lines 4 and 6 are in same parallel relationship. God heard and answered Jonah.

Reduction statement 1 (lines 2 and 4): I spoke to God and He heard me.
Reduction statement 2 (lines 3 and 5): From the belly of the great fish, in desperation, I cried out to God.

These two reduction statements are in an other parallelism relationship. Statement 2 tells of the desperate situation which prompted the desperate cry to God of statement 1.

Line 6 is in an other parallelism relationship with Reduction statement 1. It explains that God heard the prayer. Obviously this is foreshadowing what happened before it happens (a retrospective perspective).

Reduction statement 3 (lines 2 and 4 with line 6): You heard me.

Relating the reduction statements and supplying connector words we get,

Reduction statement 1 BECAUSE Reduction statement 2 AND Reduction statement 3.

<u>Stanza 1 Summary Statement</u>
I spoke to God and He heard me BECAUSE from the belly of the great fish, in desperation, I cried out to God WITH THE RESULT that you heard me.

<u>Analyzing Stanza 2</u>
Lines 7 through 20 make up stanza 2. This stanza is in other relationship to stanza 1. It explains the desperate situation in detail and more of the prayer and promise that Jonah made.

Lines 7, 8, and 9 are all in same relationship with each other.
Reduction statement 4: You threw me into the depths of the ocean.

Lines 10, 11 (same) are in different relationship with line 12. The sense of this is that in spite of this situation YET something will happen in response to my prayer.
Reduction statement 5: Though in this situation I will pray to you where you will be heard.

Lines 13 and 14 are in same relationship with each other.
Reduction statement 6: I was buried deep in the ocean.

Lines 15 and 16 are in other relationship with each other. Line 16 progressively shows the desperation situation at the bottom of the sea.
Reduction statement 7: I was very deep, at the bottom of the sea.

Lines 17 and 18 are in opposite relationship with each other. Line 18 gives a futuristic (post reflective) resolution to the desperate situation of line 17.
Reduction statement 8: I thought I was finished BUT you delivered me.

14. Jonah, Hebrew Poetry   page 99

Lines 19 and 20 are in other relationship.
Reduction statement 9: At death's door I prayed and got through to you.

The flow of stanza 2 goes like this: *Reduction statement 4*: WHICH FORCED *Reduction statement 5*. REPEATED FOR EMPHASIS *Reduction statement 6*. WHERE *Reduction statement 7* YET *Reduction statement 8* AND SUMMARIZED *Reduction statement 9*.

<u>Stanza 2 Summary Statement</u>
From the depths of the sea in a desperate life or death situation I prayed to you and you delivered me.

<u>Stanza 3 Analyzed</u>
Lines 21 through 25 make up stanza 3 which concludes the poetic section.

Lines 21 and 22 are in different relationship. Jonah contrasts himself and those who relate to God to those, perhaps like the Assyrians. God will show mercy to his own but not to those who worship worthless idols.[43]
Reduction statement 10: Idolaters miss your mercy but I sacrifice to you (implication and receive your mercy).

Lines 23 and 24 are in other relationship. Line 23 gives the result of what Jonah will do because of his promies of line 24.
Reduction statement 11: I will thankfully fulfill my vow to worship you (implied because you showed mercy and delivered me).

Line 25 then summarizes the whole poetic section. The Lord is the one who delivers.

Reduction statement 10 BUT Reduction 11.

<u>Stanza 3 Summary Statement</u>
Unlike idolaters those who worship God will know his mercy and deliverance.

The three stanzas relate to each other as follows:

Stanza 1 introduces the desperate situation. Stanza 2 is in other relationship to stanza 1, explaining in detail more of the desperate situation. Stanza 3 gives the results of Stanzas 1 and 2.

SUMMARY STATEMENT OF WHOLE POETIC SECTION:
I spoke to you, God, and you heard me BECAUSE from the belly of the great fish, in desperation, I cried out to You WITH THE RESULT that you heard me. FURTHER From the very depths of the sea in a desperate life or death situation I prayed to you and you delivered me.

Closure
This life crisis shaping of Jonah clearly brings out both Jonah's desperate situation and his realization that dependence upon God was his only solution. It also reveals clearly his exclusive view of God being only for Israel. But it also shows Jonah as a person of prayer

---

[43] This reinforces the notion of Jonah's worldview that saw God as exclusively for Israel and not for the Assyrians. This is the paradigm that God will change in chapter 4.

14. Jonah, Hebrew Poetry

and integrity. Jonah prays desperately and God answers. In the Old Testament a prime indicator of integrity was the keeping of promises made. Jonah makes a desperate promise to sacrifice to God in Jerusalem if God will save him. This Jonah does. The retrospective poetic section has allusions, futuristic foreshadowing, of the completion of Jonah's vow. This poetic section, heartfelt as it is, and given with deep emotion is difficult to analyze since it goes beyond the simple parallelism normally seen.

Article 15

15. Jonah, Eight Important Ideas to Communicate

Introduction

G. Campbell Morgan, in his book, **Living Messages of the Books of the Bible**, studied each book of the Bible for its contribution to the flow of truth in the Bible as a whole. He specifically identified truth from each book, which was applicable to present day situations. I have capitalized on that notion for Habakkuk, Jonah, and Malachi. These books have some important ideas for leaders today. Jonah, especially deals with crucial obedience ideas.

The Book of Jonah is peculiar among the prophetic writings in that it contains no message delivered to the people of God by the prophet whose name it bears. The book is a story, and the story is the message. It was not written for Nineveh. It was written for Israel, using that word in its narrower application to the Northern kingdom. Even so, its moral values and leadership lessons apply equally well to many of our modern day leadership situations.

We are invited in to see the response of a prophet who is not happy with his ministry assignment.[44] One who was seeing his ministry assignment from a different perspective than God. We are allowed to see how God changes a person's major perspective on issues. God's dealings are complex. We don't get the end result of these dealings but the implications are that Jonah began to see God's perspective. In technical terms we are talking about what missiologists call a paradigm shift.

In order to identify those ideas, we need to know the background of the book. We need to know the situation of the leader, Jonah. We need to know the message of the book. We need to know the structure of the book that develops that message. We need to know the purposes of the book. From such an understanding, we can transfer the truth implied in that situation to similar situations today. From such an analysis, we can then pinpoint several ideas worth communicating today. I have noted 8 ideas from the book of Jonah. But first the background analysis needed to see the basis for getting the 8 ideas.

Understanding Jonah—The Story Line

Jonah, a prophet (2 Kings 14:25), received a commission from the Lord to go and preach to the Assyrians in Nineveh. This great warlike nation was an enemy of Israel (and eventually defeated them and took them into captivity). Jonah did not want to obey this word from the Lord.

---

[44] Sound familiar. I hear this from many leaders today. They are not happy with the ministry situations they find themselves in.

15. Jonah, Important Ideas to Communicate

So he determined to run away—go somewhere where he was not known. He took passage on a ship. The Lord brought a storm. The crew determined that someone on the ship was the cause of their trouble. They cast lots and it fell on Jonah. When questioned he admitted he was running away from God. He and they determined that to save the ship the best thing to do would be to throw Jonah overboard. This they did.

God sent a large fish which swallowed Jonah whole. During the three days Jonah was in the fish's stomach he desperately called on the Lord for deliverance. He made promises to God that he would keep if God delivered him.

The fish vomited Jonah onto dry land. Again the Lord gives the command to go and preach to Nineveh. This time Jonah obeys (with some reluctance in his heart). His message is well received. The Assyrians repent.

Jonah is displeased because he had hoped they wouldn't and that God would destroy them. Jonah waits to see if anything will happen to the Assyrians. God shows Jonah that He is sovereign and has concern for the Assyrians as well as the Jewish people. The narration ends here but it is clear Jonah got the message since he actually wrote up the testimony,[45] which certainly puts himself in a bad light.

Understanding Jonah—The Structure of the Book
The book naturally breaks up into 4 sections as it weaves its story.

Structure

I.	(ch 1:1-17)	Jonah's Disobedience and Discipline
II.	(ch 2:1-10)	Jonah's Deliverance
III.	(ch 3:1-10)	Jonah's Obedience
IV.	(ch 4:1-11)	Jonah's Reaction

Understanding Jonah—The Theme of the Book
The overall message of the book can easily be synthesized from analysis of its structure. One way of integrating the overall message flowing from the four major sections is as follows:

JONAH'S RELUCTANT OBEDIENCE
- was prefaced by initial disobedience,
- was necessitated by God's discipline,
- brought about timely deliverance for Nineveh and
- was used by God to show His concern for non-Jewish peoples.

Understanding Jonah—Some Purposes of the Book
While it is not easy to derive purposes for a book, when they are not stated explicitly by the author, some purposes can tentatively be identified. Some purposes of the book include the following. God wanted,

- to illustrate God's missionary purpose, i.e. to show Israel's true purpose as typified by Jonah,
- to show God's concern for individuals and His intervention in their lives for their good: the sailors, the Assyrians, Jonah,
- to cause a major shift in thinking about God being exclusively just for Jewish people,
- to demonstrate God's processes for bringing about a major shift in thinking.

---

[45] Or related his experience to someone who did write it.

15. Jonah, Important Ideas to Communicate

Implications for Us Today

All leaders will face obedience issues in their lives. Most leaders will need to go through paradigm shifts as God directs them toward His purposes for their peoples. Most leaders will need to be spurred on to go with God in terms of the Great Commission and its implications for their own ministry. Most leaders will be shaped by God with the very same kind of process items that Jonah faced: ministry task, obedience check, crisis or life crisis, isolation, and/or paradigm shift.

Identifying Ideas From Jonah To Present Day Leadership Situations

When I teach the book of Jonah, I first give the information that I have just written above. When folks understand Jonah's situation and God's shaping of him, then they can see how the following 8 ideas are transferable to present day times. I usually choose 3 or 4 of these ideas to use in a short series. Table Jnh 15-1 lists those ideas and gives a brief explanation about each one. I am applying these ideas directly to leaders since that is the thrust of this commentary. But these ideas could well apply to individual followers of God as well.

Table Jnh 15-1. 8 Key Ideas From the Book of Jonah

Idea	Topic	STATEMENT/Discussion
1.	Importance of Biographical information in the Bible	**EFFECTIVE LEADERS LEARN VICARIOUSLY FROM OTHER LEADERS' LIVES./** Biblical leaders' biographical information should be studied to learn lessons vicariously (see Hebrews 13:7,8; 1 Co 10:6, 11; Ro 15:4). <u>Vicarious learning</u> refers to the method of learning from someone else's life. The principle of intentional selectivity plays a vital role here. That something of a biographical nature is included in Scripture, out of all that could be included, signifies something special about the entry. It should be studied carefully. The Holy Spirit superintended the shaping of what is put in the Bible and what is left out. We can be assured that things are included in the Bible for important reasons. Such is the case with biographical information. It is there for a reason. The book of Jonah was important enough to be included. It has some very important lessons for us. This book is not about what a prophet prophesied. It is about the shaping of that prophet. You can learn negative lessons, hard lessons, without going through the deep processing or tragic things the leader you are studying did to learn them. You can learn through the positive things, the blessings, the gains the good things that leader experienced. You can gain valuable long-term perspective that you can not get until you have lived a whole lifetime. In fact, as a leader, you will never learn enough leadership lessons, just from what you experience personally, to have an effective and successful ministry. You need to learn from other leaders.

15. Jonah, Important Ideas to Communicate

		See **Article**, *3. Biographical Study in the Bible, How To Do*.
2.	Responding to God's Shaping Experiences	**LEADERSHIP EMERGENCE CAN BE THWARTED OR IT CAN BE RESPONDED TO IMMEDIATELY. TIME OF DEVELOPMENT WILL VARY DEPENDING ON THE RESPONSE OF THE LEADER./** The flow of this pivotal point in Jonah's life illustrates an obedience continuum[46] moving from a combination of misperceived obedience and willful disobedience to reluctant obedience to willful obedience. Jonah moves as far as reluctant obedience in the book itself but to willful obedience in post-reflective analysis (at least in attitude). Two Patterns are typically seen which enhance or thwart the development time involved in some shaping activities of God. *Positive Testing Pattern* Test and positive response to it and resulting expansion of the leader being shaped. *Negative Testing Pattern* (Jonah's initial reaction) Test and refusal of test (disobedience) and remedial shaping activity to re-enforce the test.
3.	God's Shaping Activity	**GOD SHAPES A LEADER OVER A LIFETIME TO MOVE THAT LEADER TOWARD INHERENT POTENTIAL TO BE AND DO—THAT IS, TO FULFULL THAT LEADER'S DESTINY./** God patiently shapes a leader. We do not have information over the whole of Jonah's life. But it is clear in this short time span in Jonah's life that God is intentionally shaping Jonah. And we can within reason assume that God continued this shaping activity with Jonah. In the book of Jonah the following kinds of shaping activities are illustrated: ministry task, obedience check, life crisis, isolation and paradigm shift. See **Glossary** for these definitions. See **Article**, *13. Jonah, God's Shaping Activities*.
4.	Brokenness And Dependence Upon God	**DEPENDENCE UPON GOD IS FUNDAMENTAL TO ALL EFFECTIVE LEADERSHIP./** Understanding Brokenness as one way of moving toward dependence upon God provides a positive asset for a leader. <u>Brokenness</u> is a state of mind in which a person recognizes that he/she is helpless in a situation or life process unless God alone works. It is a state of mind in which a person acknowledges a deep dependence upon God and is open for God to break through in new ways, thoughts, directions, and revelation of Himself that was not the case before the brokenness experience. Jonah went through a brokenness experience that was the precursor to the important paradigm shift he needed. See **Article**, *9. Jonah, Brokenness*.

---

[46] See **Article**, *17. Jonah, Obedience Testing*.

15. Jonah, Important Ideas to Communicate

5.	God's Sovereignty/ Guidance	**LEADERS WHO HAVE EFFECTIVE MINISTRY, LIKE JONAH, MUST LEARN TO BE SENSITIVE TO GOD'S WORKING IN CIRCUMSTANCES. GOD'S SOVEREIGN ACTIVITY, INCLUDING GUIDANCE, IS VIVIDLY DEMONSTRATED IN JONAH./** The book clearly shows that God is behind the scenes in the shaping of a leader. Numerous sovereign interventions are pointed out: there was a boat ready, a storm comes up, Jonah is chosen by the lots, there is a fish ready, there is an overwhelming response by the Assyrians, there is the sun, the vine. All leaders must learn to see God in the experiences of their life and to believe that He is using them to shape his/her leadership. A leader is a person with God-given capacity and a God-given responsibility who is influencing a specific group of people toward God's purposes for them. For a leader to do this, that leader must be able to get guidance from God. A stepping stone for a leader to get guidance for a group is learning how to get guidance for himself/herself. One aspect of guidance, seen so vividly in Jonah, is that of sovereign guidance through circumstances. It is a tremendous asset for a leader to believe in a sovereign God who can control circumstances. Now guidance through circumstances alone is not totally safe. But it is part of the process. Note how God sovereignly intervenes in human affairs to accomplish His purpose. This sovereign power can be manifested: • in circumstances (vs 3 found a ship) • in control of nature (vs 4 the great wind and violent storm) • in decision making (vs 7 the lots) • in the animal kingdom (vs 17 a great fish, timing) Note the fish does not destroy him—even goes from Tarshish to Nineveh • in nature (supernatural overriding—provided vine, vs 7 east hot wind (like Santa Anas), worm to destroy the vine, then used the whole thing as an object lesson See **Article**, *16. Jonah, Sovereign Guidance.*
6.	God's Concern for the Nations	**GOD WANTS TO REACH OUT TO ALL PEOPLES./** Jonah is the top Old Testament Illustration of God's concern for the nations. The New Testament highlights this important concept through the notion of spreading the Gospel to all peoples—see the five emphases on the Great Commission.[47]
7.	Paradigm Shift	**GOD OFTEN MUST TAKE A LEADER THROUGH A MAJOR PARADIGM SHIFT IN ORDER FOR THAT LEADER TO UNDERSTAND GOD'S WORKING AND TO CONTINUE IN LEADERSHIP./** A paradigm shift, that is, seeing the same reality through new eyes, is a very necessary process through which leaders will go several times over their lifetimes. Taking followers through paradigm shifts is a major function of all leaders. They, themselves, must experientially know this process. A most important paradigm shift

---

[47] See Mt 28:19,20; Mk 16:15; Lk 24:46,47; Jn 20:21; Ac 1:8.

15. Jonah, Important Ideas to Communicate

		occurred for Jonah. He was able to see the Ninevites from God's perspective, after going through the paradigm shift. Jonah studied comparatively with other leaders helps us see some major Lessons about paradigms, paradigm shifts and leaders in the Bible: 1. Paradigms can change slowly (Jonah). 2. Paradigms can change piece by piece (Peter). 3. Paradigms can also change rapidly (Paul). 4. Crisis usually speeds up the process (Jonah, Peter, Paul). See **Article**, *25. Paradigms and Paradigm Shifts*.
8.	Obedience/ Disobedience Continuum	**IMPORTANT LESSONS ON OBEDIENCE ARE ILLUSTRATED BY JONAH'S RESPONSES./** Jonah's responses viewed along a disobedience/obedience continuum (misperceived obedience on the far left; willful disobedience mid-left; reluctant obedience mid-right; willful obedience far right) yields some valuable leadership insights especially when done comparative with other Bible leaders: 1. Willful disobedience can be rooted in greed (Saul of Kish; Achan). 2. Willful disobedience can be rooted in personal desire contrary to God's will (Samson). 3. Misperceived obedience (disobedience) can be rooted in sin (blinded -- Ninevites), our paradigms (traditions . . . Jonah, Israel toward nations), wrong perspectives (2 Co 5 Paul), and/or fear of results (Jonah). 4. Misperceived obedience (disobedience) can be rooted in impatience with God's timing (Saul of Kish). 5. Reluctant obedience can result from God's negative processing (Jonah). 6. Willful obedience is the GOAL of God for a mature follower. (Jesus)

Conclusion

There are great lessons in the book of Jonah; lessons, which apply today. Jonah is such a short book that you can read the whole thing and then teach any of the above lessons that you want to emphasize. I have not exhausted all the ideas that can be applied today from Jonah. But the ones listed above are certainly important ones. And they can make a difference in a leader who wants to finish well.

Article 16

16. Jonah, Sovereign Guidance

Introduction

A leader is a person with God-given capacity and God-given responsibility who is influencing a group of followers towards God's purposes for the group. The central element of this definition of a leader is influencing toward God's purposes. Leaders must know how to get corporate guidance for the groups they are leading. How do they do that? The basic guidance pattern is simple. A leader first learns about personal guidance for his/her own life. Having learned to discern God's direction for his/her own life in numerous crucial decisions, the leader can then shift to the leadership function of determining guidance for the group that is being led. I assume that much guidance will come through one's on-going, obedient, daily walk with God. The guidance seen in the book of Jonah is beyond these routine aspects. Jonah experiences unusual guidance means, not the norm.

Definition <u>Leadership Guidance</u> refers to the process whereby a leader learns to discern from God the perspective needed to make decisions concerning his/her leadership.

In Jonah's case, he did not even want this guidance. As a matter of fact he deliberately avoided the guidance.

Definition <u>Sovereign guidance</u> is the general category of guidance which refers both to the superintending of God over a leader's guidance as well as the direct intervention of God into a leader's guidance choices through divine revelation or circumstantial arrangement of affairs and events so that it is unmistakably clear that God is directing.

Examples of God's sovereign Guidance

In Genesis 12:1-3 we see divine revelation as God's direct intervention into the guidance process for Abraham.

In Genesis 24:12-67 (see especially verses 12-14) God providentially directs circumstances as Abraham's servant selects Rebecca.

Repeatedly in the life of Moses, God gave divine revelation to guide Moses as he led the people. See especially Ex 3 for Moses' call to leadership.

Guideon's fleece in Judges 6:36-40 is an example of divine guidance.

In Acts 8:26 Phillip received sovereign guidance concerning witnessing to the Ethiopian Eunuch.

16. Jonah, Sovereign Guidance

In Acts 9 God's direct intervention channeled Paul into a life of ministry. His direct revelation to Paul to go unto the Gentiles became the touchstone for all that Paul did.

Acts 16:6-10 contains 3 different sovereign guidance instances.

And then we have the book of Jonah in which God is sovereignly at work making sure Jonah gets guidance and understands the reasoning behind it. More on this later.

Essential Characteristic of God's Guidance

All guidance processing assumes the intervention of the living unseen God in the lives of leaders at special points in their lives to provide external guidance for leadership. Such especially was the case with Jonah.

Major Purposes

In general God's intervention, whether sovereign (more direct) or providential (less direct), has a number of important leadership purposes:

1. Give certainty guidance on critical decisions.
2. Give assurance that the leader as a person is pleasing God.
3. Give assurance that the leader's ministry is pleasing God.
4. Give indications that a change in ministry assignment is imminent.
5. Give discernment lessons on the aspects of God's will (what, how, when).

General Guidance Diagram

In my study of leaders, Biblical, historical, and contemporary, I have arrived at a basic approach for getting guidance, both personal and for ministry. Diagram Jnh16-1 below illustrates the basic components that I look for in guidance. The diagram is broken up into a foundational portion and a superstructural portion. The foundation carries the more weight in decision making. However, the more agreement there is with more of the components the more sure is one of the guidance. Glance at the diagram. Then I will describe the various components.

Component 1. God's Voice in **CIRCUMSTANCES**	Component 2. God's Voice in the **HEART**	Component 3. God's Voice in the **CHURCH**

Component 3. God's Voice in the **WORD**
a. Rhema—contemporary revelation via self or others b. Written Scripture—contemporary revelation applying some Scripture c. Written Scripture—general principles, day by day moral guidance, biblical standards.
Items b and c are foundational and have priority over item a. That is, any rhema word needs to be judged by Items b, c. God's contemporary word will never violate principles of His written word.

Diagram Jnh 16-1. Guidance Diagram

16. Jonah, Sovereign Guidance

Table Jnh 16-1 describes the components of the Guidance Diagram.

Table Jnh 16-1 Components of the Guidance Diagram.

Component	Label	Description/ Example
1	God's Voice in Circumstances	Leaders use the phrases "open doors" and "closed doors" to indicate that God sovereignly or providentially controls circumstances to give direction concerning guidance. *Open doors* mean: special opportunities appear; something becomes available at a timely moment; the way to do something is clear and unhindered. *Closed doors* mean: the opportunity to do something is not available; something desired becomes unavailable; the way to do something is blocked. By this they mean, there are circumstantial things happening touching the guidance issues they are assessing./ e.g. a piece of property comes available at the right price for a church that has been seeking to buy property to build on.
2	God's Voice in the Heart	Leaders use the phrase "God's voice in the heart" to mean convictions or feelings or desires assumed to be from God. A leader usually gets inner convictions about guidance. There is a desire to do something. But the question is, where does this come from: God, Satan, self. So we have to be cautious about inner desires about guidance. But without conviction guidance will usually be weak and not followed through on with any certainty.
3	God's Voice in the Church	The Church, in this diagram, stands for counsel from Christians as corporate groups to whom the leader is responsible or has accountability relationship[s as well as individual believers who can give wise counsel.
4	God's Voice in the Word	The Word is used here to mean both the written Word and revelatory Word. Hearing God's voice in the written Word means knowing and applying Bible truth on a given guidance matter.
4a	Contemporary— Rhema	This is a contemporary revelatory Word coming directly from God to the leader or via someone else. People with giftedness including Word of Knowledge, Word of Wisdom, Discernings of Spirits, Prophecy, Word of Faith frequently hear from God directly. This could be the leader himself/herself. Or it could be some gifted person with whom the leader comes in contact. Sometimes these contemporary Word take on the form of inward impressions, audible voice, dreams, pictures, angelic visitations, etc.
4b	Contemporary— Application of Written Word	Sometimes a leader is reading from Scripture and senses that God is making a portion "come alive." He or she senses that God is speaking through that Word to give special direct guidance. This is akin to the contemporary rhema word except it comes through the written word.
4c	Contemporary—	The biblical thrust in guidance is moral guidance and not

16. Jonah, Sovereign Guidance

	General Principles/ Values, etc. from the Written Word	decision-making guidance. The majority of admonitions toward guidance reflect conduct for living. A basic framework for viewing guidance is given in the following diagram first introduced to me by Frank Sells, one of my Bible college instructors. A daily obedient walk with God will allow for guidance to come via these four channels. This will include guidance drawn from direct teaching on the matter, principles derived from teaching and illustration in the written Word (the Old and New Testaments).

Leaders seeking **GUIDANCE** both for personal decisions and for leadership must learn to discern God's voice via these basic guidance channels.

Some basic cautions are in order. Let me give four.

Caution 1. God's voice in the written Word is foundational. A revelatory Word should never contradict the written Word. Revelatory word for major decisions should be confirmed. Once confirmed, revelatory word and written word are foundational and carry priority over the superstructural factors.

Caution 2. Circumstances can be engendered both by God and Satan. Major decisions should never be made on circumstances alone. However, timely circumstances do give a tremendous boost to confidence especially when one is praying along the exact lines and the circumstance happens.

Caution 3. What God is saying to us inwardly must be tested. The desires of the heart can not always be trusted. What we think God is saying may be confused with what we wish He would say. Inner convictions must be honored unless they violate biblical principles—that is a major biblical principle.

Caution 4. While we want to take every advantage of what God has taught others, we must remember that we alone will be responsible for our decisions. Where counsel shows biblical principle, of course, we need to take that in to account. And in general, we will heed wise counsel. But others are not responsible for understanding God's will for us. However, it is good when such counsel lines up with the other components.

Normally major decisions should not have any contradictions between guidance via the different factors. On some decisions there may be silence from some of the factors. But at least there shouldn't be contradictions. If there are, wait for clarification. In fact, a safe guideline is this. **On major decisions the guidance via all the factors should line up and confirm each other.**

Most leadership guidance comes via this model. A leader should be thoroughly familiar with the model experientially as well as cognitively. It is useful in counseling others.

Jonah's Guidance

How does Jonah's guidance in the book of Jonah line up with this guidance model? Table Jnh 16-2 describes the guidance model in terms of Jonah's experience.

16. Jonah, Sovereign Guidance

Table Jnh 16-2 Jonah and Components of the Guidance Diagram.

Component	Label	Description/ Example
1	God's Voice in Circumstances	Jonah wanted to run away. A boat was there ready to take him. You can't always trust circumstances.
2	God's Voice in the Heart	Jonah's inward desires were not to go and preach to the Ninevites. However, he knew this was not what God wanted.
3	God's Voice in the Church	Nothing indicated. Church here in the O.T. context would be fellow prophets, etc.
4	God's Voice in the Word	Nothing indicated from the written Word. There was much there that should have spoken to Jonah including God's mandate to bless the world through Abraham's descendants.
4a	Contemporary—Rhema	Jonah got contemporary revelation from God—we do not know in what form. However, he did not want to heed it and ran from it. After Jonah reluctantly obeyed, we see him getting contemporary revelation via circumstances (hot desert wind; plant providing shade; God killing the plant) and directly from God. Either audible or impressions in the heart and mind.
4b	Contemporary—Application of Written Word	None.
4c	Contemporary—General Principles/ Values, etc. from the Written Word	Same as 4 in general. Our paradigms can keep us from seeing or at least agreeing with guidance we get. Jonah's exclusive view of God for Israelites only made it difficult for him to obey a guidance direction that would help Assyria.

The major thing we learn about guidance in Jonah is that, if one doesn't want to follow God's guidance, he or she can choose to do so. In Jonah's case God gave a second chance. He continued to give further guidance. It is clear through the book that God was sovereignly intervening. The storm, the sailors casting of lots, the big fish. The second clear word to go. And then after the powerful ministry response, God explains the purposes behind His guidance. Deep processing brought Jonah around to reluctantly follow God's guidance. We can't guarantee that if we receive guidance and disobey it, that God will give us a second chance. But we can believe with all our hearts that God will guide us if we want that guidance.

Closure

In our personal lives and ministry situations we will need guidance. We should recognize the ways that guidance comes. And we should follow God's clear guidance. We should also be warned from Jonah of the consequences of disobeying God's guidance.

Article 17

17. Jonah, Obedience Testing

Introduction

Although the total events of Jonah's life are underrepresented, the book of Jonah gives a glimpse of God's intervention to develop him as a leader. God is involved in shaping Jonah's attitude about the Assyrians so that it conforms to God's. What is striking about this occasion is God's persistence in developing his character through different shaping processes[48] and critical incidents.[49]

The shaping macro lesson[50] was first seen in the Patriarchal Leadership Era in God's intervention in Abraham's life and continues to be observed through the Church Leadership Era. It is a simple lesson:

God shapes leaders' lives and ministry through critical incidents.

The key shaping process is a paradigm shift. Jonah needs a change in his thinking about non-Jewish nations and his assumptions about God's concern, specifically for the Assyrians. Jonah must go through a paradigm shift in order to see that God is not exclusively for Israel. However, several other shaping processes are seen: ministry task, obedience check, isolation, and life crisis. This article will touch on all these shaping activities.

The First Two Shaping Activities in Jonah's Life

Jonah's first critical incident is the call to preach to the Ninevites. This incident illustrates two major processes that are common to God's shaping of many leaders. These

---

[48] Technically, in leadership emergence theory, shaping activities are called process items (since God's uses these items to process or shape a person). Fifty-one common process items have been identified, defined, described and illustrated in leadership emergence theory. These were derived from comparative study of many leader's case studies. Jonah illustrates several of these. Familiarity with process items can help a leader be proactive about responding to God's shaping through them. See **Article**, *6. God's Shaping Processes With Leaders*.

[49] A critical incident is a special intervention (could be a series over time) in which God gives a *major value* that will flow through the life or will give *strategic direction* to narrow the leader's life work.

[50] A macro-lesson is a high level generalization of a leadership observation (suggestion, guideline, requirement), stated as a lesson, which repeatedly occurs throughout different leadership eras, and thus has potential as a leadership absolute. See **Articles**, *22. Macro Lessons—Defined; 23. Macro Lessons—List of 41 Across Six Leadership eras*.

17. Jonah, Obedience Testing

two are:

- Ministry Task
- Obedience Check

Let me define each of these and suggest some of the purposes behind them.

Definition A <u>ministry task</u> is an assignment from God which primarily tests a person's faithfulness and obedience but often also allows use of ministry gifts in the context of a task which has closure, accountability, and evaluation.

Figure Jnh 17-1 depicts how a ministry task is used by God to shape a leader.

```
Little                                                              Much
|------------------------------------------------------------------------|

Primarily for              JONAH                         Primarily For
Person Doing               ABOUT HERE                    Doing the Task
The Task
```

Luke 16:10 The Little/Big Principle
The one who is faithful in little things will be faithful in big things. The one who is unfaithful in little things will be unfaithful in bigger things.

Figure Jnh 17-1 Ministry Task Continuum—Luke 16:10 in Action

definition An <u>obedience check</u> refers to that special category of process items in which God tests personal response to revealed truth in the life of a person.

There are two kinds of patterns of response to an obedience check. Table Jnh 17-1 and Table Jnh 17-2 shows show pictorially the two patterns.

Table Jnh 17-1 Positive Testing Pattern

Stage 1. The Test	Stage 2. The Response	Stage 3. The Follow-Up
God brings the test into the life of a leader.	The leader discerns the test and positively responds to it with a God-honoring and pleasing obedient response.	God expands the leader is some way or moves the leader on to the next level of responsibility.

Table Jnh 17-2 Negative Testing Pattern

Stage 1. The Test	Stage 2. The Response	Stage 3. The Follow-Up
God brings the test into the life of a leader.	The leader either does not discern the test and fails to obey God in it or sees the challenge but does not want to obey. So the leader chooses not to obey.	God brings remedial shaping to try to correct the leader.

17. Jonah, Obedience Testing

It is easy to see which of these patterns was Jonah's. Obviously, it was the Negative Testing Pattern. Later on in ch 3 we will see that Jonah did discern this as a test but didn't want to obey because he feared God would be merciful to the Ninevites. And later we shall see Jonah going through the positive test pattern.

So then God uses this ministry task, which was concurrently an obedience check to begin a paradigm shift in Jonah. While other prophets in the Old Testament were asked by God to preach against other countries, Jonah is the only one who was asked to physically go to the foreign country to preach the message that God gave him. In addition to this challenge, Jonah likely holds the common view of the day that God exclusively blesses Israel. The call to preach to the Ninevites required a shift in Jonah so that he would act differently from other prophets and think differently than other Israelites.

The Third Shaping Activity in Jonah's Life

Jonah's remedial training, stage 3 of the negative testing pattern, occurs when he disobeys and runs away looking for a ship to escape on. The second critical incident that God intended for Jonah's growth was the life crisis, which came as a result of the storm and the sailors throwing Jonah overboard.

Definition The life <u>Crisis process item</u> refers to those special intense situations of pressure in human situations which are life threatening and are used by God to test and teach dependence and other ancillary values.

This time of life crisis in the belly of a great fish forced Jonah to reflect on his near death experience, his relationship with God and his disobedience to the call to preach in Assyria. The poem in Jonah 2:1-9 described Jonah's reckoning with his immortality. He wasn't sure he was going to survive. So it makes sense that Jonah also worshipped God for being a rescuing, merciful, and holy God. The prophet recognized God's providence in sending a fish to rescue him and His sovereignty over all that He created. Finally, there is indication in the poem that Jonah recommits himself to God. He makes a fox-hole[51] committal to God. He vows to follow through on what he has promised. Jonah emerges from the belly of the fish with greater conviction about his call and deeper gratitude for God.

The Fourth Shaping Activity—Obedience Check, Passed

The next critical incident involved in the shaping of Jonah was God's second commissioning of the prophet. Having secured Jonah's attention during his isolation processing, the Lord states his intentions a second time that he wants Jonah to "go to Nineveh, that great city, and preach to it the message that I tell you."

Jonah responds positively this time to God's call on his life. This illustrates the Positive Obedience Pattern. The third stage results of the pattern have an unusual expansion and one Jonah did not want. He has almost instant success to his preaching. The Ninevites repent and God shows them mercy. Jonah has shown greater obedience this second time around but, as we will discover later in the book, his obedience comes with some reluctance. This repeated call sets the stage for the reflection that will bring the paradigm shift that is happening for Jonah regarding how he views the Assyrians. This critical incident demonstrates God's commitment to and patience in developing leaders.

---

[51] So called because in war situations where a soldier feels death is imminent he/she often calls on God to get them out of the situation with some sort of vow or promise. Usually the promise or vow is forgotten. The question is, "Will Jonah follow through?" And we see that he does.

17. Jonah, Obedience Testing

A Final Shaping Time

Jonah has gone outside the city and is sitting alone waiting to see if God is going to bring judgment or not. This time of reflection along is an illustration of a process item known as isolation.

Definition   Isolation processing[52] refers to the setting aside of a leader from normal ministry involvement in its natural context usually for an extended time involving reflective thinking so as to experience God in a new or deeper way.

In Jonah's case it was not an extended time but concluded a long time of reflection concerning this whole ministry task to preach to the Ninevites.

This critical incident in the ministry of Jonah involved a turning point—the birth and death of the plant that shaded him from the sun. It was used by God to teach an important point. God prepared a plant to protect Jonah from the sun and subsequently prepared a worm to damage the plant. The creation of the plant brought joy to Jonah while the destruction of the plant incensed him. God used the creation and destruction of the plant as an object lesson relating to the creation and destruction of the Ninevites. The creation of the Ninevites brought joy to God while the possibility of Nineveh's destruction was a concern to God. God prefers to be gracious, merciful, slow to anger and abundant in lovingkindness to his creation and for this reason he was eager to relent from destroying the Ninevites once they repented of their wickedness. The creation and destruction of the plant is crucial in advancing the paradigm shift that Jonah goes through to embrace God's perspective toward non-Jewish nations. It is this turning point that makes the difference in the paradigm shift Jonah goes through.

Definition   A paradigm shift[53] is a process item, which refers to God's use of an incident or series of incidents to impress upon the leader a major new perspective (for use in ministry, for viewing things, etc.)

It is clear that Jonah went through this shift since we have the book telling about this. The book itself reflecting Jonah's negative experience and the positive experience of the non-Israelites is itself evidence that Jonah got God's perspective on this. One of the major leadership observations we have learned from comparative study of leaders lives is this,

> **The difference between leaders and followers is perspective. The difference between leaders and more effective leaders is better perspective.**

Jonah, after the paradigm shift, is a much more effective leader. He has God's view concerning the world outside of Israel. Paradigm shifts are the major way that God breaks through a leader's worldview to give new perspective.

Some General Observations Drawn From Jonah

In addition to our discussion about shaping in particular, there are also some other observations worth noting:

1. God processes individuals so that they can learn about Him. This was certainly Jonah's experience.

---

[52] See **Article**, *7. Isolation Processing —Learning Deep Lessons from God.*
[53] See **Article**, 25. *Paradigms And Paradigm Shifts.*

17. Jonah, Obedience Testing

2. Humankind can choose to go against God's purposes. Jonah willingly chose to go against God's purposes, at least initially.
3. God may after initial failure reprocess an individual toward his purposes. Jonah received remedial training concerning obedience. The second time he responded.
4. Crises experiences are God's call to know him deeply and to pursue His purposes. Jonah went deep (no pun intended) with God in his crisis experience. And it took for him. He did follow through on his vow.
5. Fasting is a sign of serious intent before God and can be a means of intensifying prayer effort. The Ninevites certainly were serious about repenting.
6. God's guidance is clear guidance. Jonah experienced God's sovereign guidance. Looking back Jonah could say, God's guidance is clear guidance.[54] Notice, God
   a. can use normal human means (lots)
   b. can use circumstances (the boat is ready)
   c. can use nature (the storm, the fish, the vine, the hot desert wind)
   d. can speak to us (directly as he did with Jonah when He explained about the destruction of the shade and His love for all peoples and creatures).

Conclusion

God shapes leaders' lives and ministry through critical incidents. This was true for Jonah and it is true today. Awareness about shaping processes and critical incidents allows a leader to participate more fully with God during the development process. Like Jonah, most leaders will face all four processes that Jonah went through. All leaders will go through paradigm shifts in order to align with God's attitudes and perspectives. The good news is that God is committed to the development of leaders. Leaders exhibit commitment to development when they submit to and learn from God's shaping activity in their lives.

---

[54] See **Article**, 16. *Jonah, Sovereign Guidance*.

Article 18

18. Learning Vicariously From Other Leaders' Lives

Introduction

I like to refer to Hebrews 13:7,8 as *The Leadership Mandate*. That is, we have the right and duty to study leaders and in fact are commanded to do so. Note my paraphrase of this famous contextual unit in Hebrews 13.

> Remember your former leaders. Imitate those qualities and achievements
> that were God-Honoring, for their source of leadership still lives -- Jesus!
> He, too, can inspire and enable your own leadership today.
> Hebrews 13:7,8 Clinton paraphrase

The Leadership Mandate carries a two-fold whammy. One, you can study leaders—biblical, historical, and contemporary—for God-honoring qualities and achievements, that is, learning leadership lessons from their lives. And you can expect Jesus to enable you to get these same things in your own life and leadership. Two, you can model leadership qualities and achievements in your own life and expect God to use them in other lives. This leads me to identify an important leadership observation.

EFFECTIVE LEADERS LEARN VICARIOUSLY FROM OTHER LEADERS' LIVES.

Passages like 1 Co 10:6, 11 and Ro 15:4 exhort us to learn from the examples of the Old Testament in general. And Hebrews 13:7,8 exhort us to learn from the examples of leaders specifically. Biblical leaders' biographical information should be studied to learn lessons vicariously.

Vicarious Learning Defined

Let me define vicarious learning and give two reasons why it is important.

Definition   <u>Vicarious learning</u> refers to the method of learning from someone else's life.

Reason 1. The principle of intentional selectivity plays a vital role here. That something of a biographical nature is included in Scripture, out of all that could be included, signifies something special about the entry. It should be studied carefully. The Holy Spirit superintended the shaping of what is put in the Bible and what is left out. We can be assured that things are included in the Bible for important reasons. Such is the case with biographical information. It is there for a reason. The book of Jonah was important enough to be included. It has some very important lessons for us. This book is not about what a prophet prophesied. It is about the shaping of that prophet.

18. Learning Vicariously From Other Leader's Lives

Reason 2. You will not have enough time nor experiences to learn first hand all of the leadership lessons you will need to have an effective ministry. You must learn to learn second hand in order to get the leadership lessons you will need for your ministry.

Biography Leadership Genre

Biographical data represents the single most important leadership source in the Old Testament and a large source in the New Testatment.[55] There is much biographical information in the Bible.

Definition — <u>Biographical</u> data refers to that large amount of information in the Scriptures, which is made up of small narrative slices of life about a person.

These narrative slices or vignettes gives information about Bible characters, which allows us to perceive processing, pivotal points, leadership acts or other such interpretations from this source material. The more slices there are the more we can build to a more complete biography. Examples of biographical information include the biblical material on Joseph, Moses, Joshua, Caleb, Jephthah, Habakkuk, and Jonah. In fact, some 288 biblical leaders are named in the Old Testament and 112 are named in the New Testament. Not all these leaders named have sufficient information for profitable biographical study. Of these 400 leaders, there is enough information to do helpful leadership studies of about 75.

Four Different Kinds of Biographical Sources

Depending on the kind and amount of information available, biographical studies can be broken into four major categories.[56]

1. **CRITICAL INCIDENT SOURCE.** A single incident or series of incidents taking place in a very short time. There may actually be a large amount of information but all focused on a short time-interval. The information can be interpreted for processing or for a leadership act or other such findings.

   example: Job, Habakkuk, Jonah

2. **MINI-SOURCES.** Multiple incidents over a period of time, which allows the creation of an abbreviated time-line and the possibility to see some patterns over time.

   example: Asa, Jehoshaphat, Hezekiah

3. **MIDI-SOURCES.** Multiple incidents over the whole lifetime, which allow not only the creation of an abbreviated time-line but some processing from the various time periods.

---

[55] Seven types of leadership source materials have been identified in the Bible. These include: 1. Biographical like Joseph, Moses, Joshua, Caleb, Jephthah, etc.; 2. Historical Leadership Acts—e.g. Samuel's final leadership act 1Samuel 12; 3. Actual leadership contexts like 1 Peter 5:1-5; 4. Parabolic leadership literature like the Stewardship parables and many others; 5. Indirect—passages dealing with Christian character or behavior, which also apply to Christian leadership as well; 6. The study of Bible books as a whole—placing them in their context hermeneutically and in terms of leadership development; 7. The Study across Books for common themes and lessons on leadership (macro lessons). See the **Article**, *20. Leadership Genre—7 Types*.

[56] These four categories are not exclusive. There is some overlap in these at the borders between them.

18. Learning Vicariously From Other Leader's Lives

example: Barnabas, Joseph, Daniel, Joshua, Peter, Jeremiah

4. **MAXI-SOURCES.** There is much information in the Scripture on the character.

example: Moses, David, Jesus, Paul, Jeremiah

Jonah—Critical Incident Source

Jonah is typical of a critical incident source of biographical information. Our study of Jonah in this commentary includes only a very few scenarios from his life that represent perhaps a few months. Yet this information has in it a number of leadership lessons.

Values of Vicarious Learning Through Biography

You can learn negative lessons, hard lessons, without going through the deep processing or tragic things the leader you are studying did to learn them.

You can learn through the positive things, the blessings, the gains the good things that leader experienced.

You can gain valuable long-term perspective that you cannot get until you have lived a whole lifetime.

In fact, as a leader, you will never learn enough leadership lessons, just from what you experience personally, to have an effective and successful ministry. You need to learn from other leaders.

How To Do Biographical Study

The **Article**, *3. Biographical Study in the Bible, How To Do* lists 12 steps for doing biographical study. I list them below to indicate what is involved in studying to learn vicariously. But you should study that article in depth. It is not the purpose of this article to teach you how to do biographical study, but to exhort you of its importance.

<u>Step 1</u>. **Identify All The Passages That Refer To The Leader.** e.g. Jonah is mentioned once outside the book of Jonah and then a number of times in the book of Jonah.

<u>Step 2</u>. **Seek To Order The Vignettes Or Other Passages In A Time Sequence.** e.g. for a critical incident source like Jonah, the book itself orders what happened.

<u>Step 3</u>. **Construct A Time-Line If You Can. At Least Tentatively Identify Major Development Phases.** e.g. this can't be done for Jonah or Habakkuk. We simply know that the critical incidents take place during the mature portion of their ministry.

<u>Step 4</u>. **Look For Process Items (Critical Events, People, Happenings) In The Life.** e.g. Jonah has 5 identifiable process items: ministry task; obedience check; life crisis; isolation; paradigm shift. Habakkuk has four: crisis; faith challenge; isolation; paradigm shift. See **Glossary** for definitions of these process items.

<u>Step 5</u>. **Identify Pivotal Points From The Major Process Items.** e.g. for both Habakkuk and Jonah the series of critical incidents describe a pivotal point in their ministries. See **Article**, *26. Pivotal Points*.

18. Learning Vicariously From Other Leader's Lives

<u>Step 6</u>. **Seek To Determine Any Lessons You Can From A Study Of These Process Items And Pivotal Points. Use The Certainty Continuum To Help You Identify The Level Of Authority For Using The Lessons You Find.** See **Article**, *Principles of Truth*. e.g. The study of Jonah and Habakkuk results in numerous leadership observations. See the **Articles**, *15. Jonah, Eight Important Ideas to Communicate; Habakkuk, Eight Important Ideas to Communicate*. See also the leadership topics and text comments which contain many leadership observations.

<u>Step 7</u>. **Identify Any Response Patterns** (or unique patterns). e.g. for Jonah, the negative and positive test patterns are seen.

<u>Step 8</u>. **Study Any Individual Leadership Acts In The Life. Use The Approach Demonstrated In This Chapter.** See *leadership act*, **Glossary**. e.g. for Jonah, this step is not applicable.

<u>Step 9</u>. **Use The Overall Leadership Tree Diagram To Help Suggest Leadership Issues To Look For.** See **Article**, *Leadership Tree Diagram*. e.g. for Jonah, this step is not applicable.

<u>Step 10</u>. **Use The List Of Major Functions (Task Functions, Relationship Functions And Inspirational Functions) To Help Suggest Insights. Which Were Done, Which Not.** See **Article**, *Leadership Functions*. e.g. for Jonah, this step is not applicable.

<u>Step 11</u>. **Observe Any N.T. Passages Or Commentary** (indirect source—anywhere in Bible) **On The Leader. Especially Be On The Lookout For** *Bent Of Life* **Evaluation.** e.g. for Jonah, Jesus validates the historicity of Jonah and the important lesson concerning truth and its response and degrees of judgment.

<u>Step 12</u>. **Use The Presentation Format For Organizing Your Display Of Findings For Steps 1-11.** e.g. for Jonah, this step is not applicable.

Closure

The difference between leaders and followers is perspective. The difference between leaders and effective leaders is better perspectives. Vicarious learning affords a leader a chance to get better perspectives. Yet, many leaders have never done any biographical study of biblical leaders, historical Christian leaders or contemporary Christian leaders. You must learn how to learn second hand.

Article 19

19. Leadership Eras In The Bible, Six Identified

Introduction

A <u>Bible Centered leader</u> refers to a leader whose leadership is informed by the Bible, who has been personally shaped by Biblical values, has grasped the intent of Scriptural books and their content in such a way as to apply them to current situations and who uses the Bible in ministry so as to impact followers. Notice that first concept again—

whose leadership is informed by the Bible.

Two of the most helpful perspectives for becoming a Bible centered leader **whose leadership is informed by the Bible** include:

(1) recognizing the differences in leadership demands on leaders throughout the Bible, i.e. seeing the different leadership eras, and
(2) Recognizing and knowing how to draw out insights from the seven genre of leadership sources in the Bible.

This article overviews the first of these helpful perspective—seeing the leadership eras in the Bible.

The Six Leadership Eras

Let me start by giving you one of the most helpful perspectives, a first step toward getting leadership eyes, for recognizing leadership findings in the Bible. That first helpful perspective involves breaking down the leadership that takes place in the Bible into leadership eras which on the whole share common leadership assumptions and expectations for the time period. These assumptions and expectations differ from one leadership era to the next, though there are commonalties that bridge across the eras.

Definition A <u>leadership era</u> is a period of time, usually several hundred years long, in which the major focus of leadership, the influence means, basic leadership functions, and followership have much in common and which basically change with time periods before or after it.

An outline of the six eras I have identified follows.

I. Patriarchal Era (Leadership Roots)—Family Base
II. Pre-Kingdom Leadership Era—Tribal Base
  A. The Desert Years
  B. The War Years--Conquering the Land,
  C. The Tribal Years/ Chaotic Years/ Decentralized Years--Conquered by the Land

19. Leadership Eras in the Bible, Six Identified

III. Kingdom Leadership Era—Nation Based
  A. The United Kingdom
  B. The Divided Kingdom
  C. The Single Kingdom--Southern Kingdom Only
IV. Post-Kingdom Leadership Era—Individual/ Remnant Based
  A. Exile--Individual Leadership Out of the Land
  B. Post Exilic--Leadership Back in the Land
  C. Interim--Between Testaments
V. New Testament Pre-Church Leadership—Spiritually Based in the Land
  A. Pre-Messianic
  B. Messianic
VI. New Testament Church Leadership—Decentralized Spiritually Based
  A. Jewish Era
  B. Gentile Era

I have used the following tree diagram[57] to provide an overview of leadership. The three overarching components of leadership include: the leadership basal elements (leader, follower, situation which make up the What of leadership); leadership influence means (individual and corporate leadership styles which make up the How of leadership); and leadership Value bases (Biblical and cultural values which make up the Why of leadership).

The Study Of Leadership
involves

Leadership Basal Elements	Leadership Influence Means	Leadership Value Bases
including	such as	including
• Leader	• Individual Means	• Cultural
• Followers	• Corporate Means	• Theological
• Situation	• Spiritual Means	

Figure Jnh 19-1. Tree Diagram Categorizing the Basics of Leadership

It was this taxonomy which suggested questions that helped me see for the first time the six leadership eras of the Bible. Table Jnh 18-1 below gives the basic questions/subjects/categories that helped me identify the different leadership eras. It is these categories that allows comparison of different leadership periods in the Bible.

Table Jnh 19-1. Basic Questions To Ask About Leadership Eras

1. **Major Focus**—Here we are looking at the overall purposes of leadership for the period in question. What was God doing or attempting to do through the leader? Sense of destiny? Leadership mandate?
2. **Influence means**—Here we are describing any of the power means available and used by the leaders in their leadership. We can use any of Wrong's categories or any of the leadership style categories I define. Note particularly in the Old Testament the use of force and manipulation as power means.

---

[57] This was derived in a research project, the historical study of leadership in the United States from the mid 18th century to the present—for further study see **A Short History of Leadership Theory**, 1986, by Dr. J. Robert Clinton. Altadena, CA: Barnabas Publishers. See **Further Study Bibliography**.

19. Leadership Eras in the Bible, Six Identified

3. **Basic leadership functions**—We list here the various achievement/ responsibilities expected of the leaders: from God's standpoint, from the leader's own perception of leadership, from the followers. Usually they can all be categorized under the three major leadership functions of task, relational, and inspirational functions. But here we are after the specific functions.
4. **Followers**—Here we are after sphere of influence. Who are the followers? What are their relationship to leaders? Which of the 10 Commandments of followership are valid for these followers? What other things are helpful in describing followers?
5. **Local Leadership**—in the surrounding culture: Biblical leaders will be very much like the leaders in the cultures around them. Leadership styles will flow out of this cultural press. Here we are trying to identify leadership roles in the cultures in contact with our Biblical leaders.
6. **Other**—Miscellaneous catch all: such things as centralization or decentralization or hierarchical systems of leadership; joint (civil, political, military, religious) or separate roles.
   Thought Questions—Here try to synthesize the questions you would like answered about leaders and leadership if you could get those answers. We are dealing here with such things as the essence of a leader (being or doing), leadership itself, leadership selection and training, authority (centralized or decentralized), etc.

Using these leadership characteristics I studied leadership across the Bible and inductively generated the Six Leadership Eras as given above.[58] Table Jnh 19-2 adds some descriptive elements of the eras.

Table Jnh 19-2. Six Leadership Eras in the Bible—Brief Characterizations

Leadership Era	Example(s) of Leader	Definitive Characteristics
1. Foundational (also called patriarchal)	Abraham, Joseph	Family Leadership/ formally male dominated/ expanding into tribes and clans as families grew/ moves along kin ship lines
2. Pre-Kingdom	Moses, Joshua, Judges	Tribal Leadership/ Moving to National/ Military/ Spiritual Authority/ outside the land moving toward a centralized national leadership
3. Kingdom	David, Hezekiah	National Leadership/ Kingdom Structure/ Civil, Military/ Spiritual/ a national leadership—Prophetic call for renewal/ inside the land/ breakup of nation
4. Post-Kingdom	Ezekiel, Daniel, Ezra	Individual leadership/ Modeling/ Spiritual Authority
5. Pre-Church	Jesus/ Disciples	Selection/ Training/ spiritual leadership/ preparation for decentralization of Spiritual Authority/ initiation of a movement/

---

[58] I have a short form of answers to each of these questions for each of the six leadership eras. See **Article 28. Six Biblical Leadership Eras, Approaching the Bible With Leadership Eyes**, where I answer these questions for each era.

19. Leadership Eras in the Bible, Six Identified

| 6. Church | Peter/ Paul/ John | decentralized leadership/ cross-cultural structures led by leaders with spiritual authority which institutionalize the movement and spread it around the world |

When we study a leader or a particular leadership issue in the Scriptures we must always do so in light of the leadership context in which it was taking place. We cannot judge past leadership by our present leadership standards. Conversely, we will find that major leadership lessons learned by these leaders will usually have broad implications for our leadership.

See **Articles**: *Leadership Genre—Seven Types; 22. Macro Lessons Defined; 23. Macro Lessons —List of 41 Across Six Leadership Eras; 28. Six Biblical Leadership Eras, Approaching the Bible With Leadership Eyes.*

Article 20

20. Leadership Genre—7 Types

Introduction
Leadership Genre—Seven Types

Introduction to the Seven Leadership Genre

A Bible Centered leader refers to a leader whose leadership is informed by the Bible, who has been personally shaped by Biblical values, has grasped the intent of Scriptural books and their content in such a way as to apply them to current situations and who uses the Bible in ministry so as to impact followers. Notice that first concept again—

whose leadership is informed by the Bible.

Two of the most helpful perspectives for becoming a Bible centered **leader whose leadership is informed by the Bible** include:

(1) recognizing the differences in leadership demands on leaders throughout the Bible, i.e. seeing the different leadership eras, and
(2) Recognizing and knowing how to draw out insights from the seven genre of leadership sources in the Bible.

This article overviews the second of these helpful perspectives—the seven leadership genres and how to get leadership information from them.

The Seven Genre—Derived From Study Across Six Leadership Eras

In a related treatment (see *Overview of Six Leadership Eras in the Bible* in **Section III**) I identified six periods of time, each of which characterized a major leadership era in the Bible. See Table Jnh 20-1 below.

Table Jnh 20-1. Six Leadership Eras in the Bible

Era	Name	Central Feature
I.	O.T. Patriarchal Era (Leadership Roots)	Family Base
II.	O.T. Pre-Kingdom Leadership Era	Tribal Base
III.	O.T. Kingdom Leadership Era	Nation Based
IV.	O.T. Post-Kingdom Leadership Era	Individual/ Remnant Based
V.	N.T. Pre-Church Leadership	Spiritually Based in the Land
VI.	N.T. Church Leadership	Decentralized Spiritually Based

20. Leadership Genre—Seven Types

Further study of each of these leadership eras resulted in the identification of seven leadership genre which served as sources for leadership findings. I then worked out in detail approaches for studying each of these genre.[59] These seven leadership genre are shown in Table Jnh 20-2.

Table Jnh 20-2. Seven Leadership Genre—Sources for Leadership Findings

Type	General Description/ Example	Approach
1. Biographical	Information about leaders; this is the single largest genre giving leadership information in the Bible/ Joseph.	Use biographical analysis based on leadership emergence theory concepts. See **Article**, 3. *Biographical Studies in the Bible— How To Do*.
2. Direct Leadership Contexts	Blocks of Scripture which are giving information directly applicable to leaders/ leadership; relatively few of these in Scripture/ 1 Peter 5:1-4.	Use standard exegetical techniques. Note the passages in 1, 2Ti and Tit which deal with leadership. These three books have more direct contexts dealing with leadership than any other books in the Bible. See my running commentary, overviews and leadership insights sections for these books.
3. Leadership Acts	Mostly narrative vignettes describing a leader influencing followers usually in some crisis situation; quite a few of these in the Bible/Acts 15 Jerusalem Council	Use three fold leadership tree diagram as basic source for suggesting what areas of leadership to look for. See Figure 1 in **Article**, *Leadership Tree Diagram* for categories helpful for analyzing.
4. Parabolic Passages	Parables focusing on leadership perspectives: e.g. stewardship parables, futuristic parables; quite a few of these in Matthew and Luke./ Luke 19 The Pounds	Use standard parable exegetical techniques but then use leadership perspectives to draw out applicational findings; especially recognize the leadership intent of Jesus in giving these. Most such parables were given with a view to training disciples.
5. Books as a Whole	Each book in the Bible; end result of this is a list of leadership observations or lessons or implications for leadership/ Deuteronomy	Consider each of the Bible books in terms of the leadership era in which they occur and for what they contribute to leadership findings; will have to use whatever other leadership genre source occurs in a given book; also use overall synthesis thinking. I have done this in the Leadership Bible Commentary in the Leadership Insights Section for each of the 8 top leadership books of the Bible. I also have done this for each book of the Bible in another manual, **The Bible and Leadership Values**.
6. Indirect Passages	Passages in the Scripture dealing with Biblical values applicable to all; more so to	Use standard exegetical procedures for the type of Scripture containing the applicable Biblical ethical findings or values

---

[59] These detailed approaches are given in my manual, **Leadership Perspectives—How To Study The Bible for Leadership Insights**.

20. Leadership Genre—Seven Types

	leaders who must model Biblical values/ Proverbs; Sermon on the Mount	
7. Macro Lessons	Generalized high level leadership observations seen in an era and which have potential for leadership absolutes/ Presence Macro	Use synthesis techniques utilizing various leadership perspectives to stimulate observations. I have made a start on this. See **Articles**, *22. Macro Lessons Defined; 23. Macro Lessons: List of 41 Across Six Leadership Eras.*

A major step in becoming informed about leadership in the Bible is to recognize the various kinds of leadership information sources, the seven genre described above. But the more important step is to start studying these sources for leadership observations, principles, guidelines, macro lessons, and absolutes.

Conclusion

The book of Jonah, as seen in this commentary, illustrates the following leadership genre:

1. Biographical (the most important one).
2. Leadership Act (minimal information on).
3. Book as a Whole (see the 8 leadership topics given in the General Reference section).
4. Macro lessons.

The *biographical* genre and *book as a whole* genre divulge the most leadership insights from Jonah.

See **Articles**, *22. Macro Lessons Defined; 23. List of 41 Macro Lessons Across Six Leadership Eras; Bible Centered Leader.*

Article 21

21. Left Hand of God

Introduction

Vertical verses in a horizontal book like Proverbs demand our attention.[60] Note Proverbs 21:1 in the several translations given below.

> 21:1 The king's heart [is] in the hand of the LORD, [as] the rivers of water: he turneth it whithersoever he will. KJV

> 21:1 The king's heart is in the hand of Jehovah as the watercourses: He turneth it whithersoever he will. ASV

> 2:1 The king's heart is [like] channels of water in the hand of the LORD; He turns it wherever He wishes. NASB

> 21:1 The king's heart is in the hand of the LORD; he directs it like a watercourse wherever he pleases. NIV

> 21:1 The king's heart [is] in the hand of the LORD, [Like] the rivers of water; He turns it wherever He wishes. NKJV

> 21:1 The king's heart is a stream of water in the hand of the LORD; he turns it wherever he will. RSV

> 21:1 The Lord controls rulers, just as he determines the course of rivers. CEV

> 21:1 The Lord controls the mind of a king as easily as he directs the course of a stream. TEV

> 21:1 The king's heart is like a stream of water directed by the Lord; he turns it wherever he pleases. NLT

---

[60] Psalms is a vertical book. That is, most of the Psalms are dealing with humans talking and/or hearing from God (vertical communication). Proverbs is dealing for the most part with humans relating to each other (horizontal relationships or activity). So then in a book dealing with horizontal relationships or activity it behooves us to note those few vertical passages. They demand our attention.

21. Left Hand of God, The

The terms used—rivers, watercourses, channels, stream, course could refer to a canal or channel of water such as an irrigation ditch. Just as the farmer directs the irrigation ditch so as to bring water where he wants it, so God directs kings and other rulers to do what He wants done.

Every missionary better learn this verse and its view of God very quickly. For missionaries operate in countries controlled by others. They must abide by decisions made by political rulers—usually not in favor of their being in the country. Missionaries learn to trust God to move in the affairs of these pagan rulers.

Glasser Phrase

Dr. Arthur Glasser uses the phrase, the *Left Hand of God*, to call attention to God's use of non-believers to accomplish His purposes. This *Left Hand of God* is seen numerous times in the Old Testament. Table Jnh 21-1 depicts just a few of them.

Table Jnh 21-1. Some Occurrences of the Left Hand of God

Passage	Persons Involved	Explanation
Genesis 20, 21	Abraham, Sarah, Abimelech	Abraham lied to Abimelech about Sarah his wife. God protects her while she is with Abimelech and gives Abimelech a dream to let him know who Sarah is.
Genesis	Joseph, Pharaoh	God sends two dreams to Pharaoh, which need to be interpreted. Joseph comes to the forefront by interpreting these dreams and suggesting a wise course of action. Joseph is elevated to high position and is in place to deliver his people when the famine hits hardest.
Daniel	Nebuchadnezzar	Daniel ch 4 is one of the clearest examples of the king's heart being in the hand of Jehovah. God humbles Nebuchadnezzar, a very powerful ruler.
Isa 45	Cyrus; Daniel et al	God predicts He will use Cyrus and He does as noted in Table Jnh 28-2 below.
Hag 1:1,2	Darius, Haggai	It is clear that Darius was used by God to help the remnant back in the land.
Ne ch 1 et al	Artaxerxes	Artaxerxes not only wrote decrees allowing the Jews to go back in the land, but he also helped fund their return.

Restoration Leaders

All the restoration leaders were very much aware of the Left Hand of God. They were rebuilding the work of God back in the land. They were there because God had moved in the hearts of pagan rulers, very powerful ones. Those rulers—particularly Cyrus, Darius, Xerxes, Artxerxes—were moved to aid God's people. Esther, Mordecai, Ezra, Nehemiah, Haggai, Zechariah, and Malachi were all aware of the Left Hand of God.

One of the astounding things is God's prediction that He will use these rulers to accomplish His purposes. A beautiful illustration of this is Isaiah's famous passage, Isa 45. Table Jnh 21-2 below illustrates just a few of the passages referring to Cyrus.

Table Jnh 21-2. God's Left Hand Working Through Cyrus

Some Passages Predicting	Some Passages Fulfilling
Isa 44:28 That saith of **Cyrus**, [He is] my shepherd, and shall perform all my pleasure: even saying to Jerusalem, Thou shalt be built; and to the temple, Thy foundation shall be laid. Isa 45:1 Thus saith the LORD to his anointed, to **Cyrus**, whose right hand I have holden, to subdue nations before him; and I will loose the loins of kings, to open before him the two leaved gates; and the gates shall not be shut; Isa 45:13 I have raised him (Cyrus) up in righteousness, and I will direct all his ways: he shall build my city, and he shall let go my captives, not for price nor reward, saith the LORD of hosts.	2Ch 36:22,23 Now in the first year of **Cyrus** king of Persia, that the word of the LORD [spoken] by the mouth of Jeremiah might be accomplished, the LORD stirred up the spirit of **Cyrus** king of Persia, that he made a proclamation throughout all his kingdom, and [put it] also in writing, saying, Thus saith **Cyrus** king of Persia, All the kingdoms of the earth hath the LORD God of heaven given me; and he hath charged me to build him an house in Jerusalem, which [is] in Judah. Who [is there] among you of all his people? The LORD his God [be] with him, and let him go up. Ezr 1:2, 7, 8 Thus saith **Cyrus** king of Persia, The LORD God of heaven hath given me all the kingdoms of the earth; and he hath charged me to build him an house at Jerusalem, which [is] in Judah. 7 Also **Cyrus** the king brought forth the vessels of the house of the LORD, which Nebuchadnezzar had brought forth out of Jerusalem, and had put them in the house of his gods; 8 Even those did **Cyrus** king of Persia bring forth by the hand of Mithredath the treasurer, and numbered them unto Sheshbazzar, the prince of Judah.

Closure

Most of us as leaders know something of the *Right Hand of God*. We have experienced God's intervention in our lives and ministries in such a way as to be awed by His power. But can we see His *Left Hand* working today. We need to be aware of this facet of God's power. And we need discernment, maybe even prophetic voices, to point out to us the *Left Hand of God*. It is especially comforting to believe we have a sovereign God in our world controlled by the most part by non-godly political leaders. May we see God turn the heart of the kings to accomplish His purposes.

See *Sovereign Mindset*; **Glossary**.

Article 22

22. Macro Lessons—Defined

Introduction to Macro lessons

Macro Lessons inform our leadership with potential leadership values that move toward the absolute. We live in a time when most do not believe there are absolutes. In my study of leadership in the Bible, I have defined a leadership truth continuum which recognizes the difficulty in deriving absolutes but does allow for them.[61] Figure Jnh 22-1 depicts this.

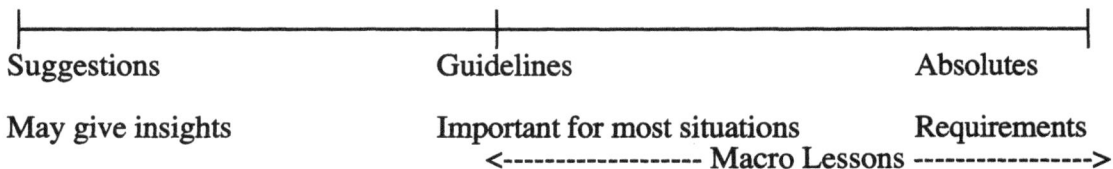

Suggestions	Guidelines	Absolutes
May give insights	Important for most situations	Requirements

<-------------------- Macro Lessons ----------------->

Figure Jnh 22-1. Leadership Truth Continuum/Where Macro Lessons Occur

In the *Complexity Era* in which we now live,[62] the thrust of leadership theory has moved, toward the importance of leadership values. The questions being asked today are not as much what is leadership (the leadership basal elements—leader, followers, and situations) and how does it operate (leadership influence means—corporate and individual) as it is why do we do what we do (leadership value bases). The first three eras (Great Man, Trait, and Ohio State) answered the question, "What is leadership?" The Contingency and early part of the Complexity Era answered the question, "How do we do it?" Now we are grappling with, "Why do we lead? or What ought we to do?" We are looking for leadership values. A leadership value is an underlying assumption which affects how a leader behaves in or perceives leadership situations. They are usually statements that have *ought* or *must* or *should* in them. Macro-Lessons are statements of truth about leadership which have the potential for becoming leadership values. These macro-lessons are observations seen in the various leadership eras in the Bible. Many of these became values for numerous Bible leaders. These macro-lessons move toward the right (requirement, value) of the leadership truth continuum.

What is a macro lesson?

Definition   A <u>macro-lesson</u> is a high level generalization
- of a leadership observation (suggestion, guideline, requirement), stated as a lesson,
- which repeatedly occurs throughout different leadership eras,
- and thus has potential as a leadership absolute.

---

[61] See Clinton, **Leadership Perspectives** for a more detailed explanation of the continuum and for my approach to deriving principles from the scriptures. See **Article**, *Principles of Truth*.

[62] A study of leadership history in the United States from 1850 to the present uncovered 6 Eras (an era being a period of time in which some major leadership theory held sway): 1. Great Man Era (1840s to 1904); 2. Trait Theory (1904-1948); 3. Ohio State Era (1948-1967); Contingency Era (1967-1980); Complexity Era (1980-present). See Clinton, **A Short History of Leadership Theory**. Altadena, Ca.: Barnabas Publishers.

22. Macro Lessons—Defined

Macro lessons even at their weakest provide strong guidelines describing leadership insights. At their strongest they are requirements, or absolutes, that leaders should follow. Leaders ignore them to their detriment.

examples **Prayer Lesson**: If God has called you to a ministry then He has called you to pray for that ministry.
Accountability: Christian leaders minister ought always with a conscious view to ultimate accountability to God for their ministry.
Bible Centered: An effective leader who finishes well must have a Bible centered ministry.

Macro Lessons are derived from a comparative study of leadership in the Six Leadership Eras. These Six Leadership Eras and number of macro lessons identified are shown in Table Jnh 22-1.

Table Jnh 22-1. Leadership Eras and Number of Macro Lessons

Leadership Era	Number of Macro Lessons
1. Patriarchal Era	7
2. Pre-Kingdom Era	10
3. Kingdom Era	5
4. Post-Kingdom Era	5
5. Pre-Church Era	9
6. Church Era	5

I have identified 41 macro lessons, roughly 5 to 10 per leadership era. When a macro-lesson is seen to occur in varied situations and times and cultural settings and in several leadership eras it becomes a candidate for an absolute leadership lesson. When that same generalization becomes personal and is embraced by a leader as a driving force for how that leader sees or operates in ministry, it becomes a leadership value.

The top three Macro Lessons for the four O.T. Leadership Eras are listed in Table Jnh 22-2.

Table Jnh 22-2. Top Three Macro Lessons in O.T. Leadership Eras

Priority	Leadership Era	Label	Statement
1	Pre-Kingdom	Presence	The essential ingredient of leadership is the powerful presence of God in the leader's life and ministry. (*Therefore a leader must not minister without the powerful presence of God in his/her life.*)
2	Patriarchal	Character	Integrity is the essential character trait of a spiritual leader. (*Therefore, a leader must maintain integrity and respond to God's shaping of it.*)
3	Pre-Kingdom	Intimacy	Leaders develop intimacy with God which in turn overflows into all their ministry since ministry flows out of being. (*Therefore a leader must seek to develop intimacy with God.*)

The top three Macro Lessons for the two N.T. Leadership Eras are listed in Table Jnh 22-3.

22. Macro Lessons—Defined

Table Jnh 22-3. Top Three Macro Lessons in N.T. Leadership Eras

Priority	Leadership Era	Label	Statement
1	Church	Word Centered	*God's Word must be the primary source for equipping leaders and must be a vital part of any leader's ministry.*
2	Pre-Church	Harvest	*Leaders must seek to bring people into relationship with God.*
3	Pre-Church	Shepherd	*Leaders must preserve, protect, and develop those who belong to God's people.*

You will notice that some of these macro lessons are already described in value language (should, must, ought) while others are simply statements of observations. I have put in italics my attempt to give the value associated with the observation.

Comparative study across the six leadership eras for macro lessons makes up one of the seven leadership genres, i.e. sources for leadership findings from the Bible.

See **Articles**, *23. Macro Lessons:List of 41 Across Six Leadership Eras; 20. Leadership Genre—Seven Types (Macro Lessons, Biographical Material, Books as A Whole, Direct Context, Indirect Context, Leadership Acts, Parabolic)*. See Clinton, **A Short History of Leadership Theory**. Altadena, Ca.: Barnabas Publishers. See also Clinton, **Leadership Perspectives**. Altadena, Ca.: Barnabas Publishers.

Article 23

23. Macro Lessons: List of 41 Across Six Leadership Eras

Introduction

Macro Lessons inform our leadership with potential leadership values that move toward the absolute. The following are the 41 lessons I have identified as I comparatively studied the six different leadership eras for leadership observations.

No.	Label	Leadership Era	Statement of Macro Lesson
1.	Blessing	Patriarchal	God mediates His blessing to His followers through leaders.
2.	Shaping	Patriarchal	God shapes leader's lives and ministry through critical incidents.
3.	Timing	Patriarchal	God's timing is crucial to accomplishment of God's purposes.
4.	Destiny	Patriarchal	Leaders must have a sense of destiny.
5.	Character	Patriarchal	Integrity is the essential character trait of a spiritual leader.
6.	Faith	Patriarchal	Biblical Leaders must learn to trust in the unseen God, sense His presence, sense His revelation, and follow Him by faith.
7.	Purity	Patriarchal	Leaders must personally learn of and respond to the holiness of God in order to have effective ministry.
8.	Intercession	Pre-Kingdom	Leaders called to a ministry are called to intercede for that ministry.
9.	Presence	Pre-Kingdom	The essential ingredient of leadership is the powerful presence of God in the leader's life and ministry.
10.	Intimacy	Pre-Kingdom	Leaders develop intimacy with God which in turn overflows into all their ministry since ministry flows out of being.
11.	Burden	Pre-Kingdom	Leaders feel a responsibility to God for their ministry.
12.	Hope	Pre-Kingdom	A primary function of all leadership is to inspire followers with hope in God and in what God is doing.
13.	Challenge	Pre-Kingdom	Leaders receive vision from God which sets before them challenges that inspire their leadership.
14.	Spiritual Authority	Pre-Kingdom	Spiritual authority is the dominant power base of a spiritual leader and comes through experiences with God, knowledge of God, godly character and gifted power.
15.	Transition	Pre-Kingdom	Leaders must transition other leaders into their work in order to maintain continuity and effectiveness.
16.	Weakness	Pre-Kingdom	God can work through weak spiritual leaders if they are available to Him.

23. Macro Lessons: List of 41 Across Six Leadership Eras

17.	Continuity	Pre-Kingdom	Leaders must provide for continuity to new leadership in order to preserve their leadership legacy.
18.	Unity	Kingdom	Unity of the people of God is a value that leaders must preserve.
19.	Stability	Kingdom	Preserving a ministry of God with life and vigor over time is as much if not more of a challenge to leadership than creating one.
20.	Spiritual Leadership	Kingdom	Spiritual leadership can make a difference even in the midst of difficult times.
21.	Recrudescence	Kingdom	God will attempt to bring renewal to His people until they no longer respond to Him.
22.	By-pass	Kingdom	God will by-pass leadership and structures that do not respond to Him and will institute new leadership and structures.
23.	Future Perfect	Post-Kingdom	A primary function of all leadership is to walk by faith with a future perfect paradigm so as to inspire followers with certainty of God's accomplishment of ultimate purposes.
24.	Perspective	Post-Kingdom	Leaders must know the value of perspective and interpret present happenings in terms of God's broader purposes.
25.	Modeling	Post-Kingdom	Leaders can most powerfully influence by modeling godly lives, the sufficiency and sovereignty of God at all times, and gifted power.
26.	Ultimate	Post-Kingdom	Leaders must remember that the ultimate goal of their lives and ministry is to manifest the glory of God.
27.	Perseverance	Post-Kingdom	Once known, leaders must persevere with the vision God has given.
28.	Selection	Pre-Church	The key to good leadership is the selection of good potential leaders which should be a priority of all leaders.
29.	Training	Pre-Church	Leaders should deliberately train potential leaders in their ministry by available and appropriate means.
30.	Focus	Pre-Church	Leaders should increasingly move toward a focus in their ministry which moves toward fulfillment of their calling and their ultimate contribution to God's purposes for them.
31.	Spirituality	Pre-Church	Leaders must develop interiority, spirit sensitivity, and fruitfulness in accord with their uniqueness since ministry flows out of being.
32.	Servant	Pre-Church	Leaders must maintain a dynamic tension as they lead by serving and serve by leading.
33.	Steward	Pre-Church	Leaders are endowed by God with natural abilities, acquired skills, spiritual gifts, opportunities, experiences, and privileges which must be developed and used for God.
34.	Harvest	Pre-Church	Leaders must seek to bring people into relationship with God.
35.	Shepherd	Pre-Church	Leaders must preserve, protect, and develop God's people.
36.	Movement	Pre-Church	Leaders recognize that movements are the way to penetrate society though they must be preserved via appropriate ongoing institutions.

23. Macro Lessons: List of 41 Across Six Leadership Eras

37.	Structure	Church	Leaders must vary structures to fit the needs of the times if they are to conserve gains and continue with renewed effort.
38.	Universal	Church	The church structure is inherently universal and can be made to fit various cultural situations if functions and not forms are in view.
39.	Giftedness	Church	Leaders are responsible to help God's people identify, develop, and use their resources for God.
40.	Word Centered	Church	God's Word is the primary source for equipping leaders and must be a vital part of any leaders ministry.
41.	Complexity	All eras	Leadership is complex, problematic, difficult and fraught with risk—which is why leadership is needed.

Conclusion

In the book of Jonah several macro lessons are seen. Jonah would not have seen them. But with today's, hindsight perspective, we can see that these macro lessons are illustrated at least remotely in the book of Jonah:

2.	Shaping	Patriarchal	God shapes leader's lives and ministry through critical incidents.
5.	Character	Patriarchal	Integrity is the essential character trait of a spiritual leader.
9.	Presence	Pre-Kingdom	The essential ingredient of leadership is the powerful presence of God in the leader's life and ministry.
10.	Intimacy	Pre-Kingdom	Leaders develop intimacy with God which in turn overflows into all their ministry since ministry flows out of being.
14.	Spiritual Authority	Pre-Kingdom	Spiritual authority is the dominant power base of a spiritual leader and comes through experiences with God, knowledge of God, godly character and gifted power.
24.	Perspective	Post-Kingdom	Leaders must know the value of perspective and interpret present happenings in terms of God's broader purposes.
25.	Modeling	Post-Kingdom	Leaders can most powerfully influence by modeling godly lives, the sufficiency and sovereignty of God at all times, and gifted power.
34.	Harvest	Pre-Church	Leaders must seek to bring people into relationship with God.

See Also **Article** *22. Macro Lessons—Defined.*

Article 24

24. Nineveh

Introduction

The city of Nineveh is made most famous by its role in the book of Jonah although it also plays a minor role in six other books in the Bible – 5 in the Old Testament, 1 in the New Testament.[63] God uses Nineveh's long-term role as an enemy to the Israelites to show his judgment of wickedness and his response of extravagant mercy to genuine repentance. In the book of Jonah, these two sides of God come to a head and are vividly exposed. An understanding of Nineveh and its people are a pre-requisite for one to understand Jonah's viewpoint and to see God's powerful truth taught to Jonah. This article will briefly describe Nineveh, including other Biblical prophets mention of it. One can well understand Jonah's reluctant obedience to preaching in this great city.

Beyond the Book of Jonah

In Biblical history Nimrod, the descendent of Cush known as the first mighty warrior, built the city of Nineveh east of the Tigris River. It later became the alternative home to many Assyrian kings most notably Sennacherib, who is credited with rebuilding the city and fortifying its water supply.

Nineveh was the last capital of Assyria. This principal city grew in stature as Assyria gained power throughout Mesopotamia particularly between 745 – 627 BC. At the peak of its success, Nineveh was home to more than 175,000 people, a population worthy of the title of a "great city." The size of the city is disputed by scholars. It was big enough that it took a long time for Jonah to traverse it.

Nineveh is the focus of the prophet Nahum's words in the book bearing his name. The prophet delineates Nineveh's wickedness and speaks of the destruction that is coming because the LORD opposes it.[64] Great shame will come upon Nineveh to the delight of other countries that have fallen prey to her evil and cruelty. Nahum ends his oracle declaring that everyone who learns of Nineveh's ruin will clap their hands for very few countries "escaped your endless cruelty."

---

[63] Biblical references to Nineveh: Genesis 10:11,12; 2 Kings 19:36; Isaiah 37:37, Nahum 1:1, 2:8, 3:7; Zephaniah 2:13; Matthew 12:41

[64] See **Articles**, *Promises of God; God The Promise Keeper*. This destruction of Nineveh is a negative illustration of God faithfully keeping his promises. There are, of course, many positive examples of God's keeping His promises. The theme of the very short book of Nahum could be expressed as, **GOD'S WRATH UPON NINEVEH** flows from His character, is certain, and will be completed. And it was. Jonah would have loved to see this happen. That is, before he went through his paradigm shift understanding about God's mercy. See also **Article**, *25. Paradigms and Paradigm Shifts*.

24. Nineveh

The prophet Zephaniah speaks against Nineveh for being overconfident and harsh. It unwisely relied on its own might instead of relying on God. This great city was destroyed in 612 BC at the hands of the Medes, Babylonians and Scythians.

On the whole, Nineveh's Assyrian warrior-like people were a violent people who did deserve what Jonah wanted to happen to them—receiving God's judgment. It is easy to side with Jonah and to want to see God's judgment fall on Nineveh. But God chooses to show His mercy. And Jonah sees this after his brokenness experience.[65]

Nineveh's reputation as an evil yet repentant people is used to Jesus' advantage in the New Testament. He makes a strong indictment against the religious leaders by promoting the people of Nineveh as models of faith.[66] Their response to the proclamation of Jonah was a true repentance and showed the greatness of God's forgiveness. Jesus declared that the Ninevites would stand and judge others for their lack of repentance.

Significance to Jonah

In the prophetic books, Nineveh represents Assyria, the country whose assaults on Israel and Judah were divinely arranged.[67] Eventually God dealt with the Assyrians for the evil they produced but not until they accomplished His purposes of Judgment on the Northern Kingdom. This dynamic could have nurtured Jonah's inclination to despise the Assyrians thus accounting for his reticence to preach repentance to Nineveh.

The book of Jonah shows the contrast between God's great power to judge or to forgive regardless of nationality. While Jonah would rather stand to the side and applaud Nineveh's destruction, God will respond to genuine repentance with mercy, forgiveness and love.

For Further Study

See the following sources for a more detailed treatment of Nineveh and the Assyrian people.

The New Bible Dictionary, 3rd edition, InterVarsity Press: Downers Grove, IL, 1996

Ellison, H.L., "Jonah." *The Expositor's Bible Commentary*. Vol. 7. Edited by Frank E. Gæberlien. Grand Rapids, MI: Zondervan Publishing, 1985, pp. 361-391.

Trible, Phyllis, "The Book of Jonah." *The New Interpreter's Bible: A Commentary in Twelve Volumes*. Vol. VII. Nashville, TN: Abingdon Press, 1996, pp. 463-529.

---

[65] See **Article**, *9. Jonah, Brokenness*.

[66] Or at least as people who discerned God's truth and obediently followed it. Jesus is showing that a people who had very little truth responded to it and contrast that with a people who had great truth and refused it.

[67] See the **Article**, *21. Left Hand of God*, which depicts God's use of other peoples to bring about His purposes.

Article 25

25. Paradigms And Paradigm Shifts

Introduction

Missionaries, pastors and other students of missiology[68] use the word paradigm and paradigm shifts like they were common words. But imagine my surprise when on a jet from Singapore to Hawaii I heard those words, in casual conversation from the person sitting next to me, a Chinese executive with IBM. I was so startled that I had to ask him where he had been introduced to them. Again I was surprised when he mentioned that IBM was showing Joel Barker's *Discovering the Future* video to all its employers in a training program. Thousands of IBM employees around the world are suddenly adding paradigm and paradigm shift to their vocabulary. We both exchanged comments on the power of that video. So the word *paradigm* and *paradigm shifts* have come a long way since Thomas Kuhn[69] first introduced them to an esoteric audience interested in philosophy and epistemology.[70]

The meaning of paradigms and paradigm shifts has also become less technical that Kuhn's use of the words. And though many of us, who have learned them sort of second hand, can generally use them in a context which roughly supports them we probably don't have a good grasp of the words. And we most certainly have not connected them with God's developmental processes in the shaping of a leader. My comparative study of many leaders has shown that paradigm shifts are a major way that *God breaks through to expand a leader*. And that is the purpose of this article. I want to define, explain, and clarify the use of the terms paradigm and paradigm shift in connection with its use in shaping leaders—For I am convinced that the *paradigm shift* is God's breakthrough processing that opens new leadership vistas. This was certainly the case for Jonah.

Let me first suggest some examples of paradigm shifts in the Bible then I will define paradigm and paradigm shifts and suggest five paradigm shifts that are needed if the church is to make an impact in the post-modern world that is upon us now. Table Jnh 25-1 lists some Biblical illustrations of paradigm shifts.

Notice that Jonah is listed as an example of a paradigm shift.

---

[68] Missiology is the science involved in studying the propagation of the Gospel across cultures.
[69] Kuhn's breakthrough 1974 work, **The Structure of Scientific Revolutions**, was studying paradigms at the higher level of the continuum. He was interested in how a whole scientific community viewed a given science.
[70] Epistemology refers to the science dealing with how we know things.

25. Paradigms and Paradigm Shifts

Table Jnh 25-1. 10 Examples of Biblical Paradigm shifts.

Who	Where in	Paradigm Before	Paradigm After
1. Job	Whole book of Job	Suffering is the result of sin and is deserved. Righteous people should not suffer.	A righteous person can suffer as a part of God's plan for him/her
2. Jonah	Jonah 1-4	God exclusively deals only with Israel in order to bless. God is basically against non-Israelites.	God is not exclusively Israel. He has concerns for all nations—to show His mercy and grace to all who repent.
3. Habakkuk	Habakkuk 1-3	God is unjust and unfaithful in His dealing with groups of people in history. He does not keep His promises.	God is just. He is complex in His dealings with nations. Ultimately His purposes and justice will be seen by all.
4. Elisha's servant	2 Kings 6:8-23; Note vs 16	Sees only natural situation. Fear of the physical warfare to come.	Sees the supernatural; sees the unseen Angelic Band protecting. Now believes in unseen world.
5. Nicodemus	John 3	Kingdom of God is external and has expected political ramifications.	Must have an inner transformation by the Spirit in order to perceive God's Kingdom (God's rule).
6. Apostles	Acts 2	No church. No one is sure of what will happen next.	Coming of Holy Spirit. Church is born. Message of salvation is for others.
7. Whole Church (example of Ananias and Sapphira)	Acts 5	Moral issues are relative; can follow cultural ethics.	Dishonesty is against God whether inward or outwardly known; integrity is a thing of the heart. God wants whole hearted obedience.
8. Saul	Acts 9	Persecuted Christians; saw Christ as a leader of a cult opposing Judaism.	Saw Christ as the resurrected Lord; loved Christians; propagated Christianity.
9. Peter	Acts 10	Gentiles not acceptable to God; Jews should not fellowship with them.	Gentiles accepted by God. All Christians are one.
10. Woman at the well	John 4	Believed Smaritans had religious views comparable with Jews. Lived an unsatisfied life. Religion not satisfying.	Saw Jesus as one sent from God who had access to supernatural revelation. Christ's religious views brought hope.

Probably the most famous paradigm shift is that of the Apostle Paul whose conversion radically turned him around from opposing Christ to serving Christ. Paradigm shifts can bring about major breakthroughs in a life or ministry.

Definition   A paradigm is a controlling perspective (symbolized by r), which allows one to perceive and understand **REALITY** ((symbolized by R).

25. Paradigms and Paradigm Shifts

Definition   A <u>paradigm shift</u> is the change of a controlling perspective and the perceptive result of that change (little **r**) so that one perceives (new little **r'**) and understands **REALITY** in a different way.

Essentially, then as we have described it a paradigm shift occurs by a changed little **r**, one's perception of reality, which in effect allows us to see more of **R** (absolute reality) or at least some different aspect of it.

A change of little **r** could be simple one like a single idea. Or it could be a change of an idea that ramifies throughout a whole group of related ideas. Not all changes of little **r** have the same impact upon our mental models.

Three Categories of Paradigm Shifts

Comparative study of real life paradigm shifts in case studies of leaders has led to the following three categories. These categories include:

1. **Cognitive**—which dominantly deals with the concept of new ideas or frameworks of thinking as the basis for a paradigm shift. These new Ideas (information, categories, etc.) allow for seeing new things. The heart of the shift has to do with a new idea for seeing things, a possibility not considered before. The cognition may also be accompanied by a volitional to use it but the heart of it is the discovery of the validity of the idea. Examples include: a mono-cultural to cross-cultural perspective; getting church growth eyes; getting new leadership style insights; learning a stewardship philosophical leadership model; learning about change dynamics theory; seeing women as fully qualified leaders in ministry.

2. **Volitional**—which dominantly focuses on the fact of committing oneself to something whether understood cognitively or not. There is a committal by an act of a will to use some idea even though it may not be fully understood or experienced. The heart of the shift is a recognition of the importance of letting go and following the new perspective whether or not it is understood. Usually there is a surrender of the will involved and an acknowledgment to God of this. Examples: radical adult conversion; leadership committal; call to ministry

3. **Experiential**—which dominantly focuses on experiences of something and an affective shift which may ramify toward a volitional and eventually a cognitive shift. These have to do with experiencing the effects of something or wanting to experience it. After the experience there may be a growing awareness of its meaning. Usually these have to do with life power or gifted power or personal experiences with the supernatural—that is, unusual experience with the Holy Spirit and supernatural power breakthroughs. Life power (the appropriation of the Holy Spirit to enable victorious living) examples include: entire sanctification—Brengle's experience; baptism of Holy Spirit—Torrey's experience; deeper life experience—McQuilkin's experience; Union life shift—Taylor's experience of the exchanged life; infilling of Holy Spirit—Luke's description of several in Acts. Gifted Power (the appropriation of God's power via the Holy Spirit to use giftedness with effective power) in ministry examples include: a major healing experience; experiences with prophetic; confirmed experiences with word of knowledge or word of wisdom or discernings of spirits; miracles; tongues or interpretation of tongues verified; anointing of Holy Spirit for a ministry; experience of unusual effectiveness with giving, helps, mercy, teaching, evangelism, apostleship, pastoral, or any of the normally considered non-supernatural gifts. Power encounters, spiritual warfare, spiritual authority, prayer power, and unusual intercessory experiences involving divine initiative praying are other miscellaneous power type experiential paradigm shifts. Some experiential paradigm shifts have to

25. Paradigms and Paradigm Shifts

do with personhood and include such things as: personality shifts through brokenness or deep processing; isolation and other maturity cluster processes.

Some General Suggestions for Follow-Up

Let me offer four rather simplistic suggestions. They seem almost anticlimactic after offering so much information on paradigm shifts. But they can make a difference.

Suggestion 1. Study Paradigms and Paradigm Shifts Thoroughly

Step 1 for having these ideas impact you is to study them thoroughly so that you understand them and can recognize in real life situations around. Study carefully each of the Biblical examples of paradigm shifts that were given. Study especially the leadership commentary notes in John. John is a *major paradigm shift book*. Study the other paradigm shift books with a view toward identifying paradigm concepts. These include: Job, Jonah, Habakkuk, Acts, and Galatians. Thorough understanding of paradigmatic concepts is a preliminary to actual positive use of them in ministry.

Suggestion 2. Be Open To Them

Recognize that most leaders are usually somewhat inflexible. That's one reason they have convictions and are willing to lead. Also recognize that God uses paradigm shifts to move an inflexible leader. So be open to paradigm shifts to help you become more flexible. Remember, one of your goals is to finish well. One means of doing that is to respond to processing by God which will break unneeded flexibility and develop your potential.

Suggestion 3. Needed Paradigm Shifts in Our Day

Table Jnh 25-3 lists some paradigm shifts I believe will be necessary if we are to minister, to lead, and to see lives changed in the post-modern era facing the church.

Table Jnh 25-3. Needed Paradigm Shifts; If Leaders Are to Impact the Post-Modern Era

Paradigm Shift	Explanation
Authentication: Power shift.	Leaders must be able to demonstrate the power of God in ministry in order to break through to post-modern people.
Ministry Base: Shift from doing to being.	Leaders must minister out of being which involves giftedness, character, intimacy with God, inner values, destiny. Success and achievement must not be the driving force. They will be by-products of the essential issue which is to minister out of being.
Social base: Demonstrate God's enablement for this.	Living victoriously as singles and marrieds must be demonstrated. Our world around us is falling apart in terms of social base issues.
Relational Empowerment: Developmental bias	Leaders must develop emerging leaders with mentoring relationships. Developing others must be a major priority.
Future Perfect Thinking: Leading with hope.	Leaders who lead with a future perfect perspective can impart hope. Hope will desperately be needed in a post-modern culture which has at best only hopelessness.

Suggestion 4. Expect Them

Paradigm shifts will come unless you are deliberately fixed in your views and perspectives for viewing things. Especially is this true for some of the needed ones I have listed under suggestion 3. We need these if we are to minister to the post-modern generation. Therefore be expecting God to challenge you with them. Be on the look out for them. Desire them. Ask for them.

25. Paradigms and Paradigm Shifts

Remember, God is full of surprises. When we get to heaven we will find out that things were not always the way we thought them to be. Be open for those surprises, which often come wrapped up in paradigm shift wrappings.

Conclusion

Strong leaders like Jonah with a paradigm set in concrete will need some radical processing by God to bring about a paradigm shift. The book of Jonah illustrates the depth to which God will go to bring about a paradigm shift.

See *Powershift, mentoring definitions, future perfect paradigm,* **Glossary**. See **Article,** *Future Perfect Paradigm.*

Article 26

26. Pivotal Points—Illustrated in Habakkuk and Jonah

Introduction
Jonah is a critical incident biographical source as is Habakkuk.[71]

Description
A <u>critical incident biographical</u> source refers to a single incident or series of incidents taking place in a very short time.

There may actually be a large amount of information but all focused on a short time-interval. The information can be interpreted for processing or for a leadership act or other such findings. Job, Habakkuk, and Jonah are all examples of critical incident biographies. As such they are prime candidates for describing a pivotal point in a life. Two definitions are important and narrow our search for leadership findings when we are looking at critical incident biographical sources—a prime critical incident and a pivotal point.

Some Basic Concepts
My preliminary study of some Bible leaders and in-depth study of others indicates that for many of them there were critical times in their lives in which decisions were made that affected all of the rest of their lives and ministries. I call these times pivotal points. A pivotal point in a leader's life is a critical time of God's dealing with that leader. The leader's response to God's processing will carry significant implications for the rest of the leadership. At the end of life one can trace back to that point in time and identify it as having done at least one of four things.

Definition   A <u>pivotal point</u> is a critical time in a leader's life in which something happens, sometimes inadvertently, or a decision is made which can,

1. curtail further use of the leader by God or at least curtail expansion of the leader's potential.
2. limit the eventual use of the leader for ultimate purposes that otherwise could have been accomplished,
3. enhance or open up the leader for expansion or contribution to the ultimate purposes in God's kingdom or
4. serve as a guidance watershed which forever changes the direction of the life.

---

[71] So too are Habakkuk and Job. Job has much more information than either Habakkuk or Jonah but takes place in a relatively short time. Because of the notion of intentional selection being what it is and the short time involved in the incidents, which happen, it will usually be the case that the incident or series of incidents describe a pivotal point in a life.

26. Pivotal Points—Illustrated in Habakkuk and Jonah   page 145

Figure Jnh 26-1 views this definition categorically.

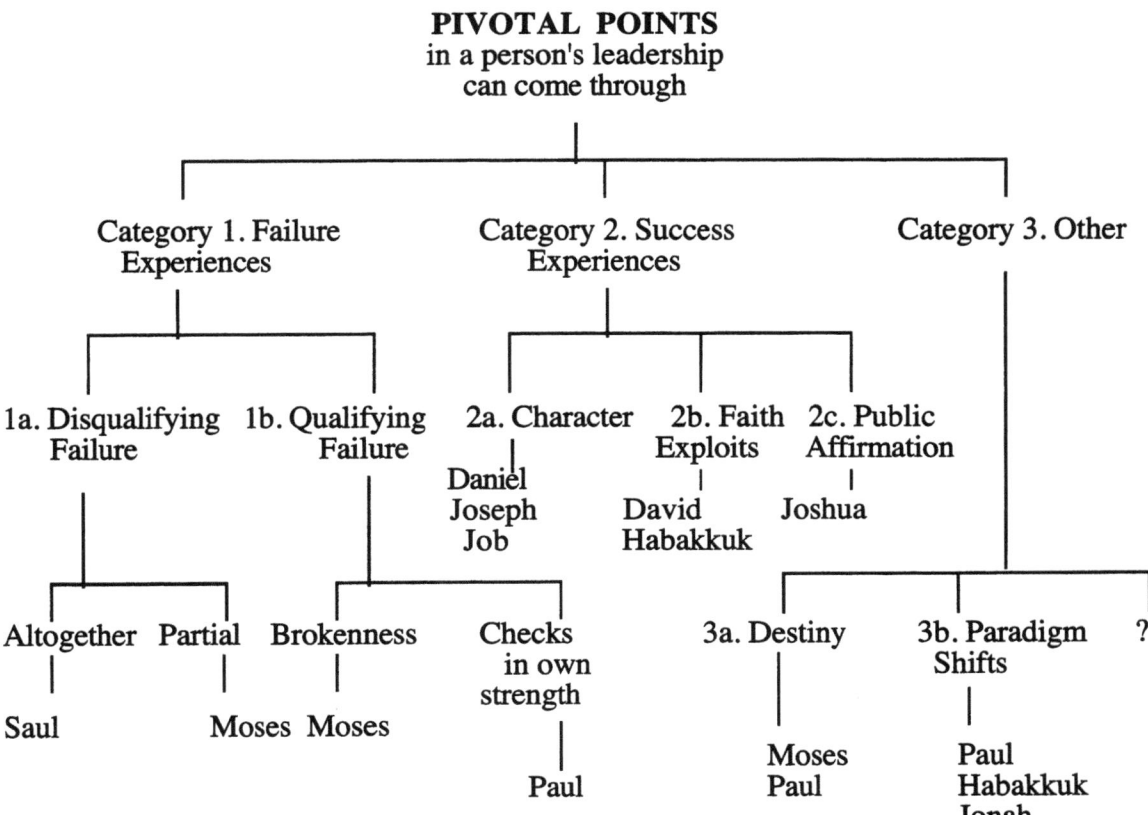

Figure Jnh 26-1. Pivotal Points Characterized

Examples of Pivotal Points

Saul typifies Category 1a. Disqualifying Failure, which eventually resulted in his being taken out of leadership by God. Two different incidents, which tested his integrity and obedience in 1 Sa 13:7-14 and 15:10-35 proved pivotal for his use as king by God.

Moses exemplifies Category 1b Qualifying failure. This shows up in two separate events in his life. One, his initial attempt to help the Israelites when he killed the Egyptian. This eventually led to his desert experience and brokenness. God was able to use Moses to deliver Israel some years later after the time of brokenness. A second event, which limited his final leadership was his act in striking the Rock to provide water in Numbers 20:11,12. This anger at his followers and disobeying God demeaned God. God prevented Moses taking the Israelites into the promised land—which should have been the culminating ultimate contribution of his ministry.

Daniel's response to the integrity check in Daniel chapter 1 illustrates a Category 2b type of pivotal point as was Joseph's response to temptation from Potiphar's wife in Genesis 39. Job's experience was filled with repeated illustrations of character testing.

Moses' burning bush experience typifies a category 3b experience as does Paul's Damascus road experience. In fact, Paul's Damascus road experience is also a type 3c pivotal point.

26. Pivotal Points—Illustrated in Habakkuk and Jonah

Since pivotal points can occur as a series of incidents over time it helps to further describe given incidents. A helpful perspective on incidents is that of the notion of a prime critical incident.

Definition   A <u>prime critical incident</u> is a special intervention (could be a series over time) in which God gives a *major value* that will flow through the life or will give *strategic direction* to narrow the leader's life work.

Prime critical incidents can be carefully distinguished in terms of their function:
1. some produce a dominant value which pervades the leader's ministry philosophy or
2. some pinpoint a key strategic directional factor or
3. some do both.

Figure Jnh 26-2 describes this concept diagrammatically.

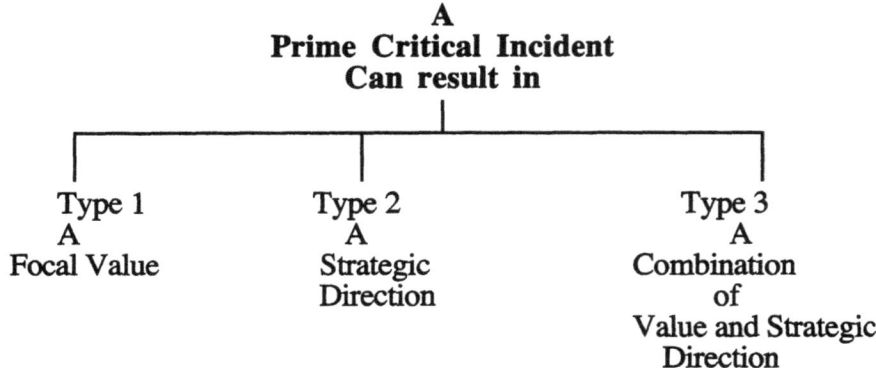

Figure Jnh 26-2. Prime Critical Incident Diagrammed Functionally

Examples of Critical Incidents

Peter's reaction to Jesus' teaching in Matthew 20 on servant leadership and then his experience in Jesus washing his feet illustrates a Type 1 Prime Critical Incident. Those shaping incidents resulted in a servant leadership value. See 1 Pe 5:1-4 where at the end of life Peter is still consistently operating on this leadership value.

Paul's Macedonian vision illustrates a Type 2 critical incident. This prime critical incident moved Paul to take the Gospel to Europe, a next step in his destiny. His Damascus road experience illustrates a Type 3. His life direction turned around. Instead of persecuting Christians he became the prime instigator of the movement—at least to the Gentile world. And he operated on a new value, the resurrected Jesus is Lord of his life.

Habakkuk and Jonah—Pivotal Experiences

In the incidents recorded about Habakkuk and Jonah both leaders illustrate a Type 3b pivotal experience. Table Jnh 26-11 indicates the paradigm shift that each went through.

Table Jnh 26-1 Before and After Paradigm Shifts

Leader	Paradigm Before Pivotal Point	Paradigm After Pivotal Point
Habakkuk	Viewed God as distant and not working in his situation particularly with reference to justice issues. He was not trusting	Viewed God as working not only in his situation but in the history of the world. He recognized that bringing justice to his situation and the world in

26. Pivotal Points—Illustrated in Habakkuk and Jonah   page 147

		God to work in his situation.	general was a complex issue that would take time. He came to joyfully trust God even though what he saw around him might deny God's working.
Jonah		Saw God as exclusively for Israel and not for other nations.	Saw God's concern for other nations, such as Assyria.

The boat/big fish incident for Jonah typifies a Type 1 Prime Critical incident. Jonah learned experientially several important values. God is omnipresent and can not be escaped by running away. God is omnipotent controlling forces of nature. God will discipline a leader who disobeys. God cares for all nations and wants justice and is against violence.

From Habakkuk we know that the incident was pivotal. His response to the paradigm shift shows he understood and embraced God's historical outworking of justice. We do not have further historical evidence of Habakkuk's leadership after the pivotal point. But his attitudinal response in the pivotal point experience bodes well for that leadership.

From Jonah we know that the incident was pivotal. We have the book. Had Jonah not accepted God's view on the Ninevite response to God's truth and mercy, you can be sure we would not even have the book. As is the case in Habakkuk's leadership we do not have further historical evidence of Jonah's leadership after the pivotal point. But we certainly know he shared his testimony with others and we can hope that he attempted to live out the rest of his ministry in light of this tremendous pivotal experience.

6 Observations On Pivotal Points
From my initial study of pivotal points I have identified some observations.

1. **RANGE.** Biblical leaders seem to have a range of from 1 to 6 pivotal points. There is frequently more than one pivotal point that serves as a "conditional road map marker" in a life. Moses giving up of his rights to the throne, his slaying of the Egyptian, his sense of destiny experience at the burning bush, his mountain top experience testing and his striking of the rock are typical examples of pivotal points.

2. **INTENTIONAL SELECTIVITY.** Due to the highly intentional selection of Bible material, the New Testament commentary on an Old Testament leader probably will signal pivotal points.

3. **PERSPECTIVE.** Pivotal points probably can't finally be evaluated except with retrospective reflection. However, even as we move through a major boundary we may well know that we have experienced a pivotal point.

4. **PURPOSE OF STUDY.** At this point studying and identifying pivotal points can furnish us with *warnings* for our own lives, can point out the ways that God frequently processes leaders at critical junctures of their lives which in turn may cause us to have a more sensitive awareness of the Spirit's daily processing in our lives. We may not be able to know at the moment if something happening to us is pivotal or not; hence we must exercise a Spirit-led caution as we respond to God. The more familiar we are with Biblical leaders and with the processes used by God in their emergence the more sensitive we will be to God's dealing with our own lives. **That a single incident in my life may be strongly determinative for the rest of a person's leadership will certainly cause one to see the importance of a daily sensitive walk with God via the Holy Spirit. Forewarned is forearmed!**

5. **BALANCE.** We must avoid two extremes. One is being afraid of running into a pivotal point every day and hence being so overcautious that we cannot freely minister as we ought. The other is assuming that since for the most part we can't control when pivotal points come we just simply ignore the truth about them and go our merry way.

6. **BARRIERS.** The six barriers[72] to finishing well usually are keyed by some negative experience and should serve to warn us. We can certainly avoid these negative pivotal points, which may cause at worst disqualifying failure and at best qualifying failure.

Closure

Both Jonah and Habakkuk illustrate pivotal points and prime critical incidents. In terms of warnings, they teach us at least two important things about leadership:

1. Leaders concerned with counting in God's purposes can expect God to bring into their lives necessary paradigm shifts so that they can see and obey God's intentions for them. Major paradigm shifts are usually pivotal in a leader's experience.

2. Frequently, a leadership value, perhaps misperceived, is the cause for a needed pivotal experience.

In addition to warnings, we should note optimistically that pivotal experience may be the springboard to great things God has in store for us. We should not fear pivotal experiences. We should take them seriously and correct what needs to be corrected. But we should also view them as opportunities for God to strategically lead us on to exploits that count for him.

---

[72] Studies of leaders who have failed to finish well has identified six major barriers to their finishing well. These include: finances—their use and abuse; power—its abuse; inordinate pride—which leads to a downfall; sex—illicit relationships; family—critical issues; plateauing. See **Article**, *Finishing Well—Six Major Barriers*.

Article 27

27. Prophetic Crises, 3 Major Biblical Times

Introduction
Years ago, when I took the class on prophets by James (Buck) Hatch, each of us was assigned a major project—do a chart on the prophets. Professor Hatch knew that the historical background was crucial to understanding the writing prophets. I still have that chart today and use it whenever I introduce any of the prophetic books. I am thankful to Professor Hatch for that project and his course that introduced me to each of the prophetic books. Getting perspective, on the times these books address, was a great leap forward in understanding them. Most of the writing prophets cluster around three major crises in the life of God's people. It is these prophetic crises, which prompted the rise of the prophetic ministry as reflected in the writing prophets.

 1. The Assyrian Crisis
 2. The Babylonian Crisis
 3. The Restoration Crisis

Let me briefly describe each of these and identify the books, which speak to them.

General Background And Some Basic Definitions
Samuel's leadership ministry transitioned the commonwealth into a kingdom that Saul ruled over. This was followed by David's rule and then his son Solomon's rule. This sets the stage for God's disciplinary work among His people.

The Assyrian and the Babylonian Crises
The story line leading to the Assyrian crisis and the Babylonian crisis hinges around the following major events:
1. Solomon goes away from the Lord providing a great warning to all leaders—He had the best start of any king yet did not finish well. A good start does not insure a good finish.
2. Rehoboam (1 Kings 12) makes an unwise decision to increase taxes and demands on people—kingdom splits as prophecy said. 10 tribes go with the northern kingdom, Judah with the southern. A poor start might not be overcome.
3. The northern kingdom under Jereboam quickly departs from God. Jereboam is used as the model of an evil king to whom all evil kings are likened; He had a good start also—God would have blessed him. Abuse of power is a major barrier to finishing well.
4. The southern kingdom generally is bad with occasional good Kings and partially good kings: Asa, Jehoshaphat, Joash, Amaziah, Uzziah, Jotham,

27. Prophetic Crises, 3 Major Biblical Times

Hezekiah, Josiah. But the trend was always downward. The extended length of life of the southern kingdom more than the northern kingdom is directly attributed to the spiritual life of the better kings. Spiritual leadership does make a difference. Lack of spiritual leadership speeds up deterioration and leads to God's bypassing of the leadership structures and even destruction of the wayward people.

5. During both the northern and southern kingdoms God sent prophets to try and correct them—first the oral prophets (many—but the two most noted were Elijah and Elisha) and then the prophets who wrote.

Now in order to understand this long period of history you should know several things:
1. The History books that give background information about the times.
2. The Bible Time-Line, need to know when the books were written.
3. Need to know the writing prophets: northern or southern kingdom, which crisis, direct or special.

The History Books

The history books covering the time of the destruction of a nation include 1, 2 Samuel, 1,2 Kings, and 1,2 Chronicles. The following chart helps identify the focus of each of these books as to major content.

Chart Jnh 27-1 The History Books—Major Content

1 Samuel	2 Samuel 1 Chronicles	1,2 Kings 2 Chronicles
Samuel, Saul, David	David	1,2 Kings: Solomon to Zedekiah (gives time oriented details on northern and southern kingdoms) 2 Chronicles exclusively on line of Judah (southern kingdom)

There are four categories of prophetical books. Prophetical books deal with three major crises: the Assyrian crisis which wiped out the northern kingdom; the Bablonian crisis which wiped out the southern kingdom; the return to the land after being exiled. There are also prophetical books not specifically dealing with these crises but associated with the time of them. The prophetical books dealing with these issues are:

Category 1. Northern—Assyrian Crisis
  Jonah, Amos, Hosea, Nahum, Micah

Category 2. Southern—Babylonian Crisis
  Joel, Isaiah, Micah, Zephaniah, Jeremiah, Lamentations, Habakkuk, Obadiah

Category 3. In Exile
  Ezekiel, Daniel, Esther

Category 4. Return From Exile—The Restoration Crisis
  Nehemiah, Ezra, Haggai, Zechariah, Malachi

27. Prophetic Crises, 3 Major Biblical Times

In addition, to knowing the crises you must know the prophets that wrote:

A. Direct to the Issue of the Crisis either Assyrian, Babylonian, or Return To The Land—The Restoration Crisis. These were:
Amos, Hosea, Joel, Micah, Isaiah, Jeremiah, Ezekiel, Haggai, Zechariah, Malachi

B. Special—These were:
Jonah, Nahum, Habakkuk, Obadiah, Zephaniah, Daniel.

The special prophets, though usually associated with one of the crisis times, wrote to deal with unique issues not necessarily related directly to the crisis. The following list gives the special prophets and their main thrust.

1. Jonah—a paradigm shift, pointing out God's desire for the nation to be missionary minded and reach out to surrounding nations. Assyria is the nation God uses to teach Jonah this important lesson.
2. Nahum—vindicate God, judgment on Assyria.
3. Habakkuk—faith crisis for Habakkuk, vindicate God, judgment on Babylon.
4. Obadiah—vindicate God, judgment on Edom for treatment of Judah.
5. Zephaniah—show about judgment, the Day of the Lord.
6. Daniel—give hope, show that God is indeed ruling even in the times of the exile and beyond, gives God's plan for the ages.

Having overviewed the story line that threads through the *Assyrian Crisis* and the *Babylonian Crisis* and briefly listed the Biblical books (both history and prophetical) that apply to these crises, we can move on to the *Restoration Crisis*.

The Restoration Crisis Overviewed

Several Bible books are associated with the return to the land from the exile. After a period of about 70 years (during which time Daniel ministered) Cyrus made a decree, which allowed some Jews (those that wanted to) to return to the land. Some went back under Zerubbabel, a political ruler like a governor. A priest, Joshua, also provided religious leadership to the first group that went back. This group of people started to rebuild the temple but became discouraged due to opposition and lack of resources. They stopped building the temple. Two prophets, after several years, 10-15, addressed the situation. These two, Haggai and Zechariah, were able to encourage the leadership and the people to finish the temple.

Another thirty or forty years goes by and then we have the events of the book of Esther, back in the land. Her book describes the attempt to eradicate the Jewish exiles—a plot which failed due to God's sovereign intervention via Esther, the queen of the land and a Jewish descendant going incognito, and her relative Mordecai.

Still another period of time passes, 20 or so years and a priest, Ezra, directs another group to return to the land. The spiritual situation has deteriorated. He brings renewal.

Another kind of leader arrives on the scene some 10-15 years later. Nehemiah, a lay leader, and one adept at organizing and moving to accomplish a task, rebuilds the wall around Jerusalem. He too has to instigate renewal.

Finally, after another period of 30 or so years we have the book of Malachi which again speaks to renewal of the people. The Old Testament closes with this final book.

27. Prophetic Crises, 3 Major Biblical Times

A recurring emphasis occurs during the period of the return. People are motivated to accomplish a task for God. They start out, become discouraged, and stop. They must be renewed. God raises up leadership to bring renewal.

Let me now introduce some important definitions before giving further detail on the *Restoration Crisis*.

Some Definitions

In my leadership literature I define two restoration terms that are important. They have some overlap but also need to be seen as distinct.

Definition	Restoration (individual leader) is the process whereby a fallen leader is transitioned back into leadership. It usually involves repentance, restitution where appropriate, correction of the aberrant leadership dysfunctionalities, and recognition by other leaders of the restoration process and their stamp of approval for the leader to renew ministry.
Definition	Corporate restoration refers to God's attempts to restore the people of God as a viable channel through whom He can work to carry out His Biblical purposes.

It is this latter definition that is important to the third major crisis—the *Restoration Crisis*.

Description	The *restoration crisis* refers to the period of time from 539 B.C. to 430 B.C. and which covers the activity of God in bringing His people back into the land and establishing a testimony there. His providential care of His people (both in the land and outside it) is also shown.

The Restoration Crisis—Further Details

While it is true that God attempts restoration efforts throughout almost all the leadership eras in both the O.T. and N.T., I define the *Restoration Crisis* as the time specifically dealing with the return of the exiles to the land and the aftermath activities that occurred. This means the time from 539 B.C. when Daniel initiated the time with his great intercessory prayer in Daniel 9 to around 430 B.C. when Malachi made a major thrust at restoration. Table Jnh 27-1 gives a brief overview of this time. The major Biblical books dealing with the *Restoration Crisis* include: Ezra, Haggai, Zechariah, Ezra, Nehemiah, Esther, and Malachi.

Table Jnh 27-1. The Restoration Era Crises And Related Biblical Material

Item	539 B.C.	536 B.C.	520-516 B.C.	486-465 B.C.	465-424 B.C.	430 B.C.
Restoration Activity	Daniel Prays	Work on Temple Begun	Work on Temple begun again and Completed	Israelites Preserved due to Esther and Mordecai's activities	Wall is constructed around Jerusalem—Ezra and Nehemiah bring about restoration movement	Malachi again engenders restoration movement
Biblical Material	Daniel 9	Ez 3:12	Ez 6:13-15 Haggai Zechariah	Esther	Nehemiah; latter part of Ezra	Malachi
Crises	1. God's Timing	2. Public Testimony Needed	3. Public Testimony Needed—Work	4. People of God Outside of	5. Protection of Jerusalem/ Public Testimony of	6. Leadership Nominality;

27. Prophetic Crises, 3 Major Biblical Times

	and Faith	Back in the Land	Stopped	Land—Danger of being Destroyed	People	follower nominality

The themes of each of the biblical books dealing with the restoration crises should be seen in terms of the crises given above in Table Jnh 27-1.

Table Jnh 27-2 gives the theme of the relevant books along with the crisis that most likely prompted the activity of the book.

Table Jnh 27-2. The Restoration Era Crises And Related Biblical Material

Crisis	Book	Theme/ Brief Explanation Relating to Corporate Restoration
1. God's Timing and Faith	Daniel	**THE MOST HIGH** (sovereign God) **RULES** in the affairs of individuals, nations, and history. **Brief Explanation:** Daniel shows how God is sovereignly working out his purposes and lays out a time table for God's future work. Included in that book is the crucial identification of the 70 years in captivity and the time to begin the restoration effort in Jerusalem.
2. Public Testimony Needed Back in the Land	Ezra	See below for explanation of Ezra theme.
3. Public Testimony Needed—Work Stopped	Ezra	See below for Ezra Theme
	Haggai	**God's Work in Rebuilding the Temple** (Under Haggai's Prophetic Impact) began when His people back in the land were renewed and reprioritized their lives in response to God's Word, initially brought discouragement and was counteracted by God's promise of His presence and blessing as the rebuilders obeyed God's Word, continued to be fueled by a God-given vision of what it could be, not what it was, and carried with it God affirmation and promise of power to the leadership inspiring this work, in an overwhelming time.
	Zechariah	**THE WORKING OF THE LORD ALMIGHTY** involves encouragement in the present to leaders, brings correction and hope to sincere followers, and reveals His future plans so as to cause anticipation and encouragement. **Brief Explanation:** Corporate restoration is an on-going process. Hope along with restoration comes when we get perspective on what God is doing and will do in the future.
4. People of God Outside of Land—Danger of being Destroyed	Esther	**THE PROVIDENTIAL WORKING OF GOD** involves foresight which includes His use of apparently natural events and responses behind the scenes in *anticipation* of later events, will test leadership in the crisis, will have timely intervention in unusual yet natural events to protect, and will accomplish His purposes in the end. **Brief Explanation:** This shows that God is still working both outside the land as well as in the land. The left hand of God is seen in the affairs of preservation that Mordecai and Esther take part in. The Left Hand of God is an important concept in the whole restoration era.
5. Protection of Jerusalem/ Public	Ezra	**EFFECTIVE LEADERSHIP IN JERUSALEM UNDER EZRA** built on a foundation of that done by Haggai, Zechariah, Zerubbabel, and Joshua, and involved a call back to Biblical standards for the people in Jerusalem.

27. Prophetic Crises, 3 Major Biblical Times

Testimony of People		**Brief Explanation:** The heart of corporate restoration is to have people understand God's revelation for them and to obey it. Ezra's ministry did this.
	Nehemiah	**NEHEMIAH'S ORGANIZATIONAL LEADERSHIP** made itself felt in the face of obstacles to rebuild the wall, was inspirational in bringing about reform and a covenant in Jerusalem, and included drastic steps of separation in order to insure an on-going meaningful religious atmosphere. **Brief Explanation:** This book emphasizes the importance of civil leadership working with religious leadership in bringing about corporate restoration.
6. Leadership Nominality; follower nominality	Malachi	**NOMINALITY**, religious form without power and meaning, reflects a lack of understanding of God's love, is manifested by half-hearted obedience which hinders God's purposes, is perpetuated by nominal leadership, and ultimately will be corrected by God. **Brief Explanation:** The heart of corporate restoration is to have people understand God's revelation for them and to obey it. Malachi, like Ezra's ministry, did this. Both Ezra and Malachi's ministries show that the people of God will tend toward nominality over time and need intervention ministries that will call them back to God.

The important macro lessons that are illustrated in the restoration crisis era include the following (numbers refer to a list of 41 macro lessons seen in the Bible):

19. **Stability** — **Preserving a ministry of God with life and vigor over time is as much if not more of a challenge to leadership than creating one.**

20. **Spiritual Leadership** — **Spiritual leadership can make a difference even in the midst of difficult times.**

21. **Recrudescence** — **Kingdom God will attempt to bring renewal to His people until they no longer respond to Him.**

22. By-pass — God will by-pass leadership and structures that do not respond to Him and will institute new leadership and structures.

23. Future Perfect — A primary function of all leadership is to walk by faith with a future perfect paradigm so as to inspire followers with certainty of God's accomplishment of ultimate purposes.

24. **Perspective** — **Leaders must know the value of perspective and interpret present happenings in terms of God's broader purposes.**

25. Modeling — Leaders can most powerfully influence by modeling godly lives, the sufficiency and sovereignty of God at all times, and gifted power.

26. Ultimate — Leaders must remember that the ultimate goal of their lives and ministry is to manifest the glory of God.

27. Prophetic Crises, 3 Major Biblical Times

| 27. Perseverance | Once known, leaders must persevere with the vision God has given. |

Of these, macro lessons 19, 20, 21, 24 and 27 directly relate to corporate restoration.

General Lessons Learned From Perspective on The There Major Crises

In observing the length of time of the northern kingdom leading to the Assyrian Crisis as compared to the length of time of the southern kingdom leading to the Babylonian Crisis, a much longer time, one can emphasize strongly the spiritual leadership macro lesson.

20. Spiritual Leadership
Spiritual leadership can make a difference even in the midst of difficult times.

In observing the intervention times in all three prophetic crises, one cannot but help notice the crucial sense of timing involved in God's activity through the prophets.

3. Timing Macro-Lesson
God's Timing Is Crucial To Accomplishment Of God's Purposes.

We should also be warned. God has by-passed leadership and structures in the past, which did not respond to His warnings. This can happen again to us in our church leadership eras. We should be warned.

22. By-pass
God will by-pass leadership and structures that do not respond to Him and will institute new leadership and structures.

In general, we note that if we are to be Bible Centered leaders who apply O.T. scriptures appropriately in our N.T. Church leadership era, we must study carefully the details of the historical background surrounding these O.T. writing. We must adhere carefully to the General Hermeneutical principle involved with historical background.

Historical Background Hermeneutical Principle
In The Spirit, Prayerfully Study The Historical Background Of The Book Which Includes Such Information As:
   a. the author of the book and the *historical perspective* from which he/she wrote.
   b. the *occasion* for the book
   c. the *purpose* for the book including where pertinent the people for whom it was intended and their situation.
   d. any geographical or cultural factors bearing on the communication of the material.

Closure
Perspective makes a difference. The difference between leaders and followers is perspective. The difference between leaders and more effective leaders is better perspective. Leaders today need perspective on how God has worked. To understand the writing prophets, the three major crises detailed in this article become very significant. Bible centered leaders who want to apply concepts from the writing prophets to today's ministry must understand the historical background associated with these major crises.

Article 28

28. Six Biblical Leadership Eras
Approaching the Bible with Leadership Eyes

Introduction
In my opinion, the Bible provides one of the richest resources that Christian leaders have on leadership. The Bible is full of leadership insights, lessons, values and principles about leaders and leadership. It is filled with influential people and the results of their influence... both good and bad.

Three assumptions undergird what I will say in this article.

1. I have a strong **conviction** that the Bible can give valuable leadership insights.
2. I have made a **willful decision** to study the Bible and use it as a source of leadership insights.[73]
3. To study the Bible for leadership insights, you need **leadership eyes** to see leadership findings in the Bible. That is, there are many leadership perspectives, i.e. paradigms, that help stimulate one to see leadership findings. I have been discovering and using these in my own study.

I want to do three things in this keynote overview. I want to introduce two most helpful perspectives for studying the Bible for leadership findings: 1. Seeing Leadership Eras; 2. Recognizing Leadership Genre. I will give more space to *the Six Leadership Eras*. These two concepts will help give one *leadership eyes*. And then I want to talk about the impact of the two most important boundary times between leadership eras, Moses desert leadership and Jesus' foundational work instigating a major movement. Both of these were fundamental and foundational times of Biblical leadership. They introduced radical macro lessons that deeply impact our own leadership today.

The Six Leadership Eras
A first step toward having *leadership eyes*, for recognizing leadership findings in the Bible involves seeing the various leadership eras in the Bible. These time periods share common leadership assumptions and expectations. These assumptions and expectations differ markedly from one leadership time period to the next. Though, of course, there are commonalties that bridge across the eras.

Definition   A <u>leadership era</u> is a period of time, usually several hundred years long,[74] in which the major focus of leadership, the influence means, basic leadership

---

[73] I have been doing this deliberately for ten years at this writing.

[74] There is one exception. Though technically, the N.T. Pre-Church Era includes the inter-testamental time, I only really focus on Jesus' ministry which lasted a short period of time. But it is so unique and so radically different from what preceded and followed it that I treat it as the essential time in this era.

functions, and followership have much in common and which basically differ with time periods before or after it.

Table Jnh 28-1 contains the outline of the six eras I have identified.

Table Jnh 28-1. Six Leadership Eras Outlined

Era	Label/ Details
I.	**Patriarchal Era** (Leadership Roots)—Family Base
II.	**Pre-Kingdom Leadership Era**—Tribal Base A. The Desert Years B. The War Years—Conquering the Land, C. The Tribal Years/ Chaotic Years/ Decentralized Years—Conquered by the Land
III.	**Kingdom Leadership Era**—Nation Based A. The United Kingdom B. The Divided Kingdom C. The Single Kingdom—Southern Kingdom Only
IV.	**Post-Kingdom Leadership Era**—Individual/ Remnant Based A. Exile—Individual Leadership Out of the Land B. Post Exilic—Leadership Back in the Land C. Interim—Between Testaments
V.	**New Testament Pre-Church Leadership**—Spiritually Based in the Land A. Pre-Messianic B. Messianic
VI.	**New Testament Church Leadership**—Decentralized Spiritually Based A. Jewish Era B. Gentile Era

The three overarching elements of leadership include: the *leadership basal elements* (leader, follower, situation which make up the **What** of leadership); *leadership influence means* (individual and corporate leadership styles which make up the **How** of leadership); and *leadership value bases* (theological and cultural values which make up the **Why** of leadership).[75] It was this taxonomy which suggested questions that helped me see for the first time the six leadership eras of the Bible. It is these categories that allow comparison of different leadership periods in the Bible. Later I will apply the taxonomy to each of the eras and give my preliminary findings.

Using these leadership characteristics I studied leadership across the Bible and inductively generated the six leadership eras as given above. Table Jnh 36-2 adds some descriptive elements of the eras.

---

[75] See the **Article**, *Leadership Tree Diagram*, which explains in details these three elements of leadership.

Table Jnh 28-2. Six Leadership Eras in the Bible—Definitive Characteristics

Leadership Era	Example(s) Leader(s)	Definitive Characteristics
1. Foundational (also called Patriarchal)	Abraham, Joseph	Family Leadership/ formally male dominated/ expanding into tribes and clans as families grew/ moves along kinship lines.
2. Pre-Kingdom	Moses, Joshua, Judges	Tribal Leadership/ Moving to National/ Military/ Spiritual Authority/ outside the land moving toward a centralized national leadership.
3. Kingdom	David, Hezekiah	National Leadership/ Kingdom Structure/ Civil, Military/ Spiritual/ a national leadership—Prophetic call for renewal/ inside the land/ breakup of nation.
4. Post-Kingdom	Ezekiel, Daniel, Ezra, Nehemiah	Individual leadership/ Modeling/ Spiritual Authority.
5. Pre-Church	Jesus/ Disciples	Selection/ Training/ spiritual leadership/ preparation for decentralization of Spiritual Authority/ initiation of a movement.
6. Church	Peter/ Paul/ John	decentralized leadership/ cross-cultural structures led by leaders with spiritual authority which institutionalize the movement and spread it around the world.

When we study a leader or a particular leadership issue in the Scripture, we must always do so in light of the leadership context in which it was taking place. We cannot judge past leadership by our present leadership standards. Yet, we will find that major leadership lessons learned by these leaders will usually have broad implications for our leadership.

Second Major Perspective for Getting Leadership Eyes—The Seven Leadership Genre

Further study of each of these leadership eras resulted in the identification of seven leadership genre which served as sources for leadership findings. I then worked out in detail approaches for studying each of these genre.[76] These seven leadership genre are shown in Table Jnh 28-3.

Table Jnh 28-3. Seven Leadership Genre—Sources for Leadership Findings

Type	General Description/ Example	Approach
1. Biographical	Information about leaders; this is the single largest genre giving leadership information in the Bible/ **Joseph**	Use biographical analysis based on leadership emergence theory concepts.
2. Direct Leadership Contexts[77]	Blocks of Scripture which are giving information directly applicable to leaders/ leadership; relatively few of these in Scripture/ **1 Peter 5:1-4**	Use standard exegetical techniques.
3. Leadership Acts[78]	Mostly narrative vignettes describing a leader influencing followers, usually in some crisis situation; quite a few of	Use three-fold leadership tree diagram as basic source for suggesting what areas of leadership to look for.

---

[76] See **Leadership Perspectives—How To Study the Bible for Leadership Findings**. Altadena: Barnabas Publishers.

[77] I have identified many of the direct leadership texts and exegetically analyzed the important ones.

28. Six Biblical Leadership Eras, Using Leadership Eyes   page 159

	these in the Bible/ **Acts 15 Jerusalem Council**	
4. Parabolic Passages[79]	Parables focusing on leadership perspectives: e.g. stewardship parables, futuristic parables; quite a few of these in Matthew and Luke./ **Luke 19 The Pounds**	Use standard parable exegetical techniques but then use leadership perspectives to draw out applicational findings; especially recognize the leadership intent of Jesus in giving these. Most such parables were given with a view to training disciples.
5. Books as a Whole	Each book in the Bible[80]; end result of this is a list of leadership observations or lessons or implications for leadership/ **Deuteronomy**	Consider each of the Bible books in terms of the leadership era in which they occur and for what they contribute to leadership findings; will have to use whatever other leadership genre source occurs in a given book; also use overall synthesis thinking.
6. Indirect Passages	Passages in the Scripture dealing with Biblical values applicable to all; more so to leaders who must model Biblical values/ **Proverbs; Sermon on the Mount**	Use standard exegetical procedures for the type of Scripture containing the applicable Biblical ethical findings or values.
7. Macro Lessons[81]	Generalized high level leadership observations seen in an era and which have potential for leadership absolutes/ **Presence Macro**	Use synthesis techniques utilizing various leadership perspectives to stimulate observations.

The Criteria For Evaluating An Era
What Are the Distinguishing Characteristics We Are Looking For? I have used the following categories:

1. Major Focus—
Here we are looking at the overall purposes of leadership for the period in question. What was God doing or attempting to do through the leader? Sense of destiny? Leadership mandate?

2. Influence means—
Here we are describing any of the power means available and used by the leaders in their leadership. We can use any of Wrong's categories or any of the leadership style categories I define. Note particularly in the Old Testament the use of force and manipulation as power means.

3. Basic leadership functions—
We list here the various achievement responsibilities expected of the leaders: from God's standpoint, from the leader's own perception of leadership, from the followers. Usually

---

[78] Many leadership acts have been identified and more than 20 have been analyzed. There is much work to do on analyzing leadership acts.

[79] I have studied every parable, exegetically, in Matthew, Mark and Luke for its central truth and applicable leadership lessons.

[80] I have done this for each book in the Bible over the past 10 years. My findings are included in **The Bible and Leadership Values** (and in the commentary series). Though I have made a good start, there is much more to be done here. I am intending other Handbooks which include all of the top 25 Bible books on leadership.

[81] This area needs the most research. Several PhD research projects are now focused on this.

they can all be categorized under the three major leadership functions of task, relational, and inspirational functions. But here we are after the specific functions.

4. Followers—
Here we are after sphere of influence. Who are the followers? What are their relationship to leaders? Which of the 10 Commandments of followership are valid for these followers? What other things are helpful in describing followers?

5. Local Leadership—
In the surrounding culture: Biblical leaders will be very much like the leaders in the cultures around them. Leadership styles will flow out of this cultural press. Here we are trying to identify leadership roles in the cultures in contact with our Biblical leaders.

6. Other:
Miscellaneous catch all; such things as centralization or decentralization or hierarchical systems of leadership; joint (civil, political, military, religious) or separate roles.

Thought Questions—
In addition to the above categories, I try to synthesize the questions that I would like answered about leaders and leadership if I could get those answers. With these thought questions I am considering such things as the essence of a leader (being or doing), leadership itself, leadership selection and training, authority (centralized or decentralized), etc.

My preliminary findings for these categories for each leadership era follows.

1st Leadership Era: Patriarchal Leadership

1. **Major Focus**—Pass on the promise and heritage of the Most High God to the family; priestly role (regularity)—intercede, sacrifice, and worship the Most High God;
2. **Influence means**—apostolic style, father-initiator, father-guardian, full range of Wrong's typology: force, manipulation, authority (coercive, inducive, positional—fatherly head, competence, personal), spiritual authority
3. **Five basic leadership functions**—(1) Godly/ priestly functions:- demonstrate absolute loyalty to God; - demonstrate reality of the unseen God; - pass on heritage of what is known (revelatory) of God and His ways and desires, very little revelation, animistic; - pass on sense of destiny; —God's prophetic promises; (2) Primarily performing the inspirational function—largely through modeling; the relational function consisted primarily of keeping the family together and obedience to the patriarch. Inspirational function -Creating hope in God -Creating sense of God's intervention in life; (3) Mediate Blessing of God: - contagious blessing; - heritage blessing; (4) Military head—protection of family; (5) Civil—judge/ justice
4. **Followers**—family members: (1) Age/masculine-oriented; (2) Almost all of 10 Followership Laws in force; (3) Oldest to receive blessing and birthright; (4) The one receiving blessing and birthright passes it on to next generation
5. **Local Leadership**—in the culture around the Patriarchs: - tribal heads; - City States / Regional heads (called kings);
   - local priests (practitioners/ animistic); - local military
6. **Other:** Highly Decentralized; each given family responsible to God

Thought Questions—1. How did other families relate to God (Melchezidek's, Labin's, etc.)? 2. What were expectations of Patriarchs as leaders? by followers? by God? by

28. Six Biblical Leadership Eras, Using Leadership Eyes

surrounding culture? 3. What was the foundational aspect of character? What was integrity to the Patriarchs? 4. What was the birthright? What was the blessing? 5. If modeling was the primary training methodology, what were the most important positive leadership qualities modeled by Abraham? by Isaac? by Jacob? by Joseph? by Job? 6. Using a modified form of the six characteristics of finishing well, how did the Patriarchs finish? Abraham? Isaac? Jacob? Joseph? Job?

2nd Leadership Era: Pre-Kingdom Leadership

1. **Major Focus**—Uniting of a people, preparing them to follow God, preparing them to invade the promised land, settling them in the land. The Desert leadership is one of discipline, a heavy time of revelation, and supernatural events backing leadership. The Challenge Era is one of stretching of faith to overcome the many obstacles involved in capturing the land. The Judges Era has the major challenge of how to unite disparate peoples, survive attacks, and degeneration of relationship to God. In each there is Charismatic Leadership: You lead because of spiritual authority, personal authority or competence not because of nepotism or birth; a formal priestly role is secondary—there is an inheritance with this role—and this leadership is weak, probably because of that.
2. **Influence means**—apostolic style, father-initiator, father-guardian, full range of Wrong's typology: force, manipulation, authority (coercive, inducive, positional—fatherly head, competence, personal), spiritual authority
3. **7 basic leadership functions** seen include: (1) Centralize Authority/ Develop Authority Structures:- military, political, religious;- tribal/ trans-tribal (elders); (2) Primarily performing the inspirational function: -Creating hope in God; -Creating sense of God's intervention in life. (3) Revelatory (Desert)/Inscribe and pass on the basic revelation of God as given in the law/how to live separated lives; (4) Military head—protection/ mobilize an on-call army distributed over the tribes; (5) Civil—judge/ justice/ set up legal system for interpreting and applying the law; (6) Fulfill Promise of Taking the Land; settling it; (7) Call to renewal; recrudescence; see God work anew.
4. **Followers**—12 large tribes:(1) Age/ masculine-oriented leadership; (2) Almost all of 10 Followership Laws in force; centralization out of balance; leadership more nepotistic than functional; reciprocal commands a legalistic thing carried by enforcement of law.
5. **Local Leadership**—in the surrounding culture:- tribal heads; - City State / Regional heads (called kings); - local priests (practitioners/ animistic); - local military
6. **Other**: Highly centralized during desert and capturing of land; highly decentralized during Judges era/ continuity of leadership a major problem except for the first transition from Moses to Joshua

Thought Questions:
1. How were leaders selected and developed? 2. What did they do at the different levels? 3. What is missing from the Judges Era that was the driving force of the Warfare Era? 4. What has happened to the Abrahamic mandate? Which of the eras, if any, are concerned with that mandate? 5. How does this era compare with the Patriarchal, spiritually?

3rd Leadership Era: Kingdom Leadership

1. **Major Focus**—The Kingdom united the dispersed tribal groups into a more cohesive nation which could provide government and military protection. The Davidic covenant was part of an on-going means to bring about Abraham's promise and to manifest the concept of God's rule on earth as well as provide resources to bring others into relationship with God. It never lived up to its ideals.
2. **Influence means**—the full range of Wrong's typology : **force, manipulation, authority** (coercive, inducive, positional)—fatherly head; competence, personal, spiritual authority.
3. **6 basic leadership functions** seen include:(1) Centralize Authority/ Develop Authority Structures:- military, political, religious; - tribal/ trans-tribal (elders); (2) Revelatory (Particularly in the Divided Kingdom and the Single Kingdom)/ Much of the

corrective revelation done by the prophets was oral. But there was also the Prophetic revelation which was inscribed. Often these writings were a call to repentance, renewal, and a return to kingdom ideals; (3) Military head—protection/ have a standing army that could defend against the attacks that were coming more frequently from the expanding empires or ambitious kings. They would also mobilize an on-call army distributed over the tribes to go along with the standing army in big crises. (4) Civil—judge/justice/set up legal system for interpreting and applying the law; (5) Call to renewal; recrudescence; see God work anew (prophetic function); (6) Persevere as a people of God; maintain a base from which God could work. Major Problems: communication and control; followership scattered over large area; -large empires on the rise
4. Followers—a. United Kingdom-12 large tribes, also the many surrounding small kingdoms that were conquered
b. Divided Kingdom—Northern-10 1/2 Large Tribes c. Southern—About 1 1/2 tribes—mostly Judah; Leadership (1) Age/ masculine oriented; (2) Almost all of 10 Followership Laws in force; centralization out of balance; leadership more nepotistic than functional;
5. Local Leadership—in the surrounding cultures: - tribal heads; - kings of territories with a number of cities; usually one dominated and was walled; - local priests (practitioners/ animistic); - military.
6. Other: Large Empires are vying for world dominion or at least for large influence: Assyria, Egypt, Babylon
Thought Questions:1. Why were the prophets raised up? 2. According to Deuteronomy what was the place of the law for the Kings? Was it followed? 3. Was the central religious function (the three yearly treks) carried out? 4. Why was the nepotistic approach to leadership selection used? Was it successful? 5. How does this era compare spiritually with the Pre-Kingdom era?

4th Leadership Era: Post-Kingdom Leadership
1. Major Focus—The nation no longer exists. It has been disciplined by God. Leadership during this time must do several things: analyze what happened and why; bring hope during this time; demonstrate the importance of godliness under oppressive conditions; demonstrate the importance of God's sovereignty; point to the future in which God is going to work.
2. Influence means—largely by modeling, spiritual authority, toward latter time in the time of the return, Jewish leaders again take up roles: political, religious, quasi-military for the Jewish people.
3. Basic leadership functions seen include: The inspirational function is dominant. The need for community in little pockets brings out the need for the relational function of leadership. The rise of the synagogues—small communities upholding their Jewish origins and religion bring about the need for scribes, and those who interpret the written scriptures.
4. Followers—Pockets of scattered Jewish people
5. Local Leadership—in the surrounding cultures: - tribal heads; - City States / Regional heads (called kings); - local priests (practitioners/ animistic); - local military; - emperors/ kings/ heads of powerful international groups formed by conquering vast territories and kingdoms/ various administrative leaders under these
6. Other: ?
Thought Questions: 1. Why did Jewish leaders prosper during these oppressive days? 2. What kinds of leadership did they participate in? 3. What has happened to the Abrahamic promise? How did the Jewish people feel about it in these days? 4. How were religious leaders selected (e.g. for the synagogues)?

5th Leadership Era: Pre-Church Leadership
1. Major Focus—Galatians 4:4. This is the acme of charismatic leadership. Jesus models servant leadership and ideal spiritual authority—all aspects of it. The end result of

28. Six Biblical Leadership Eras, Using Leadership Eyes

this leadership is revelation, redemption, and a movement to universalize the redemption to all humankind.

2. Influence Means—the entire range of Pauline leadership styles are demonstrated. The whole range of Wrong's Typology is seen.

3. Leadership Functions: (1) Provide the redemptive base reconciling God and humankind and its major ramifications, the revelation and enabling power for human beings to realize their idealized human potential. (2) Provide a leadership mandate that will utilize all three major leadership functions in its fulfillment. Task, relational, and inspirational functions are essential to the accomplishment of the mandate. (3) Create a movement that will institutionalize the leadership functions for on-going effective leadership. (4) Provide a call for renewal to Israel. (5) Present the Kingdom of God in concept and power. (6) Provide a revelatory base, model, and standards for future revelation.

4. Followers—In the land there were remnants of the tribes, mixed ethnic groups (like Samaritans), religious leadership like the Pharisees, Saducees, and the political leaders of the Roman empire along with garrisons of Roman Military to give authority as well as the Jewish Religious leaders the Sanhedrin.

5. Local Leaders: Sanhedrin, Saducees, Pharisees, Lawyers, Roman Military, Synagogues/ elders, Rabbis.

6. Other: This is a mixed era of centralized and decentralized means and authority. Jerusalem provided some means of religious centralization. There was political centralization in a number of centers. But Jesus leadership was not centralized.

Thought Questions: 1. What renewal aims did Christ specifically focus on? 2. What were the leadership selection and development processes in existence in the culture? 3. What were Jesus' leadership selection and development processes? How different? 4. How does Christ leadership compare or contrast with essential characteristics of each of the previous eras?

6th Leadership Era: Church Leadership

1. Major Focus—When Barnabas and Paul give their report to the elders back in Jerusalem at the Jerusalem conference described in Acts 15, there is much discussion. Finally, James summarizes the essence of the major focus of the Church leadership era, "Simon has declared how God at the first did visit the Gentiles, to take out of them a people for his name (Acts 15;14)." The central message of the book of Acts emphasizes this thrust in more detail. THE GROWTH OF THE CHURCH which spreads from Jerusalem to Judea to Samaria and the uttermost parts of the earth is seen to be of God, takes place as Spirit directed people present a salvation centered in Jesus Christ, and occurs among all peoples, Jews and Gentiles. During this leadership era, God is developing an institution that will carry His salvation to all cultures and all peoples. The development of this decentralized institution which can be fitted to any culture and people, the church, with its nature its leadership and its purposes for existing will be at the heart of this leadership era. Paul is a major architect of this leadership era. The book of 2 Corinthians is especially helpful to give us insights into early church leadership.

2. Influence Means—My past leadership studies have identified a number of leadership styles. In particular, I have categorized ten Pauline leadership styles. The entire range of Pauline leadership styles are demonstrated during the Church Leadership Era. The whole range of Wrong's Typology is seen including force, manipulation, authority, and persuasion power forms.

3. Leadership Functions—All three of the generic leadership functions are prominent: task oriented leadership, relationship oriented leadership and inspirational leadership. The major models for this era include Peter, John, and Paul with much more information given about Paul. Paul is dominantly a task-oriented leader with a powerful inspirational focus. He sees the necessity of relationship oriented leadership but that is not his strength. John is more of a relationship-oriented leader who also has a powerful inspirational thrust. Peter is

28. Six Biblical Leadership Eras, Using Leadership Eyes   page 164

dominantly a task oriented leader with inspirational thrust. As each matures they become more gentle—that is, relational leadership begins to come to the front. But always they are dominantly inspirational. God is creating new forms through which to reveal Himself to the world and followers must be inspired to participate and carry it all over the world in the face of persecution and obstacles.

4. Followers—The beauty of the church lies in its ability as an institutional form to fit into any culture. Since leadership in a given culture is defined in part by the followers expectations of what a leader is, we will have distinctive differences in various cultures as to leadership and followership. Each cultural situation will be different and hence have its unique demands. But there are commonalties in Biblical church leadership across cultures. This is seen especially in the values which determine why leaders operate and the standards by which they are judged. The book of 2 Corinthians helps us understand key leadership values.

5. Local Leaders—Various kinds of models of leadership existed in the various cultures. Paul, the main architect of local church leadership, gives us various descriptions of qualitative characteristics of leaders in his various epistles. The essential trait that flows throughout all of them is integrity. But Paul having described key character traits recognizes that these will manifest themselves differently in different cultures and situations.

6. Other—The church leadership era is a highly decentralized period of time. Churches are to exist in all cultures and peoples. They will be spread far and wide. Because of the decentralized nature of the church it is especially important to ask what unites it? What is common? Particularly is this important for leadership. And one of the answers is leadership values. 2 Corinthians helps us see some of the values that Paul modeled.

The Findings—The Best of Each Era

Table Jnh 28-4 summarizes the more important aspects of each of the leadership eras.

Table Jnh 28-4. Six Leadership Eras, On-Going Impact Items, Follow-Up

Era	On-Going Impact Items And Areas For Follow-Up Study
1. Patriarchal	Destiny leadership; Introduction of biographical study of leadership (Abraham, Isaac, Jacob, Joseph, Job); God's shaping processes introduced; intercession macro lesson introduced; character strength highlighted (Abraham, Jacob, Joseph); leadership responsibility to God instigated (accountability); leadership responsibility to followers introduced (blessing); leadership intimacy with God introduced (Abraham—friend of God, Job—trusting in deep processing). **Key Macro Lesson**: Destiny—Leaders must have a sense of destiny.
2. Pre-Kingdom	Seven Macro lessons from Moses' desert leadership (Timing; Intimacy; Intercession; Burden; Presence; Hope; Transition); Spiritual authority highlighted in Moses' and Joshua's ministries; pitfalls of centralized leadership seen; pitfalls of decentralized leadership seen; roots of inspirational leadership seen (Moses, Joshua, Caleb, Deborah, Jephthah, Samuel, David); outstanding biographical genre material. **Key Macro Lesson**: Presence—The essential ingredient of leadership is the powerful presence of God in the leader's life and ministry.
3. Kingdom	Five macros carry a warning for all future leadership (Unity; Stability; Spiritual Leadership; Recrudescence; By-Pass). Excellent biographical material both positive and negative examples (Saul, David, Asa, Josiah, Uzziah, Hezekiah, Elijah, Elisha, Jonah, Habakkuk, Ezekiel, Jeremiah and many others). **Key Macro Lesson**: Spiritual leadership can make a difference in the midst of difficult times.
4. Post-Kingdom	All five macros stress revelational perspective (Future Perfect; Perspective; Modeling; Ultimate, Perseverance). Excellent biographical genre available (Ezekiel, Daniel, Ezra, Nehemiah). **Key Macro Lesson**: Future Perfect—A primary function of all leadership

28. Six Biblical Leadership Eras, Using Leadership Eyes

	is to walk by faith with a future perfect paradigm so as to inspire followers with certainty of God's accomplishment of ultimate purposes.
5. Pre-Church	Selection/ Training/ spiritual leadership/ preparation for decentralization of Spiritual Authority/ initiation of a movement. Major Biographical— Jesus' and his movement leadership. **Key Macro Lesson**: Focus—Leaders must increasingly move toward a focus in their ministry which moves toward fulfillment of their calling and their ultimate contribution to God's purposes for them.
6. Church	Decentralized leadership/ cross-cultural structures led by leaders with spiritual authority, which institutionalize the movement and spread it around the world. Excellent biographical (Peter, Barnabas—a bridge leader, Paul, John); numerous leadership acts. **Key Macro Lesson:** Universal—The church structure is universal and can fit any culture. It must be propagated to all peoples.

The Foundational Transitions—Moses' And Jesus' Leadership Eras

Three figures give perspectives on Biblical leadership. Figure Jnh 28-1 illustrates the relative time involved in the six leadership eras. Figure Jnh 28-2 pinpoints distinctive features of leadership across the time-line. Figure Jnh 28-3 focuses on the two major transitions—Moses' Desert Leadership; Jesus' Movement Leadership.

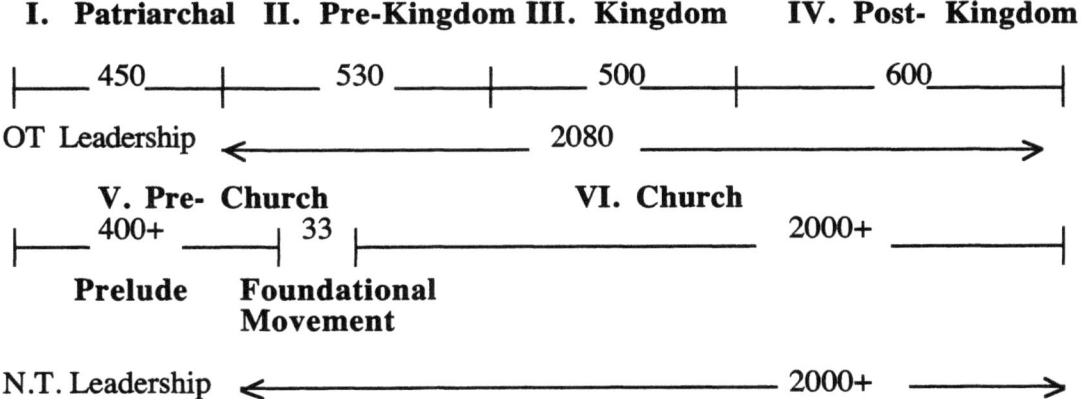

Figure Jnh 28-1. Leadership Eras— Rough Chronological Length In Years

28. Six Biblical Leadership Eras, Using Leadership Eyes

I. Patriarchal Leadership Roots	II. Pre-Kingdom Leadership	III. Kingdom Leadership	IV. Post-Kingdom	V. N.T. Pre-Church Leadership	VI. Church Leadership
A. Abraham B. Isaac C. Jacob D. Joseph E. Job	A. Desert B. Conquering The Land C. Conquered By the Land	A. United B. Divided C. Single	A. Exile B. Post Exile C. Interim	A. Pre-Messianic B. Messianic	A. Jewish B. Gentile
Family	Revelatory Task Inspirational	Political Corrective	Modeling Renewal	Cultic Spiritual Movement	Spiritual Institutional
Blessing Shaping Timing Destiny Character Faith Purity	(Timing) Presence Intimacy Burden Hope Challenge Spiritual Authority Transition Weakness Continuity	Unity Stability Spiritual Leadership Recrudescence By-Pass	Hope Perspective Modeling Ultimate Perseverance	Training Focus Spirituality Servant Steward Shepherd Movement	Structure Universal Giftedness Word Centered Harvest

Figure Jnh 28-2. Overview Time-Line of Biblical Leadership

In Figure Jnh 28-2 above, macro lesson labels occur at the bottom in the six columns. Just above the macro lesson labels are given distinctive characteristics of each of the eras. Finally, above that occurs the outline of the sub-time periods and the major time-line with the six eras.

28. Six Biblical Leadership Eras, Using Leadership Eyes

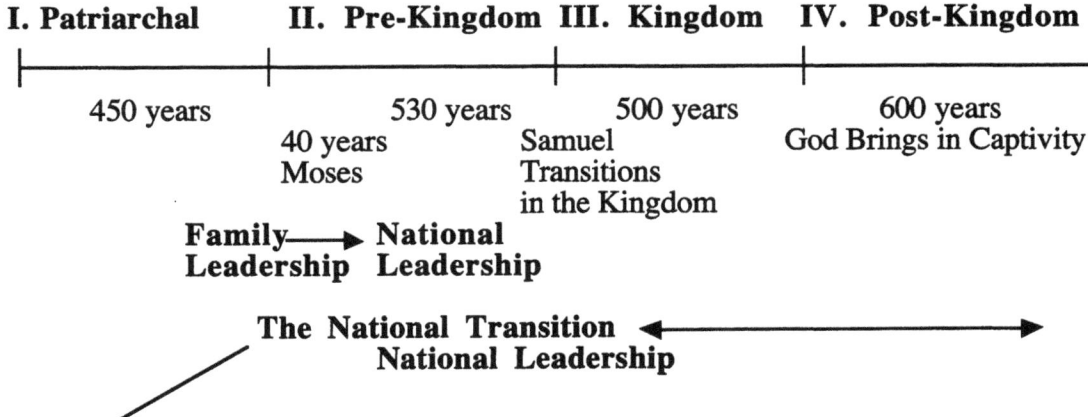

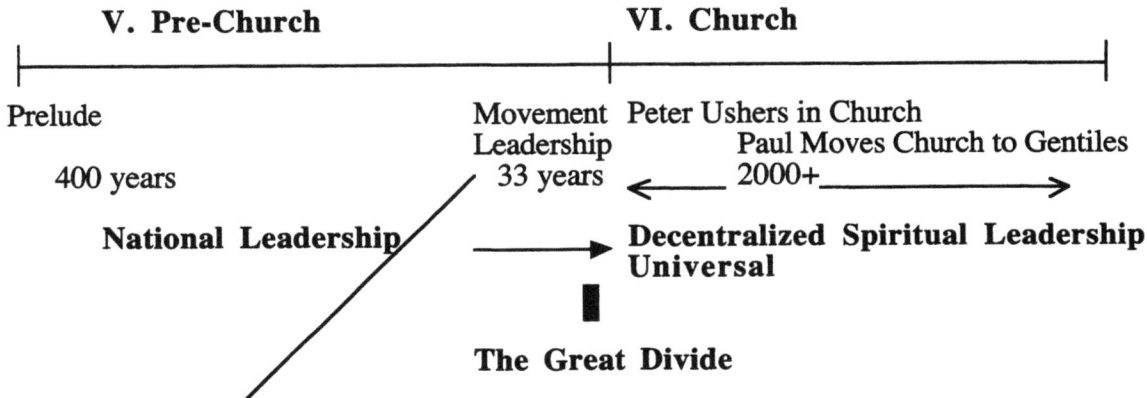

Figure Jnh 28-3. Two Major Transitions—The National Transition and The Great Divide

Note two things. These major transition times were short. God brought in major changes in a short period of time. Both transition times contain a large number of important macro lessons. For such short periods of time these are relatively large numbers of important leadership lessons.

Table Jnh 28-5 lists the transitions and key figures and the result of the transition.

Table Jnh 28-5. Transitions Along the Biblical Leadership Time-Line

Transition	Eras Involved	Key Figure/ Results
To God Directed Leadership	Begin Patriarchal Era	Abraham/ a God directed destiny involving an ethnic group and leaders from that group hearing God, getting revelation from Him, and obeying God.
Tribal to National	From the Patriarchal Era to the Pre-Kingdom Era	Moses/ A nation is established. God established concept of influential leader with spiritual authority to direct the nation; God reveals truth about Himself, life, and destiny for this nation. Major leadership guidelines

		(important macro lessons) flow through this transitional leadership.
Federation to Kingdom	Pre-Kingdom to Kingdom	Samuel/ A dispersed geographical/tribal society, each doing its own thing and basically not following God-given truth, is moved toward a centralized, unified national entity directed by one major leader—a king, who is to direct the nation with God's direction.
Babylonian Captivity	From Kingdom to Post-Kingdom	God/ God dismantles the kingdom structure. He disperses the followers. God by-passes the kingdom leadership altogether and begins a long preparation that will eventually emerge in spiritual leadership. In this era, individual spiritual leadership is highlighted in which God's perspective is crucial.
The Great Divide	From Post-Kingdom to Pre-Church. From a defunct national leadership to spiritual leadership which can be decentralized anywhere.	Jesus/ Jesus re-established God-directed leadership—the concept of the Kingdom of God. God by-passes the Jewish national leadership when they reject Him—i.e. His message through Jesus. Jesus at the same time of offering the kingdom also builds the foundational roots of a movement which will eventually contextualize the Kingdom of God in an institutional church form which can move into any culture on earth.
Universal Invitation	From Pre-Church to Church	Peter, Paul/ Peter ushers in the church to the Jewish followers of Jesus. Paul takes the church to the Gentiles. God's invitation of salvation and His truth for living God-directed lives become available (decentralized) to any people on the earth.

Note that that there are transition times between all the eras. Each of these are important in themselves but two stand out: Moses' Desert-Leadership; Jesus' Movement-Leadership. As is sometimes the case crucial transitions in the Bible are foundational. God focuses intently in these times and usually reveals foundational truth. Such is the case with all the transitions.

Tables Jnh 28-6 and Jnh 28-7 give the macro lessons discovered in these key transition times with suggested implications for today.

Table Jnh 28-6. Moses' Transition/ Lessons/ Implications

Timing— God's timing is crucial to accomplishment of God's purposes. **Implication**(s): Leaders today, especially in their complex ministries involving multi-cultural settings, must be more sensitive to the timing of God than ever before.
Intercession— Leaders called to a ministry are called to intercede for that ministry. **Implication**(s): Various prayer movements have gained tremendous momentum in our day testifying to the fact that God sees this as a very important aspect of leadership in our day.
Presence— The essential ingredient of leadership is the powerful presence of God in the leader's life and ministry. **Implication**(s): Much present day leadership misses the balance of this—God both in powerful ministry and in powerful life changing impact in the leader himself/herself.
Intimacy— Leaders develop intimacy with God which in turn overflows into all their ministry since ministry flows out of being. **Implication**(s): Doing and achievement dominate present day leadership. God through the various spirituality movements is

28. Six Biblical Leadership Eras, Using Leadership Eyes

calling leaders back to spirituality and beingness as the core of their ministries.

Burden— Leaders feel a responsibility to God for their ministry. **Implication**(s): Accountability is missing altogether in most cultures. This is true of Christian leadership as well. Sensitivity to this needed ingredient would avoid many of the leadership gaffes that are seen.

Hope— A primary function of all leadership is to inspire followers with hope in God and in what God is doing. **Implication**(s): This is especially true for leaders trying to reach Xers—generally without hope. But it is needed in all ministries as complex situations tend to take away hope for most Christians.

Challenge— Leaders receive vision from God which sets before them challenges that inspire their leadership. **Implication**(s): A leader must hear from God if that leader is to influence specific groups of people toward God's purposes—the basic definition of a leader. This is deeply needed especially in the many small churches which are floundering in our day.

Spiritual Authority—Spiritual authority is the dominant power base of a spiritual leader and comes through experiences with God, knowledge of God, godly character and gifted power. **Implication**(s): Abuse of power is one of the five major barriers facing leaders today. There are lots of leaders with all kinds of authority but few who exercise spiritual authority as a primary power base (with all its implications).

Transition—Leaders must transition other leaders into their work in order to maintain continuity and effectiveness. **Implication**(s): Every work of God is just one generation away from failure if it does not transition emerging leaders into its decision-making influential positions.

Table Jnh 28-7. Jesus' Transition/ Lessons/ Implications

Selection— The key to good leadership is the selection of good potential leaders which should be a priority of all leaders. **Implication**(s): Leadership selection is desperately needed in church and parachurch organizations. Recruitment is often haphazard at best, especially in local church situations.

Training—Leaders should deliberately train potential leaders in their ministry by available and appropriate means. **Implication**(s): If emerging new leaders are not developed they will exit organizations and go somewhere else, depriving churches and parachurch organizations of on-going leadership. Leading with a developmental bias is the key to seeing on-going recruitment and longevity in organizational life.

Focus— Leaders should increasingly move toward a focus in their ministry which moves toward fulfillment of their calling and their ultimate contribution to God's purposes for them. **Implication**(s): Focused leaders are few and far between. Most leaders are faddish leaders jumping on the bandwagon of other apparently successful leaders. What is needed is leaders, knowing their own focus, and following it. Focused leaders are the need of the hour.

Spirituality— Leaders must develop interiority, spirit sensitivity, and fruitfulness in accord with their uniqueness since ministry flows out of being. **Implication**(s): As previously seen with the intimacy lesson from Moses' era, spirituality is crucial to leadership. And what is true of intimacy, one aspect of spirituality, is true as leaders develop balanced spirituality. Doing and achievement dominate present day leadership. God through the various spirituality movements is calling leaders back to spirituality and beingness as the core of their ministries.

Servant— Leaders must maintain a dynamic tension as they lead by serving and serve by leading. **Implication**(s): Servant leadership is not naturally found in any culture. It requires a paradigm shift for any leader to move into this leadership model—which is what Jesus intended for leaders he developed. Because of accepted leadership patterns in some cultures (great power distance) this is really difficult for emerging leaders to see or

accept.
Steward— Leaders are endowed by God with natural abilities, acquired skills, spiritual gifts, opportunities, experiences, and privileges which must be developed and used for God. **Implication**(s): Accountability is greatly needed in our generation where successful leaders dominantly self-authenticate their own ministries and heed little or nothing from outside resources which could hold them accountable.
Harvest— Leaders must seek to bring people into relationship with God. **Implication**(s): The outward aspect of the Great Commission must be carried out. God is focusing on this as He continues to raise up missionary movements from all over the world. The impetus of the missionary movement has already moved from the western world to the non-western world. We need to support this while at the same time bringing about renewal of missionary thinking in the western world.
Shepherd— Leaders must preserve, protect, and develop God's people. **Implication**(s): God still gets most of the leadership business done at local church level. Leaders who hold to the shepherd model concepts must in fact carry local church ministries—especially as cultures become more radically opposed to Gospel values. This means that more pastoral work will be necessary if we are winning those from deteriorating cultures.
Movement— Leaders recognize that movements are the way to penetrate society though they must be preserved via appropriate on-going institutions. **Implication**(s): New life can be instilled in parachurch organizations and churches when movement ideals are focused on. We see all around us movement leaders being raised up by God who are creating new ministries which God is blessing. This can be done more deliberately and proactively when movement dynamics are heeded.

Conclusion

The Six Leadership Eras and the seven leadership genre provide major perspectives for studying leadership in the Bible. The leadership commentary series analyzes Bible books and applies these perspectives. Of particular importance are two of the leadership genre—the *macro lessons* across each leadership era and the Bible *books as a whole*. The macro lessons flowing from Moses' desert leadership and Jesus' movement foundations are particularly instructive. They apply with great force to today's leadership challenges.

See **Articles**, *3. Biographical Study in the Bible—How To Do; Bible Centered Leader; Leadership Act; 19. Leadership Eras in the Bible—Six Identified; 20. Leadership Genre—Seven Types; 22. Macro Lessons Defined; 23. Macro Lessons—List of 41 Across Six Leadership Eras; Principle of Truth.*

Article 29

29. Spiritual Authority Defined—Six Characteristics

A Biblical leader is a person with God-given capacities and with God-given responsibility who is influencing specific groups of God's people toward God's purposes for them. To influence, a leader must have some power base. I am indebted to Dennis Wrong[82] for helping me identify a taxonomy of concepts dealing with power. Wrong has influence as the highest level on his taxonomy, power next, and authority third. Influence can be unintended or intended. In terms of leadership we are interested in intended influence. Intended influence can be subdivided into four power forms, the second level: Force, Manipulation, Authority, and Persuasion. All of these are important for Christian leaders with the final two being the most important—authority and persuasion—since spiritual authority is related to both. Authority, the third level, can further be sub-divided into coercive, inducive, legitimate, competent, personal. A leader will need to use various combinations of these power forms to influence people. However,

> **Effective leaders value spiritual authority as a primary power base.**

This is one of seven major leadership lessons that I have identified from comparative study of effective leaders. This article defines spiritual authority and gives some guidelines about its use.

Spiritual Authority—What Is It?

Spiritual authority is the ideal power base for a leader to use with mature believers who respect God's authority in a leader. A simplified definition focusing on the notion of maturity of believers is:

Definition   <u>Spiritual authority</u> is the
- right to influence,
- conferred upon a leader by followers,
- because of their perception of spirituality in that leader.

An expanded definition focusing on how a leader gets and uses it is:

---

[82] See Dennis H. Wrong, **Power—Its Forms, Bases, and Uses**. 1979. San Francisco, CA: Harper and Row.

29. Spiritual Authority Defined—Six Characteristics

Definition **Spiritual Authority** is that
- characteristic of a God-anointed leader,
- developed upon an experiential power base (giftedness, character, deep experiences with God),

that enables him/her to influence followers through
- persuasion,
- force of modeling, and
- moral expertise.

Spiritual authority comes to a leader in three major ways. As leaders go through deep experiences with God they experience the sufficiency of God to meet them in those situations. They come to know God. This experiential knowledge of God and the deep experiences with God are part of the experiential acquisition of spiritual authority. A second way that spiritual authority comes is through a life which models godliness. When the Spirit of God is transforming a life into the image of Christ those characteristics of love, joy, peace, long suffering, gentleness, goodness, faith, meekness, temperance carry great weight in giving credibility that the leader is consistent inward and outward. A third way that spiritual authority comes is through gifted power. When a leader can demonstrate gifted power in ministry—that is, a clear testimony to divine intervention in the ministry via his/her gifts—there will be spiritual authority. Now while all three of these ways of getting spiritual authority should be a part of a leader, it is frequently the case that one or more of the elements dominates. From the definitions and description of how spiritual authority comes you can readily see that a leader using spiritual authority does not force his/her will on followers.

What Are Some Guidelines—To Maximize Use and Minimize Abuse

The following descriptive characteristics about spiritual authority sets some limits, describe ideals, warn against abuse and in general gives helpful guidelines for leaders who desire spiritual authority as a primary means of influence.

Six Characteristics And Limits Of Spiritual Authority

These six descriptions were derived from my own observations of leaders and from adaptations made from several writers on power such as Watchman Nee, R. Baine Harris, and Richard T. De George. Nee was a Chinese Christian leader. The other two are secular authorities on power and authority in leadership.

Table Jnh 29-1. Six Characteristics of Spiritual Authority

Characterization	Statement
1. Ultimate Source	Spiritual authority has its ultimate source in Christ. It is representative religious authority. It is His authority and presence in us which legitimates our authority. Accountability to this final authority is essential.
2. Power Base	Spiritual authority rests upon an experiential power base. A leader's personal experiences with God and the accumulated wisdom and development that comes through them lie at the heart of the reason why followers allow influence in their lives. It is a resource which is at once on-going and yet related to the past. Its genuineness as to the reality of experience with God is confirmed in the believer by the presence and ministry of the Holy Spirit who authenticates that experiential power base.
3. Power Forms	Spiritual authority influences by virtue of persuasion. Word gifts are dominant in this persuasion. Influence is by virtue of legitimate authority. Positional leadership carries with it recognition of qualities of leadership which are at least initially recognized by followers. Such authority must

29. Spiritual Authority Defined—Six Characteristics

	be buttressed by other authority forms such as competent authority, and personal authority.
4. Ultimate Good	The aim of influence using spiritual authority is the ultimate good of the followers. This follows the basic Pauline leadership principle seen in 2Co 10:8.
5. Evaluation	Spiritual authority is best judged longitudinally over time in terms of development of maturity in believers. Use of coercive and manipulative forms of authority will usually reproduce like elements in followers. Spiritual authority will produce mature followers who will make responsible moral choices because they have learned to do so.
6. Non-Defensive	A leader using spiritual authority recognizes submission to God who is the ultimate authority. Authority is representative. God is therefore the responsible agent for defending spiritual authority. A person moving in spiritual authority does not have to insist on obedience. Obedience is the moral responsibility of the follower. Disobedience, that is, rebellion to spiritual authority, means that a follower is not subject to God Himself. He/she will answer to God for that. The leader can rest upon God's vindication if it is necessary.

Remember,

Effective leaders value spiritual authority as a primary power base.[83]

See *power forms* (various definitions), **Glossary**. See **Articles**, *Influence, Power, and Authority Forms; Leadership Lessons—Seven Major Identified*.

---

[83] They also know that it will take varied forms of power including coercive, inducive, positional, personal, competence and others to influence immature believers toward maturity. But the ideal is always there to use spiritual authority with mature believers.

Article 30

30. Testing Patterns

Introduction
The prophet Jonah illustrates a negative response to God's testing pattern and the effects of such a response. His deliberate disobedience to the commission to preach is unique among the prophets and results in his being set aside from ministry. Jonah is an apt example of how leaders should <u>not</u> respond to tests of their character and call to ministry. But he also demonstrates a positive response to God's 2nd call to preach. And with it comes God's blessing. Both these testing patterns are worth noting.

Defining Testing Patterns
Leadership Emergence Theory [84] delineates many common patterns [85] in the development of leaders. Pattern is the term used to describe a repetitive cycle of happenings. A Testing Pattern is a fairly regular pattern and it includes three aspects: a test, a response, and a resulting action. Depending on the leader's response, two results take place. The positive testing pattern implies a test, positive response and growth or expansion. A negative testing pattern entails a test, negative response and remedial action.

Here are the two patterns described in more detail:

Definition	The <u>positive testing pattern</u> describes God's uses of process items to form character in a leader through a three-step process, which includes:
Stage 1	a test of the leader's character through a given incident,
Stage 2	a positive response of the leader to recognize God's special dealing with him/her and then the positive response of acting in a way that honors inner convictions and God's desires in the situation,
Stage 3	expansion in which God honors the response by confirming the inner conviction as an important leadership value and by increasing the leader's capacity to influence.
Definition	The <u>negative testing pattern</u> describes God's use of process items to point out lack of characters through a three set process, which includes:
Stage 1	a test of the leader's character through a given incident,

---

[84] This is the phrase to denote the developmental theory of a leader that has resulted from Clinton's research.
[85] More than 20 common patterns have been identified and described. See **Leadership Emergence Theory**.

30. Testing Patterns

Stage 2   a failure response in which the leader either does not perceive the incident as a test from God and makes a poor choice or the leader deliberately chooses to go against inner convictions or that which pleases God,

Stage 3   remedial action by God that tests the leader again on the same or similar issue, restricts the leader's development until the lesson is learned, or disciplines the leader.

Jonah's Testing Patterns Analyzed

In the opening of the book, Jonah is given an obedience check[86] by God to test his response to the truth that God wants his word preached to the Ninevites. An obedience check is one of the process items that God uses to shape a leader. Will a leader obey something when God tells him/her to. That is the bottom line of an obedience check. In Jonah's development, God used this process item to reveal Jonah's disdain for non-Jewish people. Thus, Jonah's call to this ministry is a test of his character.

Jonah responds by deliberately choosing to go against that which pleases God. Instead of obeying his commission to preach to the Ninevites, Jonah boarded a ship to Tarshish (Spain?), a country in the opposite direction of Nineveh. Jonah's reaction is to run from the presence of God and the call to preach to non-Jewish people. His response reveals that he is not a leader whose inner convictions match God's love for all that He created. This begs the question about what will happen to leaders who disobey the Lord?

The Lord's remedial work starts while Jonah is on the ship to Spain.[87] Jonah will not be allowed to flee from God or the commission to preach to the Ninevites because the Lord is interested in shaping his character. Initially, the Lord sends a great wind upon the sea and causes a terrific storm. When this does not gain the attention of Jonah, the Lord causes the lot to fall on Jonah showing that he was the reason for the storm. Eventually the Lord prepares a great fish to swallow Jonah and isolate him for a few days. Jonah emerges from isolation with new conviction about obeying the Lord although later it's revealed that his inner convictions still do not match God's desires.

Implications for Leaders Today

Leaders today need to recognize God's shaping activities in the incidents of their own lives because they will be tested too. Leaders would do well to learn from the negative testing pattern of Jonah instead of learning from their own experience. Here are some lessons for leaders today:

1. Correction – The good news about Jonah is that the Lord is committed to growth in leaders' lives. This growth sometimes happens through the corrective actions of God. God holds in tension his desire to develop leaders and his desire for ministry that will happen through those leaders. He is not only focused on the ministry task. He is also committed to developing character in leaders so that they can embody his values as they lead. Oftentimes this character development comes through remedial actions in the form of discipline, isolation or retesting.

2. Discernment – This lesson requires a leader to be discerning about the incidents in their life and to see them as part of God's shaping activity. In particular, the Testing Pattern is one that is repeated in the lives of leaders and is used by God to shape a leader's character, enhance inner convictions, and honor God's desires. Sensitivity to integrity

---

[86] See **Glossary** for the notion of *process items* in general and specifically for *obedience check*. Check is used in the sense of test. Jonah went through a test of obedience.

[87] The Good News Bible translates the KJV Tarshish by the word Spain.

checks, obedience checks, word checks, faith checks and ministry tasks will increase one's ability to respond positively to the God ordained pattern.

3. Vicarious learning – The story of Jonah gives leaders an example to avoid. His actions along with the corresponding remedial training serve as a vivid warning. Many leaders may be tempted to shun a particular call to ministry. Jonah brings a caution that rejecting a commission from God could eventuate in corrective actions by God until the leader embodies godly values. We can learn this from Jonah's life instead of from our own failure to respond well to God's words.

So when you read Jonah in your Bible learn for your own life.

See *integrity checks, obedience checks, word checks, faith checks, ministry tasks,* **Glossary.**

Article 31

31. Transparency With God—Jonah Contrasted with Habakkuk

Introduction

In the small four-chapter book of Jonah, the prophet Jonah is facing a difficult task, which he does not want to do. Go and preach to the Ninevites, that violent enemy nation which would eventually destroy his kingdom. In Jonah's story we see a strong leader with integrity. God has to break that strong leader to get him to obey. The interesting thing to observe in the book is Jonah's honest transparency with God. I want to point out this transparency and then compare and contrast Jonah's transparency with Habakkuk's transparency. Both of these leaders certainly illustrate the following two leadership observations:

A leader can be absolutely honest with God in prayer concerning how he/she feels or thinks.

A leader who is transparent, with God and others, can impact lives via his/her modeling of transparency.[88]

Jonah's Transparency With God

Notice the ways that Jonah is transparent with God.

Way #1 He openly rebels against God's command because he differs with God concerning the salvation of the Ninevites (ch 1 and ch 4:2).

Way #2 He isolates himself to see if God will indeed bring judgment or not (ch 4).

Way #3 In his dialog with God he openly shows God his anger at what God is doing (ch4).

Jonah's Transparency With Others

Way #1 Openly admitting to sailors that he is the cause of the judgment seen in the storm.

Way#2 Sharing his testimony with the Ninevites (implied; not seen directly in the text but certainly a real reason why the Ninevites might listen to him and respond the way they did).

Way #3 We have the book. Jonah wrote this down or told it to someone who did. The way the gentiles are compared so favorably in their response to God as compared to Jonah's

---

[88] See 2nd Corinthians for the most powerful demonstration of this second observation on transparency. Paul is transparent with others about his dealings, motivation, values, etc.

negative responses to God reveals real transparency. Jonah wanted us to get the message of his paradigm shift. He wanted us to know God is concerned for the nations.

Habakkuk's Transparency With God[89]

<u>Way #1.</u> He attacks God's character—especially holiness and justice. He is accusing God

<u>Way #2.</u> Challenges what God is doing.

<u>Way #3.</u> Now Habakkuk challenges God about his justice—concerning the Babylonians.

Way #4 And finally Habakkuk flat out rebukes God

But Habakkuk is also transparent to us, the readers of this little book. And to those who would be singing its final chapter in their public words. I see Habakkuk as being transparent with us in three ways.

Habakkuk's Transparency With The Readers

<u>Way #1.</u> We have the book. If Habakkuk were a person who kept his cards close to his chest[90] we would never have gotten the book in the first place. Habakkuk would never have written this for public use, if he was not a transparent person.

<u>Way #2.</u> Habakkuk shares the downer side of his feelings. He is fearful. He knows that trouble is coming his way. He does not look forward to his personal suffering but does look forward to the process of God's justice being worked out. Notice the boldfaced below.

<u>Way #3.</u> Habakkuk also shares the upbeat side of his feelings written for public use. Habakkuk wanted to have this openly sung in public worship. That's being transparent.

Comparisons and Contrasts Seen in Transparency of these Two Leaders

Both Habakkuk and Jonah wanted others to know their stories, even though the stories reflected their challenging of God and His purposes. Both isolate themselves with God to express to Him their challenges of God and His ways. Both are freely emotional as they do so. Habakkuk is more logical in his approach to transparency with God while Jonah is more emotional. Habakkuk uses prayer as a weapon to negotiate with God concerning what he is seeing or not seeing. Jonah uses prayer for his own personal deliverance as well as showing the deep despair he was in when in the depths of the ocean. But both men certainly illustrated the leadership observations with which I opened this article.

A leader can be absolutely honest with God in prayer concerning how he/she feels or thinks.

A leader who is transparent, with God and others, can impact lives via his/her modeling of transparency.

---

[89] See the **Article**, *Transparency With God*, in the Habakkuk commentary for an exhaustive treatment of these ways.

[90] I am using an idiom here. "Keeping one's cards close to the chest" means not being very open about how one feels about things or not letting people in on one's secrets or thoughts.

Closure

One of the reasons Jonah and Habakkuk are such a powerful books is that they illustrate the power of modeling for us. They exemplify one of the important Old Testament macro lessons, which is also powerfully seen in the lives of Jesus and Paul.

25. Modeling First seen vividly in the Post-Kingdom Leadership Era
Leaders can most powerfully influence by modeling godly lives, the sufficiency and sovereignty of God at all times, and gifted power.

Habakkuk and Jonah deliberately share with us their pivotal experiences with God, so we can learn from them. The more a leader can be transparent with others about his/her deep relationship with God the more the impact in others lives. Transparency is the hallmark of modeling as a means of powerful influence. Transparency for Habakkuk involved honest sharing in prayer, challenging God personally about his holiness and justice, challenging God about His justice, both in Judah and with the Babylonians (and by extension over the whole world). But once Habakkuk deeply responded to those powerful faith words, "the just shall live by faith," he went through a paradigm shift in recognizing that God's way are right and that God would be vindicated over all the earth.

Transparency for Habakkuk also involved sharing with others. He wrote this book in order that we may learn from his experience. He wrote this closing testimony so that it could be sung in public worship. He shared his bad feelings and his good feelings. Habakkuk's final modeling is his most powerful. He shares his innermost feelings at the hard things to come but rejoices in his trust of God to do things right—to deliver, God of my salvation.

Transparency for Jonah involved openly admitting he was the cause of the storm, sharing of his testimony with the Ninevites and most importantly writing his testimony in book form so that it could have lasting impact on leaders. He wrote his book in order that we may learn from his experience. He shared his testimony with its rebellion against God. He shared with us hid deep dependence on God to deliver. He shared with us his anger with God at the results of his ministry to the Ninevites.

I have noted in my leadership emergence case studies of leaders that there are a few people who are truly free to be transparent. There are also a few who can not be very transparent at all. And then there are the larger majority who have a tendency to become transparent in their leadership, but have a long way to go.

Which one of these three categories are you? (1) Not transparent; (2) a lot to learn about transparency and its place in leadership influence; (3) Very transparent and have seen God use it in leadership influence.

Jonah

CLINTON'S BIBLICAL LEADERSHIP COMMENTARY SERIES

Seeing God's Perspective—
A Crucial Paradigm Shift

Glossary and Bibliography

Glossary—Leadership Definitions

The following leadership related definitions occur throughout the **Habakkuk Leadership Commentary**. They are listed here alphabetically for convenience in referencing. SRN stands for Strong's Reference Number. These numbers can be used to look up the definitions of these words in the **Strong's Exhaustive Concordance** containing Hebrew and Greek dictionaries. These numbers are now also used by many other Bible study aids.

Item	Definition
Affect	a learning domain, that is, a term describing learning which primarily moves the feelings and emotions.
Aftermath	Aftermath refers to the after effects and ramifications of some past act or event which has continuing influence of the present.
Authority	a Dennis Wrong concept. Authority is the legitimate use of power resources involving one or more of the following authority components: coercive, inducive, positional, competence, personal.
Authority Insights	from leadership emergence theory. One of 51 process items that God uses to shape a leader. Authority insights describe those instances in ministry in which a leader learns important lessons, via positive or negative experiences, with regards to: submission to authority, authority structures, authenticity of power bases underlying authority, authority conflict, how to exercise authority.
Beforemath	Beforemath refers to the effects and implications of some future event or state which has influence reaching back into the present, at least to the eye of the leader holding the future perfect vision by faith.
Brokenness	a state of mind in which a person recognizes that he/she is helpless in a situation or life process unless God alone works. It is a state of mind in which a person acknowledges a deep dependence upon God and is open for God to break through in new ways, thoughts, directions, and revelation of Himself that was not the case before the brokenness experience. Example: Jacob in Genesis 32 faced a life threatening situation in which he was forced to desperately depend upon God.
Capture	a technical term used when talking about figures of speech being interpreted. A figure or idiom is said to be captured when one can display the intended emphatic meaning of it in non-figurative simple words. e.g. not ashamed of the Gospel = captured: completely confident of the Gospel.
Celebration	Celebration refers to a corporate time, a gathering of a group of God's people, who recognize God for who He is and what He does, and worships Him, in such a way as to honor Him and to renew their committal to follow this God.
Cognitive	a learning domain, that is, a term describing learning which primarily focuses on the transmittal and understanding of knowledge and ideas.
Conative	a learning domain, that is, a term describing learning which affects the will or the decision making aspect of the learner. The learner will opt to use the learning in life.

Glossary of Leadership Definitions

Conflict	from leadership emergence theory. One of 51 process items that God uses to shape a leader. The conflict process item refers to those instances in a leader's life-history in which God uses conflict, whether personal or ministry related to develop the leader in dependence upon God, faith, and inner-life.
Connector words	In Hebrew Poetry analysis, a connector word(s) is a word(s) such as *but*, *and*, *nevertheless*, which connects two phrases or two couplets or a line with a couplet and serves to help interpret the relationships between the things connected.
Connector phrase	In Hebrew Poetry analysis, a connector phrase is a phrase placed between reduction statements or lines (inserted by the interpreter) to indicate the flow of thought in the extended parallelism.
Corporate crisis	A corporate crisis refers to those special intensive situations of pressure in human situations, which are used by God to test groups as a whole, like the Northern Kingdom, Southern Kingdom, a local church, etc. Just as individuals are tested so too with groups.
Corporate restoration	Corporate restoration refers to God's attempts to restore the people of God as a viable channel through whom He can work to carry out His Biblical purposes.
Crisis Process Item	from leadership emergence theory. One of 51 process items that God uses to shape a leader. Crisis process items refer to those special intense situations of pressure in human situations, which are used by God to test and teach dependence.
Critical Incident	A critical incident is a special intervention (could be a series over time) in which God gives a *major value* that will flow through the life or will give *strategic direction* to narrow the leader's life work.
Destiny, 4 types	Leadership Emergence Theory has identified 4 basic destiny types: (1) Awe Inspiring Encounters with God (some including revelation; others not so); (2) Indirect (things are done by others that affect our destiny and over which we have little control); (3) Providential: God has set up things in our past experience which will later come together and have meaning; could also involve repeated opening and shutting doors of as we are led on to our destiny; (4) Blessing: God's Hand of blessing repeatedly seen so as to assure us of His Destiny for us
Destiny pattern	A three stage pattern involving an accumulation of knowledge about one's destiny given by God over a lifetime: (1) Stage 1. Destiny preparation (hints at one's destiny); (2) Stage 2. Destiny revelation (clarification); (3) Stage 3. Destiny Fulfillment (God brings the destiny to completion).
Different parallelism	*Hebrew Poetry* is said to be different parallelism when one or more members of one phrase is in different correspondence with its related member of the parallel.
Divine Contacts	from leadership emergence theory. One of 51 process items that God uses to shape a leader. A divine contact is a person whom God brings in contact with a leader at a crucial moment in a development phase in order to

Glossary of Leadership Definitions

	accomplish one or more of the following to: affirm leadership potential, encourage leadership potential, give guidance on a special issue, give insights which may indirectly lead to guidance, challenge the leader God-ward, open a door to a ministry opportunity, other insights helping the emerging leader to make guidance decisions.
Double Confirmation	from leadership emergence theory. One of 51 process items that God uses to shape a leader. Double confirmation refers to the unusual guidance in which God makes clear His will by giving the guidance directly to a leader and then reinforcing it by some other person totally independent and unaware of the leader's guidance.
Experiental	a learning domain which integrates learning into practice in life situations.
Extended parallelism	Extended parallelism describes any unit of *Hebrew Poetry* larger than a couplet in which three or more phrases are placed in parallel. There exits the possibility of thought relationships between any of the phrases in parallel.
Exteriority	One of eight spirituality factors. Describes the outward testimony of a person as perceived by others.
Faith challenge	from leadership emergence theory. One of 51 process items that God uses to shape a leader. A faith challenge refers to those instances in ministry where a leader is challenged to take steps of faith in regards to ministry and sees God meet those steps of faith with divine affirmation and ministry affirmation and often with guidance into on going ministry leading to a focused life.
Figure	A figure is the unusual use of a word or words differing from the normal use in order to draw special attention to some point of interest.
Flesh act	from leadership emergence theory. One of 51 process items that God uses to shape a leader. A flesh act refers to those instances in a leader's life where guidance is presumed and decisions are made either hastily or without proper discernment of God's choice. Such decisions usually involve the working out of guidance by the leader using some human manipulation or other means and which brings ramifications which later negatively affect ministry and life. See Genesis 16 for an example in Abraham's life. See Joshua's treaty with Gibeonites in Jos 9. See Isa 39:4 for Hezekiah's action with Babylonian envoys.
Future perfect paradigm	The future perfect paradigm refers to a way of viewing a future reality as if it were already present which in turn, inspires one's leadership, challenges followers to the vision, affects decision making, and causes one to persevere in faith, which finally results in the future reality coming into being. For leaders who move in revelatory gifts, especially futuristic prophecy and apostolic types, especially with the gift of faith, who must get vision and motivate followers toward it, this is a very necessary paradigm.
Gifted Power	refers to the empowerment of the Holy Spirit when using giftedness; 1Pe 4:11 gives the basic admonition for this to the use of word gifts. It is naturally extended to other areas of giftedness.
Giftedness Discovery	from leadership emergence theory. One of 51 process items that God uses to shape a leader. Giftedness discovery refers to instances in which a leader

Glossary of Leadership Definitions

	becomes aware of natural abilities, or acquired skills, or spiritual gifts so as to use them well in ministry. This is a significant advance along the giftedness development pattern.
Giftedness Set	a term describing natural abilities, acquired skills, and spiritual gifts which a leader has as resources to use in ministry. Sometimes shortened to giftedness.
Guidance	from leadership emergence theory. One of 51 process items that God uses to shape a leader. Guidance is the general category which refers to the many ways in which God reveals information that informs a leader about decisions to be made.
Habakkuk's Dilemma	a phrase describing the situation in which Habakkuk's situation seemed to deny the existence and work of God. In general, a situation in which a leader's perspective on a situation he/she faces seems to deny God's existence and working.
Hebrew Poetry	Hebrew Poetry is a way of expressing relationships between parallel thoughts in an emotional language. Usually it is the repetition of phrases in which member of one phrase relate to the members of the other phrase.
Idiom	the use of words to imply something other than their literal meanings. An idiom is a group of words, which have a corporate meaning that cannot be deduced from a compilation of the meanings of the individual words making up the idiom. People in the culture know the idiomatic meaning of the words. Example, I smell a rat. Some idioms are patterned in which case you can reverse the pattern to get the meaning. Others must simply be learned in the culture from contextual usage of them.
Inspirational leadership	At the highest levels of leadership there are three crucial leadership functions that must be accounted for: Inspirational, Task Oriented, Relational. Inspirational dominantly deals with motivational effort.
Integrity	the top leadership character quality. It is the consistency of inward beliefs and convictions with outward practice. It is an honesty and wholeness of personality in which one operates with a clear conscience in dealings with self and others.
Integrity Check	from leadership emergence theory. One of 51 process items that God uses to shape a leader. The integrity check refers to the special kind of process test which God uses to evaluate heart –intent, consistency between inner convictions and outward actions, and which God uses as a foundation from which to expand the leader's capacity to influence. The word check is used in the sense of test—meaning a check or check-up. See also testing patterns.
Interiority	One of eight spirituality factors. Describes the inward life and relationship with God of a person.
Isolation Processing	from leadership emergence theory. One of 51 process items that God uses to shape a leader. Isolation processing refers to the setting aside of a leader from normal ministry involvement in its natural context usually for an extended time in order to experience God in a new or deeper way.

Glossary of Leadership Definitions

Issachar Factor	The Issachar Factor refers to that special needed leadership aspect—clarity as to what is happening in the complex situation currently facing a leader and options for addressing the situation.
Leadership act	A leadership act is the specific instance at a given point in time of the leadership influence process between a given influencer (person said to be influencing) and follower(s) (person or persons being influenced) in which the followers are influenced toward some goal.
Leadership Backlash	from leadership emergence theory. One of 51 process items that God uses to shape a leader. The leadership backlash process item refers to the reactions of followers, other leaders within a group, and/or Christians outside the group, to a course of action taken by a leader because of various ramifications that arise due to the action taken. The situation is used in he leader's life to test perseverance, clarity of vision, and faith.
Leadership Challenge	a leadership emergence theory term referring to the shaping process God uses to give a leader an on-going renewal experience about leadership and to direct that leader to some new leadership task.
Leadership Committal	a special shaping activity of God observed in leadership emergence theory which is usually a spiritual benchmark and produces a sense of destiny in a leader. It is the call to leadership by God and the wholehearted response by the leader to accept and abide by that call. Paul's Damascus road experience, the destiny revelation given by Ananias, and Paul's response to it as a life calling provide the New Testament classic example of leadership committal.
Leadership Era	A leadership era is a period of time, usually several hundred years long, in which the major focus of leadership, the influence means, basic leadership functions, and followership have much in common and which basically change with time periods before or after it.
Learning domains	Educational technologists refer to the overall learning process by breaking it up into 4 learning components, which the call learning domains. Affect learning refers to learning which touches the feelings; cognitive learning refers to the acquisition and understanding of new ideas; conative learning refers to learning which affects one's decisions (the will); experiential learning refers to the integration of learning from any of the domains so that the learning actually affects everyday behavior.
Left hand sensitivity	Left hand sensitivity refers to gaining a perspective on God's use of other nations and groups, apart from those dedicated to His service, to accomplish His purposes.
Life Crisis	A special form of the general crisis process item in which an individual faces the threat of loss of life. This drives the individual deep into dependence upon God for deliverance.
Macro lesson	A macro-lesson is a high level generalization of a leadership observation (suggestion, guideline, requirement), stated as a lesson, which repeatedly occurs throughout different leadership eras, and thus has potential as a leadership absolute.
Mentoring	a relational experience in which one person, the mentor, empowers another person, the mentoree, by sharing God-given resources. See the 9 mentor

Glossary of Leadership Definitions

roles: mentor discipler, mentor spiritual guide, mentor coach, mentor counselor, mentor teacher, mentor sponsor, mentor contemporary model, mentor historical model, mentor divine contact. e.g. The apostle Paul demonstrated many of these roles in his relationships with team members and others in his ministry. See Stanley and Clinton **Connecting** for a popular treatment of mentoring. See Clinton and Clinton **The Mentor Handbook** for a detailed treatment of mentoring.

Mentor Coach	one of nine mentor roles. Coaching is a process of imparting encouragement and skills to succeed in a task via relational training.
Mentor Discipler	one of nine mentor roles. A mentor discipler is one who spends much time, usually one-on-one, with an individual mentoree in order to build into that mentoree the basic habits of the Christian life. It is a relational experience in which a more experienced follower of Christ shares with a less experienced follower of Christ the commitment, understanding, and basic skills necessary to know and obey Jesus Christ as Lord.
Mentor Divine Contact	one of nine mentor roles. A person whose timely intervention is perceived of as from God to give special guidance at an important time in a life. This person may or may not be aware of the intervention and may or may not have any further mentoring connection to the mentoree.
Mentor Spiritual Guide	one of nine mentor roles. A spiritual guide is a godly, mature follower of Christ who shares knowledge, skills, and basic philosophy on what it means to increasingly realize Christlikeness in all areas of life. The primary contributions of a Spiritual guide include accountability, decisions, and insights concerning questions, commitments, and direction affecting spirituality (inner-life motivations) and maturity (integrating truth with life).
Mentor Sponsor	one of nine mentor roles. A mentor sponsor is one who helps promote the ministry (career) of another by using his/her resources, credibility, position, etc. to further the development and acceptance of the mentoree.
Mentor Teacher	one of nine mentor roles. A mentor teacher is one who imparts knowledge and understanding of a particular subject at a time when a mentoree needs it.
Mentor Model (contemporary)	one of nine mentor roles. A mentor contemporary model is a person who models values, methodologies, and other leadership characteristics in such a way as to inspire others to emulate them.
Mentor Model (historical)	one of nine mentor roles. A mentor historical model is a person whose life (autobiographical or biographical input) modeled values, methodologies, and other leadership characteristics in such a way as to inspire others to emulate them.
Metaphor	a figure of speech which involves an implied comparison in which two unlike items (a real item and a picture item) are equated to point out one point of resemblance. e.g. The Lord is my shepherd. These can be simple (all elements present) or complex (verbal metaphor, some element may be missing and has to be supplied). 2Ti 1:6 stir up the gift is complex, a verbal metaphor. Gift is compared to a flame which has gotten low. Timothy is urged to develop and use with power that gift.

Glossary of Leadership Definitions

Ministry Task	one of 51 process items that God uses to shape a leader. A ministry task is an assignment from God which primarily tests a person's faithfulness and obedience but often also allows use of ministry gifts in the context of a task which has closure, accountability, and evaluation. e.g. Barnabas trip to Antioch; Titus had 5 ministry tasks.
Modality	a structural time definition. A modality is a structured fellowship, which is a permanent institution reflecting God's work in a given geographical location(s) in which membership is broadly seen as inclusive and makes no distinction between age or sex or whatever.
Negative Preparation	from leadership emergence theory. One of 51 process items that God uses to shape a leader. Negative preparation refers to the special guidance process involving God's use of events, people, conflict, persecution, or experiences, all focusing on the negative, so as to free up a person from the situation in order to enter the next phase of development with a new abandonment and revitalized interest.
Negative testing pattern	See testing pattern, negative.
Networking Power	a leadership emergence theory term. One of 51 processing items used by God to shape a leader's ministry. It describes how God can connect a leader to resources of all kinds which can come from contacts with people. People provide a bridge, connecting a given leader with other persons or needed resources.
Obedience Check	from leadership emergence theory. One of 51 process items that God uses to shape a leader. An Obedience checks refer to that special category of process items in which God tests personal response to revealed truth in the life of a person.
Other Parallelism	Other parallelism relates to the broad classification of *Hebrew Poetry* not specifically same or different.
Paradigm	a controlling perspective in the mind which allows one to perceive and understand REALITY.
Paradigm Shift	a change of a controlling perspective so that one perceives and understands REALITY in a different way than previously.
Pivotal Point	A pivotal point is a critical time in a leader's life in which processing going on will be responded to in such a way that one of three typical things may happen: The response to this processing can: 1. curtail further use of the leader by God or at least curtail expansion of the leader's potential. 2. limit the eventual use of the leader for ultimate purposes that otherwise could have been accomplished, 3. enhance or open up the leader for expansion or contribution to the ultimate purposes in God's kingdom, that is, it may be a springboard to future expanded use by God of the leader.
Power Encounter	A power encounter identifies a situation in which the power of God is tested over against some other god's power.

Glossary of Leadership Definitions

Power forms	A term arising from Dennis Wrong's research. Power refers to the intential use of various resources to influence others. Power forms include: force, manipulation, and authority. See also authority.
Power Gifts	a category of spiritual gifts which authenticate the reality of God by demonstrating God's intervention in today's world. These include: tongues, interpretation of tongues, discernings of spirits, kinds of healings, kinds of power (miracles), prophecy, faith, word of wisdom, word of knowledge.
Power Ministry	refers to use of the power gifts to demonstrate God's intervention and often to validate or vindicate a leader's spiritual authority in a situation.
Powershift	a term describing the paradigm shift in which a leader moves from not believing in God's supernatural intervention in ministry to believing it and using it. See Jn 6:1-15; 16-21.
Prayer Power	from leadership emergence theory. One of 51 process items that God uses to shape a leader. Prayer power refers to the specific instance in which God uses the situation to answer prayer and demonstrate the authenticity of the leader's spiritual authority.
Prayer Challenge	One of 51 process items identified in Leadership Emergence Theory. It represents a God-given challenge to trust God concerning some crucial prayer item.
Process item	A process item is the technical name in leadership emergence theory describing actual occurrences in a given leader's life including providential events, people, circumstances, special divine interventions, inner-life lessons and other like items which God uses to develop that leader by shaping leadership character, leadership skills, and leadership values.
Progressive calling	the recognition that most leaders will receive on-going leadership challenges from God throughout their lifetimes and not just some initial call; such challenges will bring renewal, divine affirmation, ministry affirmation and will continue to give strategic guidance to a leader's ministry. Peter illustrates this very strongly.
Promise from God	A *promise from God* is an assertion from God, specific or general or a truth in harmony with God's character, which is perceived in one's heart or mind concerning what He will do or not do for that one and which is sealed in our inner most being by a quickening action of the Holy Spirit and on which that one then counts.
Prophecy	*Prophecy* refers to the genre of Scripture in which the thrust of the passage is an authoritative revelation from God usually through a spokesperson, called a prophet or prophetess, to correct a given historical situation or to warn of a future situation.
Prophetic past	an idiom; prophetic past—in the prophetic past idiom the past tense is used to describe or express the certainty of future action. See Ge 15:18; Jn 13:31; Ro 8:29,30.
Providential guidance	This refers to guidance that God gives indirectly by controlling guidance via circumstances or contextual factors. In Christian speak, we use the term open doors or closed doors to refer to providential guidance.

Glossary of Leadership Definitions

Reduction statement	A reduction statement (sometimes shortened to reduction) is a one line summary statement representing the emphatic meaning of a Hebrew Poetic couplet.
Relational leadership	At the highest levels of leadership there are three crucial leadership functions that must be accounted for: Inspirational, Task Oriented, Relational. Relational leadership dominantly deals with setting the ambiance so that followers want to follow and contribute.
Restoration	Restoration (individual leader) is the process whereby a fallen leader is transitioned back into leadership. It usually involves repentance, restitution where appropriate, correction of the aberrant leadership dysfunctionalities, and recognition by other leaders of the restoration process and their stamp of approval for the leader to renew ministry.
Restoration crisis	The restoration crisis refers to the period of time from 539 B.C. to 430 B.C. and which covers the activity of God in bringing His people back into the land and establishing a testimony there. His providential care of His people (both in the land and outside it) is also shown.
Rhetorical question	an idiom; A rhetorical question is a figure of speech in which a question is not used to obtain information but is used to indirectly communicate, (1) an affirmative or negative statement, or (2) the importance of some thought by focusing attention on it, or (3) one's own feeling or attitudes about something. See 1 Ti 3:5. See Nehemiah for numerous examples noted in the commentary explanation.
Same parallelism	Same parallelism refers to the type of *Hebrew Poetry* in which members of one phrase relate to members of the parallel phrase in basically the same way.
Simile	a figure of speech, which involves a stated comparison of two unlike items (one called the real item and the other the picture item) in order to display one graphic point of comparison. The words like or so or as or than are used to indicate the stated comparison between the real and picture items. e.g. 1 Pet 2:24 All flesh is as grass.
Sovereign guidance	This refers to guidance that God gives by directly intervening in some way.
Sovereign mindset	an attitude demonstrated by the Apostle Paul in which he tended to see God's working in the events and activities that shaped his life, whether or not they were positive and good or negative and bad. He tended to see God's purposes in these shaping activities and to make the best of them.
Spiritual Authority (short)	Spiritual authority is the right to influence, conferred upon a leader by followers, because of their perception of spirituality in that leader.
Spiritual Authority (longer)	Spiritual Authority is that characteristic of a God-anointed leader, developed upon an experiential power base (giftedness, character, deep experiences with God), that enables him/her to influence followers through persuasion, force of modeling, and moral expertise.
Spiritual disciplines	Spiritual disciplines are activities of mind and body purposefully undertaken to bring personality and total being into effective cooperation with the Spirit of God so as to reflect Kingdom life.

Glossary of Leadership Definitions

Spiritual gifts	a God-given unique capacity which is given to each believer for the purpose of releasing a Holy Spirit empowered ministry either in a situation or to be repeated during the Church Leadership Era. I identify 19 such gifts from a comparative analysis of the 8 major and 16 minor passages about gifts in Scripture. I categorize these 19 in terms of major purposes for the church as Word gifts, Power gifts, and Love gifts. The 19 include: teaching, exhortation, pastoring, evangelism, apostleship, prophecy, ruling, word of wisdom, word of knowledge, faith, miracles, gifts of healings, governments, helps, giving, mercy, tongues, interpretation of tongues, discernings of spirits. All leaders have at least one word gift. See word gifts. See Clinton and Clinton **Unlocking Your Giftedness** for detailed explanation of leadership and spiritual gifts.
Structural time	Structural time refers to an overall perspective for analyzing a work of God in terms of built-in cycles of existence by viewing events, states of development, or some discernible stages from initiation of the cycle until completion of the cycle.
Summary statement	In Hebrew Poetry analysis, a summary statement is a condensed statement of the entire poetic unit. It consists of the subject of the unit and each major idea developed about the subject.
Task Leadership	At the highest levels of leadership there are three crucial leadership functions that must be accounted for: Inspirational, Task Oriented, Relational. Task oriented leadership dominantly deals with getting the job done, that is, accomplishing the mission of the organization.
Testing Pattern, negative	A three stage pattern involving God's development of character in a leader via a test. (1) There is the test which may refer to obedience of some command or a recognition that God is challenging toward some faith exploit; (2) then there is the response by the leader—in this case negative, meaning not properly responding to God in the test; (3) usually if a leader fails, God will bring some remedial training to rework the issue.
Testing Pattern, positive	A three stage pattern involving God's development of character in a leader via a test. (1) There is the test which may refer to obedience of some command or a recognition that God is challenging toward some faith exploit; (2) then there is the response by the leader—in this case positive, meaning the leader has an appropriate response to God in the test; (3) a proper response is usually followed by some sort of expansion of the leader (successful ministry or development to a broader level of leadership, etc.).
Ultimate contribution set	An ultimate contribution is a lasting legacy of a Christian worker for which he or she is remembered and which furthers the cause of Christianity by one or more of the following: setting standards for life and ministry; impacting lives by enfolding them in God's kingdom or developing them once in the kingdom; serving as a stimulus for change which betters the world; leaving behind an organization, institution, or movement that will further channel God's work; the discovery of ideas, communication of them, or promotion of them so that they further God's work. 13 common category types have been identified and labeled in leadership emergence theory.
Volitional	also called conative; a learning domain, that is, a term describing learning which primarily focuses on the influencing a person to commit to the things

Glossary of Leadership Definitions

being learned; it wants to bring about volitional compliance—a willingness to use what is being learned. Jesus stresses this emphasis in Jn 7:17 and Jn 13-17.

Word Check — from leadership emergence theory. One of 51 process items that God uses to shape a leader. A <u>word check</u> is a process item which tests a leader's ability to understand or receive a word from God personally and to see it worked out in life with a view toward enhancing the authority of God's truth and a desire to know it.

Glossary of Leadership Definitions

Jonah Bibliography

American Bible Society, General Editors
    2001   **The Learning Bible, contemporary English Version.** New York: American Bible Society.

(Bratcher, Robert G. et al)
    n.d.   **Good News Bible—Today's English Version.** New York: American Bible Society.

Bullinger, E. W.

Clinton, Dr. J. Robert
    1977   **Interpreting The Scriptures: Figures and Idioms.** Altadena, Ca: Barnabas Publishers.

    1983   **Interpreting The Scriptures: Hebrew Poetry.** Altadena, CA: Barnabas.

    1986   **Coming to Conclusions On Leadership Styles.** Altadena,Ca: Barnabas Publishers.

    1986   **Short History of Leadership Theory**, 1986, by Dr. J. Robert Clinton. Altadena, CA: Barnabas Publishers.

    1989   *The Ultimate Contribution.* Altadena,Ca: Barnabas Publishers.

    1989   **The Making of A Leader.** Colorado Springs: NavPress.

    1989   **Leadership Emergence Theory.** Altadena,Ca: Barnabas Publishers.

    1993   **The Bible and Leadership Values.** Altadena,Ca: Barnabas Publishers.

    1993   **Leadership Perspectives.** Altadena,Ca: Barnabas Publishers.

    1995   *The Life Cycle of a Leader.* Altadena,Ca: Barnabas Publishers.

    1997   **Having A Ministry That Lasts.** Altadena,Ca: Barnabas Publishers.

    2000   **Clinton's Biblical Leadership Commentary CD.** Altadena,Ca: Barnabas Publishers.

    2001   **Titus—Apostolic Leadership.** Altadena,Ca: Barnabas Publishers.

    2002   **Habakkuk—Hope For A Leader In Troubled Times.** Altadena,Ca: Barnabas Publishers.

    2002   **Haggai—Restoring a Work of God, Inspirational, Task-Oriented Leadership.** Altadena,Ca: Barnabas Publishers.

Clinton, Dr. J. Robert and Dr. Richard W.
    1993   **Unlocking Your Giftedness—What Leaders Need To Know To Develop Themselves and Others.** Altadena,Ca: Barnabas Publishers.

Bibliography

Davis, Stanley B. Davis,

    1987   **Future Perfect**. New York: Addison-Wesley, 1987.

Ebor, Donald (Chairman of the Joint Committee)
    1970   **New English Bible**. Oxford: Oxford University Press.

Ellison, H.L.,
    1985   "Jonah." *The Expositor's Bible Commentary*. Vol. 7. Edited by Frank E. Gæberlien. Grand Rapids, MI: Zondervan Publishing.

InterVarsity Press, General Editors
1996 *The New Bible Dictionary*, 3rd edition, InterVarsity Press: Downers Grove, IL.

Kuhn, Thomas
    1970   **The Structure of Scientific Revolutions**. Chicago: University of Chicago Press.

Mickelsen, A. Berkley
    1963   **Interpreting The Bible**. Grand Rapids: Eerdmans Publishing Company.

Phillips, J.B.
    1958   **The New Testament in Modern English**. USA: The Macmillan Company.

Pusey, E. B. D.D.,
    1907   **The Minor Prophets With a Commentary, Vol. VI, Habakkuk and Malachi**, London: James Nisbet and Co.

Strong, James
    1890   **The Exhaustive Concordance of the Bible** (with Dictionaries of the Hebrew and Greek Words). Nashville: Abingdon Press.

(Taylor, Ken did original version; other Bible scholars the new version)
    1996   **Holy Bible—New Living Translation**. Wheaton, Il: Tyndale house Publishers, Inc.

Terry, Milton S. (2nd edition)
    1964   **Biblical Hermeneutics**. Grand Rapids: Zondervan.

Trebesch, Shelley
    1997   **Isolation—A Place of Transformation in the Life of A Leader**. Altadena, Ca: Barnabas Publishers.

Trible, Phyllis,
    1996   "The Book of Jonah." *The New Interpreter's Bible: A Commentary in Twelve Volumes*. Vol. VII. Nashville, TN: Abingdon Press.

Wrong, Dennis
    1979   **Power—Its Forms, Bases, and Uses**. San Francisco, CA: Harper and Row.

BARNABAS PUBLISHER'S MINI CATALOG

Approaching the Bible With Leadership Eyes: An Authoratative Source for Leadership Findings — Dr. J. Robert Clinton
Barnabas: Encouraging Exhorter — Dr. J. Robert Clinton & Laura Raab
Boundary Processing: Looking at Critical Transitions Times in Leader's Lives — Dr. J. Robert Clinton
Connecting: The Mentoring Relationships You Need to Succeed in Life — Dr. J. Robert Clinton
The Emerging Leader — Dr. J. Robert Clinton
Fellowship With God — Dr. J. Robert Clinton
Finishing Well — Dr. J. Robert Clinton
Figures and Idioms (Interpreting the Scriptures: Figures and Idioms) — Dr. J. Robert Clinton
Focused Lives Lectures — Dr. J. Robert Clinton
Gender and Leadership — Dr. J. Robert Clinton
Having A Ministry That Lasts: By Becoming a Bible Centered Leader — Dr. J. Robert Clinton
Hebrew Poetry (Interpreting the Scriptures: Hebrew Poetry) — Dr. J. Robert Clinton
A Short **History of Leadership Theory** — Dr. J. Robert Clinton
Isolation: A Place of Transformation in the Life of a Leader — Shelley G. Trebesch
Joseph: Destined to Rule — Dr. J. Robert Clinton
The Joshua Portrait — Dr. J. Robert Clinton and Katherine Haubert
Leadership Emergence Theory: A Self Study Manual For Analyzing the Development of a Christian Leader — Dr. J. Robert Clinton
Leadership Perspectives: How To Study The Bible for Leadership Insights — Dr. J. Robert Clinton
Coming to Some Conclusions on **Leadership Styles** — Dr. J. Robert Clinton
Leadership Training Models — Dr. J. Robert Clinton
The Bible and **Leadership Values:** A Book by Book Analysis— Dr. J. Robert Clinton
The Life Cycle of a Leader: Looking at God's Shaping of A Leader Towards An Eph. 2:10 Life — Dr. J. Robert Clinton
Listen Up Leaders! — Dr. J. Robert Clinton
The Mantle of the Mentor — Dr. J. Robert Clinton
Mentoring Can Help—Five Leadership Crises You Will Face in the Pastorate For Which You Have Not Been Trained — Dr. J. Robert Clinton
Mentoring: Developing Leaders...Without Adding More Programs — Dr. J. Robert Clinton
The Mentor Handbook: Detailed Guidelines and Helps for Christian Mentors and Mentorees — Dr. J. Robert Clinton
Moses Desert Leadership—7 Macro Lessons
Parables—Puzzles With A Purpose (Interpreting the Scriptures: Puzzles With A Purpose) — Dr. J. Robert Clinton
Paradigm Shift: God's Way of Opening New Vistas To Leaders — Dr. J. Robert Clinton
A Personal Ministry Philosophy: One Key to Effective Leadership — Dr. J. Robert Clinton
Reading on the Run: Continuum Reading Concepts — Dr. J. Robert Clinton
Samuel: Last of the Judges & First of the Prophets–A Model For Transitional Times — Bill Bjoraker
Selecting and Developing Those Emerging Leaders — Dr. Richard W. Clinton
Social Base Processing: The Home Base Environment Out of Which A Leader Works — Dr. J. Robert Clinton
Starting Well: Building A Strong Foundation for a Life Time of Ministry — Dr. J. Robert Clinton
Strategic Concepts: That Clarify A Focused Life – A Self Study Guide — Dr. J. Robert Clinton
The Making of a Leader: Recognizing the Lessons & Stages of Leadership Development — Dr. J. Robert Clinton
Time Line —Small Paper (What it is & How to Construct it) — Dr. J. Robert Clinton
Time Line: Getting Perspective—By Using Your Time-Line, Large Paper — Dr. J. Robert Clinton
Ultimate Contribution — Dr. J. Robert Clinton
Unlocking Your Giftedness: What Leaders Need to Know to Develop Themselves & Others — Dr. J. Robert Clinton
A **Vanishing Breed:** Thoughts About A Bible Centered Leader & A Life Long Bible Mastery Paradigm — Dr. J. Robert Clinton
The Way To Look At Leadership (How To Look at Leadership) — Dr. J. Robert Clinton
Webster-Smith, Irene: An Irish Woman Who Impacted Japan (A Focused Life Study) — Dr. J. Robert Clinton
Word Studies (Interpreting the Scriptures: Word Studies) — Dr. J. Robert Clinton

(Book Titles are in Bold and Paper Titles are in Italics with Sub-Titles and Pre-Titles in Roman)

BARNABAS PUBLISHERS

Unique Leadership Material that will help you answer the question:
"What legacy will you as a leader leave behind?"

"The difference between leaders and followers is perspective. The difference between leaders and effective leaders is better perspective."
Barnabas Publishers has the materials that will help you find that better perspective and a closer relationship with God.

BARNABAS PUBLISHERS
Post Office Box 6006 • Altadena, CA 91003-6006
Fax Phone (626)-794-3098